DIRECTORY OF UNITED NATIONS DOCUMENTARY AND ARCHIVAL SOURCES

Prepared in co-operation with
the United Nations Dag Hammarskjöld Library

Compiled with annotations and an introduction by

PETER I. HAJNAL

Co-published by

The Academic Council on the United Nations System
Kraus International Publications
United Nations

1991

Reports and Papers are produced by the
Academic Council on the United Systems
as part of its program to expand our
understanding of the problems of
international institutions.
The individual authors, however,
remain responsible for the content
of the work that is presented.

The opinions expressed in this book
are solely those of the compiler and
do not necessarily reflect the views
of the co-publishers. All information
is provided "as is" without warranty
of any kind by the United Nations.

© 1991 by the United Nations
© 1991 by Peter I. Hajnal
for the compilation, annotations and Introduction

Library of Congress Cataloging-in-Publication Data

Hajnal, Peter I., 1936-
  Directory of United Nations documentary and archival sources /
compiled with annotations and an introduction by Peter I. Hajnal.
  p. cm. — (Reports and papers / the Academic Council on the
United Nations System ; 1991-1)
  "Prepared in co-operation with the United Nations Dag Hammarskjold
Library."
  Includes biographical references and index.
  1. United Nations — Archival resources. I. Title. II. Series:
Reports and papers (Academic Council on the United Nations System) ; 1991-1.

JX1977.8.D6H34 1991
026'.34123 — dc20   91-61735
                                              CIP

United Nations Sales # 91.I.14
ISBN 92-1-100455-1 (United Nations)
ISBN 0-527-37321-4 (Kraus International Publications)

TABLE OF CONTENTS

Foreword	iii
Preface	v
Typical Entries in the Directory	vi
Abbreviations and Acronyms	ix
Introduction	
Publication vs. Document	xiii
Volume, Subject Matter and Physical Form	xviii
Distribution Policies and Practices of Organizations of the UN System	xx
Depository Libraries	xxi
Bibliographic Tools	xxiii
Subjects	
Structural and Institutional Issues	1
Peace and Security, Disarmament and Arms Control	20
Economic and Social Issues	23
International Law	34
Human Rights	39
Environment	42
Other Topics and General Information	44
Research Resources	
Collections of Documents	50
Statistics	55
Archival Resources	62
Catalogs, Indexes, Guides, and Other Bibliographic Tools	65
Index	91

FOREWORD

In June 1987, a group of forty scholars, teachers and other specialists from Canada, Mexico and the United States, active in the work and study of international organizations, founded the Academic Council on the United Nations System (ACUNS). In the report of this meeting, entitled "Strengthening the Study of International Organization", ACUNS' major purpose was conceived as "encouraging teaching and research which broaden and deepen understanding of the bases and effectiveness of international cooperation, and which give special attention to the role of organizations of the United Nations System and the emergence of new problems on the global agenda." Specifically, ACUNS undertook to pursue a program that included: "1) projects to support teaching and broad public understanding of international organizations; 2) activities to enhance scholarly research and build closer links between scholars and policy-makers; and 3) documentation and information services that support teaching and research projects." The report noted that "Documentation and information services are indispensable resources in strengthening the study of international organization." A Committee on Documents and Archives was established to implement ACUNS' commitment in the field of documentation.

Since its inception, ACUNS, through its Committee on Documents and Archives, has undertaken several projects that share the common objective of making UN documentation more accessible and serviceable to scholars and practitioners. Most noteworthy among these is the innovative series of documentary essays that selects, systematically organizes and annotates the most salient documents generated in recent years on a single major issue. Two such essays, *Administrative and Financial Reform of the United Nations* by John de Gara and *Strengthening the United Nations Economic and Social Programs* by Jacques Fomerand have already appeared, and a documentary essay on peacekeeping will appear shortly. In addition, the preparation of a special bibliography on the occasion of the forthcoming fiftieth anniversary of the founding of the United Nations is being prepared.

As the Committee on Documents and Archives probed more deeply into its task, it became firmly convinced that considerably more attention had to be paid to the matter of the accessibility of UN documentation -- that is to provide information to scholars and others working in the field as to what documentary collections and sources are available, what these collections contain and where they are located. During the forty-five years of its existence, the United Nations and its affiliated agencies have generated an extraordinary volume of documents, reports, records and statistical data scattered in diverse depositories, libraries, archives and electronic data banks.

Today, there is widespread renewed interest in the United Nations due in large part to the political successes emanating from the resurgent effectiveness of the Security Council, the movement towards resolving a number of heretofore intractable regional disputes, and UN peacekeeping operations. However, this represents only a small part of United Nations activities and concerns. The work of the United Nations in the non-political fields may very well be of equal if not greater significance because it is concerned with long-term human survival issues that must be addressed. As the United Nations system has been dealing with every aspect of human existence -- social, economic, cultural as well as political -- a wealth of information on all of these areas has been accumulated within the many organs that constitute the United Nations system. The importance and utility of this information extends not only to the international relations specialists concerned with contemporary developments and current issues but also to scholars in all the social sciences as well as in many of the physical sciences. The broad scope of United Nations documentation is attested to by the "global agenda" which includes balancing development and a sustainable environment, promoting human rights and the democratization process, coping with human disasters of famine and forced population migrations, planning for the conservation of the earth's water resources and controlling the depletion of the ozone layer, etc. The massive accumulation of information and documentation within the United Nations system is of particular interest to historians, who are becoming increasingly aware of the historical importance of the United Nations in understanding the post-World War II period.

Convinced that the United Nations documentary and archival collections represent an invaluable resource and in keeping with its original commitment to strengthen the study of international organization, ACUNS decided that it was most important to draw attention to this largely hidden and untapped set of resources. To carry out this important task, ACUNS commissioned Peter Hajnal of the University of Toronto Library to prepare a volume that would help orient teachers, researchers, students and practitioners to the riches buried in the United Nations archives and documentary collections. The end result is this *Directory of United Nations Documentary and Archival Sources* which does not merely list, but annotates some 500 entries of material originating from within the United Nations system and from other sources as well. ACUNS was fortunate in enlisting Peter Hajnal for this task. Author of *The United Nations and Its Publications: A Bibliographical Guide* (Toronto: University of Toronto Library, 1976) and *Guide to United Nations Organization, Documentation and Publishing* (Dobbs Ferry, N.Y.: Oceana, 1978), Hajnal's long experience as a librarian, working on international documents both inside and outside the United Nations uniquely qualified him to prepare this volume with his usual initiative, thoroughness and meticulous care.

Benjamin Rivlin
Chair
ACUNS Committee on Documents and Archives

PREFACE

The purpose of this *Directory* is to assist teaching, research, and documentation and library work in the field of international relations as well as in a wide variety of subject fields in the purview of the United Nations system of organizations. The *Directory* provides to concerned individuals and organizations an annotated guide to major documentary and archival sources of those organizations. In addition to material originating from organizations of the UN system itself, the *Directory* includes entries for items of reference or informational value published commercially, academically or by governments.

Following an introduction describing the patterns, characteristics and problems of the documentation of the UN system, the *Directory* presents 524 entries covering major titles, collections such as microform sets and compendia of resolutions, archival collections and reference sources; annotations refer also to many additional important titles. Entries are presented in two sections: Subjects, and Research Resources. Entries provide: names of corporate and personal authors, title (and titles in languages other than English when applicable), publisher, place and date of publication, date(s) of coverage for serials, pagination, sales number, document series symbol or other document number, ISBN or ISSN, and, in most cases, annotation. The *Directory* ends with an alphabetical index of authors and titles.

I acknowledge with thanks the material and intellectual assistance I received from the Academic Council on the United Nations System (ACUNS), which enabled me to compile and edit the *Directory*. I am particularly grateful to Professors Benjamin Rivlin of the Ralph Bunche Institute and Gene Lyons of the Dickey Foundation, Dartmouth College; to Robert W. Schaaf and Marjorie Browne of the Library of Congress for their valuable suggestions and constructive criticism; to Patti McSherry of the Ralph Bunche Institute for her conscientious research assistance; and to Alanna Kalnay for her speedy and conscientious indexing. The rich holdings of published and unpublished material in the Dag Hammarskjöld Library of the United Nations provided an essential source of information for many of those entries in the *Directory* that cover documents and publications of the UN system, and I gratefully acknowledge my indebtedness to these sources. I would like to thank for their help the staff of the Dag Hammarskjöld Library, especially Maureen Ratynski and Maritina Paniagua, and Britt Kjölstad of the Legal Reference Collection of that Library. Alf Erlandsson and Marilla B. Guptil of the UN Archives were also most helpful. I am grateful to my wife Edna for thoughtful editorial assistance, and to my son Mark for help in inputting and organizing the material. All these organizations and individuals (and others too numerous to name here) deserve credit for a significant contribution to this effort. Any inaccuracies, important omissions or needless inclusions are my sole responsibility.

Peter I. Hajnal   Toronto, May 1991

TYPICAL ENTRIES IN THE DIRECTORY

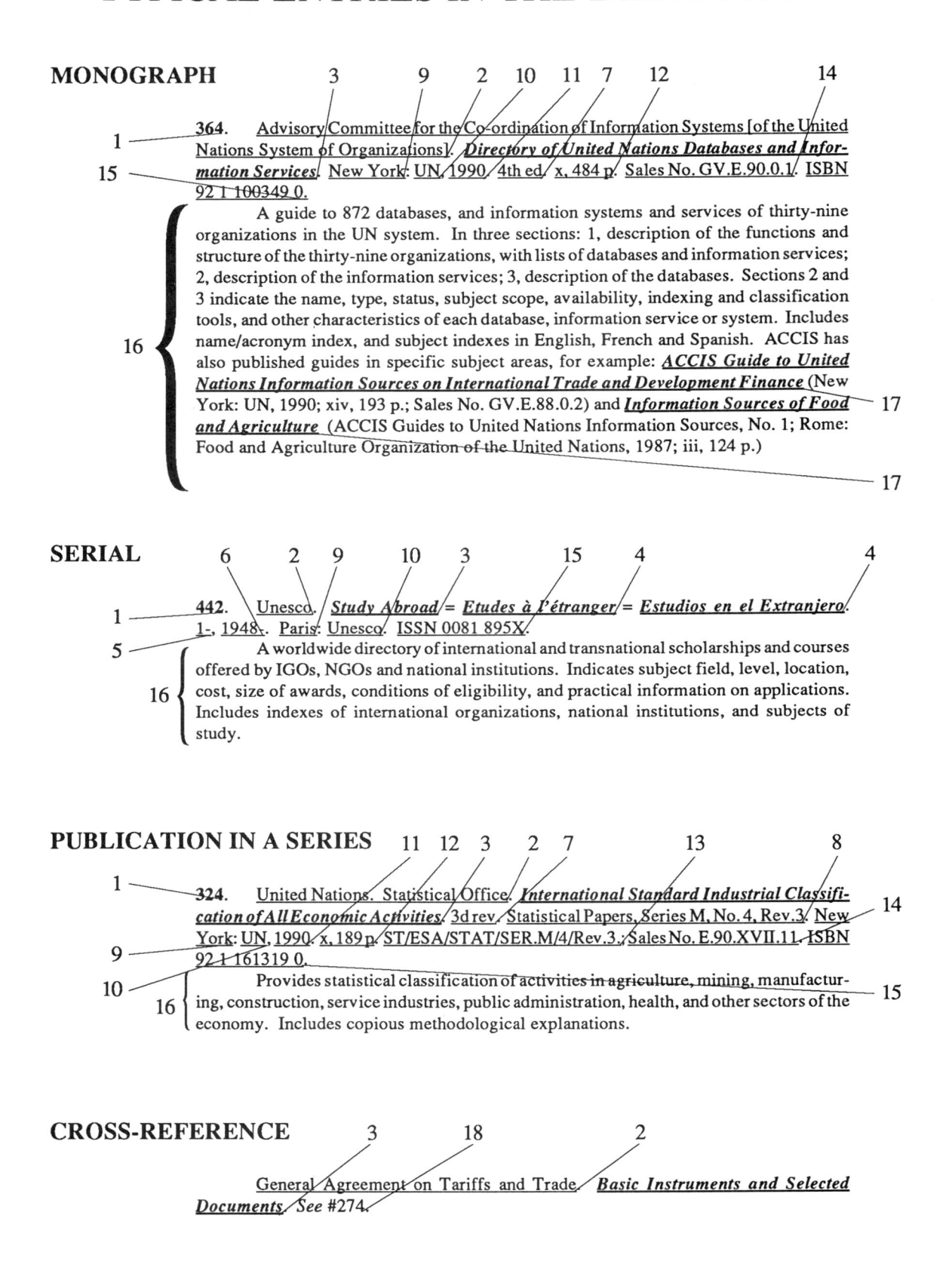

MONOGRAPH 3 9 2 10 11 7 12 14

1 — 364. Advisory Committee for the Co-ordination of Information Systems [of the United Nations System of Organizations]. *Directory of United Nations Databases and Information Services*. New York: UN, 1990. 4th ed. x, 484 p. Sales No. GV.E.90.0.1. ISBN 92 1 100349 0.

15

16 {
A guide to 872 databases, and information systems and services of thirty-nine organizations in the UN system. In three sections: 1, description of the functions and structure of the thirty-nine organizations, with lists of databases and information services; 2, description of the information services; 3, description of the databases. Sections 2 and 3 indicate the name, type, status, subject scope, availability, indexing and classification tools, and other characteristics of each database, information service or system. Includes name/acronym index, and subject indexes in English, French and Spanish. ACCIS has also published guides in specific subject areas, for example: *ACCIS Guide to United Nations Information Sources on International Trade and Development Finance* (New York: UN, 1990; xiv, 193 p.; Sales No. GV.E.88.0.2) and *Information Sources of Food and Agriculture* (ACCIS Guides to United Nations Information Sources, No. 1; Rome: Food and Agriculture Organization of the United Nations, 1987; iii, 124 p.)
— 17

— 17

SERIAL 6 2 9 10 3 15 4 4

1 — 442. Unesco. *Study Abroad* = *Etudes à l'étranger* = *Estudios en el Extranjero*. 1-, 1948-. Paris: Unesco. ISSN 0081 895X.

5

16 {
A worldwide directory of international and transnational scholarships and courses offered by IGOs, NGOs and national institutions. Indicates subject field, level, location, cost, size of awards, conditions of eligibility, and practical information on applications. Includes indexes of international organizations, national institutions, and subjects of study.

PUBLICATION IN A SERIES 11 12 3 2 7 13 8

1 — 324. United Nations. Statistical Office. *International Standard Industrial Classification of All Economic Activities*. 3d rev. Statistical Papers, Series M, No. 4, Rev.3. New York: UN, 1990. x, 189 p. ST/ESA/STAT/SER.M/4/Rev.3. Sales No. E.90.XVII.11. ISBN 92 1 161319 0.
— 14

9

10

16 {
Provides statistical classification of activities in agriculture, mining, manufacturing, construction, service industries, public administration, health, and other sectors of the economy. Includes copious methodological explanations.
— 15

CROSS-REFERENCE 3 18 2

General Agreement on Tariffs and Trade. *Basic Instruments and Selected Documents*. See #274.

EXPLANATION OF ELEMENTS OF DESCRIPTION

1. Entry number
2. Corporate author (author organization) or personal author
3. Primary title
4. Titles in additional languages
5. Beginning issue or volume number
6. Beginning date or year of coverage
7. Edition statement
8. Series statement
9. Place of publication
10. Publisher
11. Date of publication
12. Pagination
13. United Nations document series symbol
14. United Nations publication sales number
15. ISBN (International Standard Book Number) or ISSN (International Standard Serial Number)
16. Annotation
17. Reference to additional titles (not described in the Directory)
18. References to [another] entry in the Directory

ABBREVIATIONS AND ACRONYMS

ACC	Administrative Committee on Co-ordination (of the United Nations System of Organizations)
ACCIS	Advisory Committee for the Co-ordination of Information Systems (of the United Nations System of Organizations) (formerly IOB)
AGRIS	International Information System for the Agricultural Sciences and Technology (FAO)
ATAS	Advance Technology Alert System (UN)
CELADE	Centro Latinoamericano de Demografía (Latin American Demographic Centre (ECLAC)
EC	European Community (Communities)
ECA	Economic Commission for Africa (UN)
ECE	Economic Commission for Europe (UN)
ECLA(C)	Economic Commission for Latin America (and the Caribbean) (UN)
ECOSOC	Economic and Social Council (UN)
ESCAP	Economic and Social Commission for Asia and the Pacific (UN)
FAO	Food and Agriculture Organization of the United Nations
GA	General Assembly (UN)
GATT	General Agreement on Tariffs and Trade
GDP	Gross domestic product
GEMS	Global Environment Monitoring System (UNEP)
GNP	Gross national product
IAEA	International Atomic Energy Agency
IBRD	International Bank for Reconstruction and Development (World Bank)
ICAO	International Civil Aviation Organization
ICJ	International Court of Justice (UN)
ICSID	International Centre for Settlement of Investment Disputes
IDA	International Development Association
IDRC	International Development Research Centre (Canada)
ICSID	International Centre for Settlement of Investment Disputes
IFAD	International Fund for Agricultural Development

IFC	International Finance Corporation
IGO	International intergovernmental organization
ILC	International Law Commission (UN)
ILO	International Labour Organisation; International Labour Office
IMF	International Monetary Fund
IMCO	Inter-Governmental Maritime Consultative Organization (now IMO)
IMO	International Maritime Organization (formerly IMCO)
INFOTERRA	International Referral System for Sources of Environmental Information (UNEP)
INIS	International Nuclear Information System (IAEA)
IOB	Inter-Organization Board for Information Systems (of the United Nations System of Organizations) (now ACCIS)
IPDC	Intergovernmental Programme for the Development of Communication Unesco)
IRO	International Refugee Organization
ISBN	International Standard Book Number
ISSN	International Standard Serial Number
ITC	International Trade Centre (UNCTAD/GATT)
ITU	International Telecommunication Union
JIU	Joint Inspection Unit (of the United Nations System of Organizations)
MIGA	Multilateral Investment Guarantee Agency
NGO	Non-governmental organization
OAS	Organization of American States
ODA	Official development assistance
OECD	Organisation for Economic Co-operation and Development
PAHO	Pan American Health Organization
PICAO	Provisional International Civil Aviation Organization
PAIS	Public Affairs Information Service
RAMP	Records and Archives Management Programme (Unesco)
TNC	Transnational corporation
UN	United Nations
UNA-USA	United Nations Association of the United States of America
UNBIS	United Nations Bibliographic Information System
UNCHC	United Nations Centre for Human Settlements (Habitat)
UNCITRAL	United Nations Commission on International Trade Law
UNCTAD	United Nations Conference on Trade and Development

UNCTC	United Nations Centre on Transnational Corporations
"UNDI"	*United Nations Documents Index*
UNDP	United Nations Development Programme
UNDRO	Office of the United Nations Disaster Relief Co-ordinator
UNEP	United Nations Environment Programme
Unesco	United Nations Educational, Scientific and Cultural Organization
UNFPA	United Nations Population Fund (former name: United Nations Fund for Population Activities)
UNHCR	Office of the United Nations High Commissioner for Refugees
UNICEF	United Nations Children's Fund (former name: United Nations International Children's Emergency Fund)
UNICRI	United Nations Interregional Crime and Justice Research Institute (formerly UNSDRI)
UNIDIR	United Nations Institute for Disarmament Research
UNIDO	United Nations Industrial Development Organization
UNISIST	World Information System for Science and Technology (Unesco)
UNITAR	United Nations Institute for Training and Research
UNOG	United Nations Office at Geneva
UNRISD	United Nations Research Institute for Social Development
UNRRA	United Nations Relief and Rehabilitation Administration
UNSDRI	United Nations Social Defence Research Institute (now UNICRI)
UNU	United Nations University
UPU	Universal Postal Union
WHO	World Health Organization
WIPO	World Intellectual Property Organization
WMO	World Meteorological Organization
World Bank	International Bank for Reconstruction and Development and International Development Association (joint name)
World Bank Group	International Bank for Reconstruction and Development, International Development Association, and International Finance Corporation
World Court	International Court of Justice (UN)

INTRODUCTION *

There is an organic relationship between international governmental organizations (IGOs) -- including those in the United Nations system -- and the source material they produce. Many documents and publications are mandated by a given agency; for example, the Security Council and other organs of the UN submit annual and special reports to the General Assembly in accordance with Article 15 of the Charter. Conference proceedings and statistical compilations appear as a result of an agency's activities. Program and budget documents govern the operations of the agency. A direct relationship exists also between teachers and researchers on multilateral issues, and IGOs -- including the UN system -- and their documentation. Any researcher exploring the future shape of an IGO must look at what has been recommended in the past and how responsive that IGO has been to those recommendations. For example, the basis for a UN peace and security role must be sought in the reports and documents of past committees and past Security Council meetings. Efforts to reform the expanding institutional structure monitoring human rights around the world must examine the documentation, including the procedures established by various UN and treaty-based bodies. An examination of the meaning and intent of a provision of the 1967 Outer Space Treaty (formally known as the Treaty on Principles Governing the Activities of States in the Exploration and Peaceful Uses of Outer Space) requires a review of documents and proceedings of both the Committee on the Peaceful Uses of Outer Space and the appropriate committee of the General Assembly. This *Directory* facilitates the search for the right document, especially if the document is more than a year or two old.

PUBLICATION VERSUS DOCUMENT

Like other IGOs, agencies in the UN system** distinguish between *documents* and *publications*, although the line between the two categories is often blurred. There are a number of definitions and characterizations of the two categories of material. According to the UN:

> The term "document" is used to designate written material officially issued under a United Nations document symbol ... regardless of the form of reproduction. In practice, the term is applied mainly to material offset from typescript and issued under a masthead ... . Most documents are intended to serve as a basis for discussion at meetings of United Nations bodies.[1]

---

* This Introduction is based on Peter I. Hajnal's "Access to Information from International Intergovernmental Organizations," in *Public Access to Government Information: Issues, Trends, and Strategies*, 2d ed., edited by Peter Hernon and Charles R. McClure (Norwood, N. J.: Ablex, 1988), 411-48; and his "Collection Development," in *International Information: Documents, Publications and Information Systems of International Governmental Organizations*, edited by Peter I. Hajnal (Englewood, Co.: Libraries Unlimited, 1988), 79-118. Used by permission of Ablex Publishing Corporation and Libraries Unlimited.

** See Figure 1 for an organization chart of the UN system and Figure 2 for names, dates of establishment and headquarters addresses of the organizations.

Documents, understood in this sense, include reports, memoranda, notes, analyses, studies, surveys, replies to questionnaires, working documents, communications, and addenda, corrigenda and revisions.[2] The UN further states:

> The term "United Nations publication" means any written material which is issued by or for the United Nations to the general public, normally under an authorization of the [UN] Publications Board. Such publications, which are usually offered for sale, include major studies, reports, statistical compilations and the proceedings of certain conferences, seminars and symposia, as well as such serial publications as yearbooks, *Official Records* of the principal organs of the United Nations, the United Nations *Treaty Series* and technical journals and bulletins ... [and publications issued by] the Department of Public Information ... designed to further public understanding of the work and purposes of the United Nations.[3]

One would wish for the simplification or, better yet, the disappearance of such unclear distinctions. A prominent writer on official publishing states sensibly that "in plain language the essence of a publication is whether it achieves a public circulation, irrespective of its internal classification or the form in which it is produced."[4]

In practical terms, however, the distinction remains important. It has implications for the originating organizations (in terms of publication programs, budget, production responsibilities, and distribution policies and practices), for libraries (in the areas of bibliographic control, collection development and reference work), and, most important, for the availability and potential use of the material.

Certain organizations in the UN system make their publications widely available but keep most of their documents internal. Some bibliographic tools cover both documents and publications, for example, the *UNDOC: Current Index, United Nations Documents Index*, and the *Unesco List of Documents and Publications*, while others, such as the World Bank's *Index of Publications*, cover publications only, and still others cover documents only.

In the hope of further clarifying the distinction between document and publication, this definition is offered:

> **Documents** are official records of meetings of IGOs and other material issued in the exercise of their functions, while **publications** are destined to inform the public about the particular organization and its activities. Documents are usually intended primarily or exclusively as working tools for internal use, although many documents are of interest to outside users and may reach a wider audience; publications are intended for wider distribution in the first place. Documents are often free of charge, while publications may be either free or priced. Documents are usually mimeographed, offset, or word-processed; publications are often printed. Documents may reappear as publications (unchanged or with modifications) if the issuing IGO does not consider them confidential and perceives a wider interest in them.[5]

(Continued on page xviii)

FIGURE 1
ORGANIZATION CHART OF
THE UNITED NATIONS DEPARTMENT OF PUBLIC INFORMATION
Courtesy of United Nations Art Department, Graphic Presentation Unit

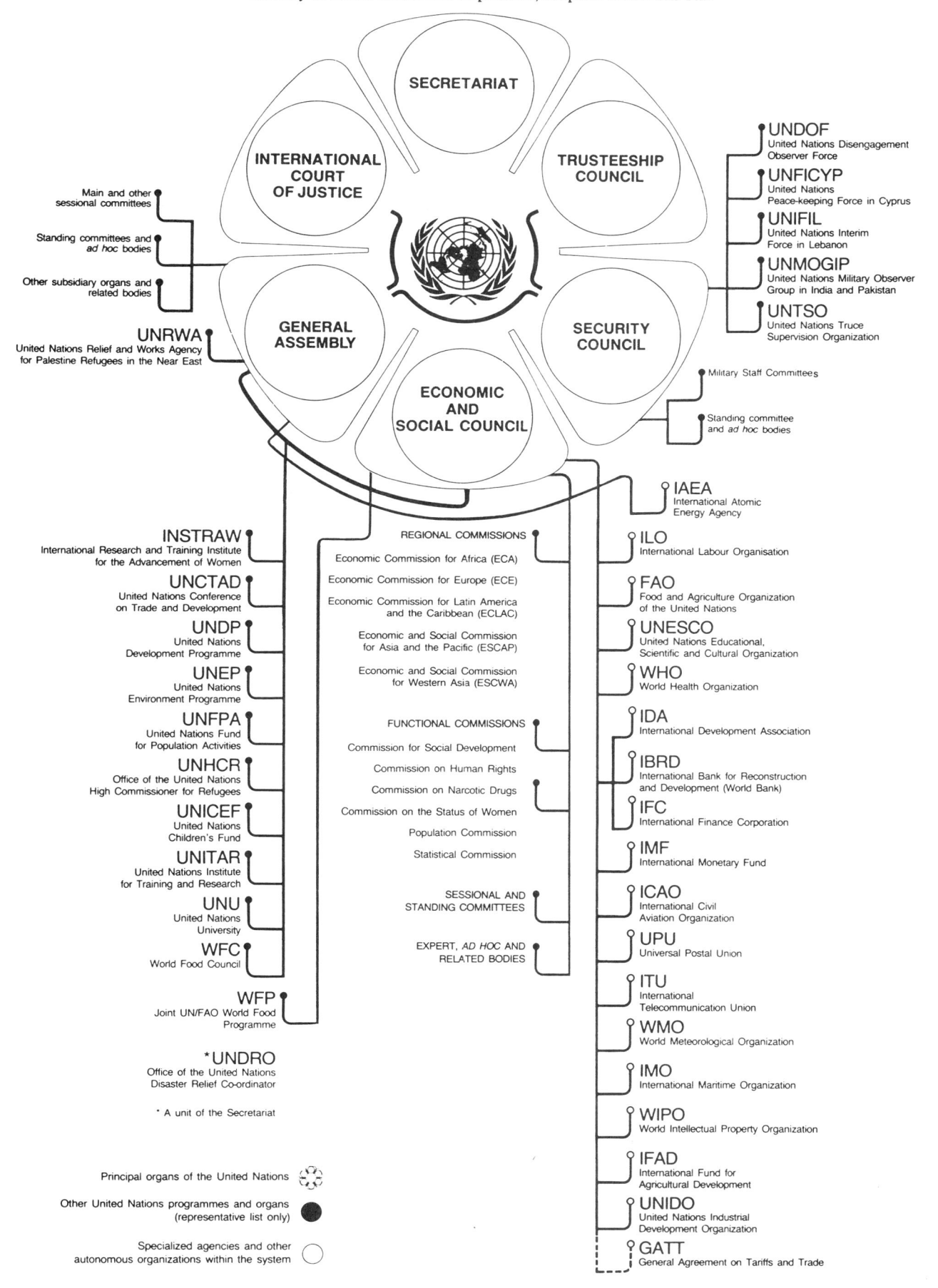

Principal organs of the United Nations:
- SECRETARIAT
- INTERNATIONAL COURT OF JUSTICE
- TRUSTEESHIP COUNCIL
- GENERAL ASSEMBLY
- SECURITY COUNCIL
- ECONOMIC AND SOCIAL COUNCIL

General Assembly related bodies:
- Main and other sessional committees
- Standing committees and *ad hoc* bodies
- Other subsidiary organs and related bodies
- UNRWA — United Nations Relief and Works Agency for Palestine Refugees in the Near East

Security Council related:
- UNDOF — United Nations Disengagement Observer Force
- UNFICYP — United Nations Peace-keeping Force in Cyprus
- UNIFIL — United Nations Interim Force in Lebanon
- UNMOGIP — United Nations Military Observer Group in India and Pakistan
- UNTSO — United Nations Truce Supervision Organization
- Military Staff Committees
- Standing committee and *ad hoc* bodies

Other United Nations programmes and organs (representative list only):
- INSTRAW — International Research and Training Institute for the Advancement of Women
- UNCTAD — United Nations Conference on Trade and Development
- UNDP — United Nations Development Programme
- UNEP — United Nations Environment Programme
- UNFPA — United Nations Fund for Population Activities
- UNHCR — Office of the United Nations High Commissioner for Refugees
- UNICEF — United Nations Children's Fund
- UNITAR — United Nations Institute for Training and Research
- UNU — United Nations University
- WFC — World Food Council
- WFP — Joint UN/FAO World Food Programme
- *UNDRO — Office of the United Nations Disaster Relief Co-ordinator

* A unit of the Secretariat

Economic and Social Council:

REGIONAL COMMISSIONS
- Economic Commission for Africa (ECA)
- Economic Commission for Europe (ECE)
- Economic Commission for Latin America and the Caribbean (ECLAC)
- Economic and Social Commission for Asia and the Pacific (ESCAP)
- Economic and Social Commission for Western Asia (ESCWA)

FUNCTIONAL COMMISSIONS
- Commission for Social Development
- Commission on Human Rights
- Commission on Narcotic Drugs
- Commission on the Status of Women
- Population Commission
- Statistical Commission

SESSIONAL AND STANDING COMMITTEES

EXPERT, AD HOC AND RELATED BODIES

Specialized agencies and other autonomous organizations within the system:
- IAEA — International Atomic Energy Agency
- ILO — International Labour Organisation
- FAO — Food and Agriculture Organization of the United Nations
- UNESCO — United Nations Educational, Scientific and Cultural Organization
- WHO — World Health Organization
- IDA — International Development Association
- IBRD — International Bank for Reconstruction and Development (World Bank)
- IFC — International Finance Corporation
- IMF — International Monetary Fund
- ICAO — International Civil Aviation Organization
- UPU — Universal Postal Union
- ITU — International Telecommunication Union
- WMO — World Meteorological Organization
- IMO — International Maritime Organization
- WIPO — World Intellectual Property Organization
- IFAD — International Fund for Agricultural Development
- UNIDO — United Nations Industrial Development Organization
- GATT — General Agreement on Tariffs and Trade

FIGURE 2
THE UNITED NATIONS SYSTEM OF ORGANIZATIONS

(A)   1. United Nations (UN). Established in 1945. Headquarters: New York, NY 10017, U.S.A.

(B)   *Specialized Agencies*

2. Food and Agriculture Organization of the United Nations (FAO). Established in 1945. Headquarters: Via delle Terme di Caracalla, 00100 Rome, Italy

3. International Civil Aviation Organization (ICAO). Established in 1947. Headquarters: 1000 Sherbrooke Street West, Montreal, Quebec H3A 2R2, Canada

4. International Fund for Agricultural Development (IFAD). Established in 1977. Headquarters: Via del Serafico, 107, 00142 Rome, Italy

5. International Labour Organisation (ILO). Established in 1919; became a specialized agency in 1946. Headquarters: 4, route des Morillons, CH-1211 Geneva 22, Switzerland

6. International Maritime Organization (IMO). Established in 1958 as Inter-Governmental Maritime Consultative Organization (IMCO). Headquarters: 4 Albert Embankment, London SE1 7SR, United Kingdom

7. International Monetary Fund (IMF). Established in 1945. Headquarters: 700 19th Street N.W., Washington, D.C. 20431, U.S.A.

8. International Refugee Organization (IRO). Established in 1948; ceased operations in 1952. Headquarters were in Geneva

9. International Telecommunication Union (ITU). Established in 1865 as International Telegraph Union; became a specialized agency in 1947. Headquarters: Place des Nations, CH-1211 Geneva 20, Switzerland

10. United Nations Educational, Scientific and Cultural Organization (Unesco). Established in 1946. Headquarters: 7, place de Fontenoy, 75007 Paris, France

11. United Nations Industrial Development Organization (UNIDO). Established in 1967; became a specialized agency in 1986. Headquarters: Vienna International Centre, A-1400 Vienna, Austria

THE UNITED NATIONS SYSTEM OF ORGANIZATIONS (Continued)

12. Universal Postal Union (UPU). Established in 1875; became a specialized agency in 1948. Headquarters: Case Postale, CH-3000 Berne 15, Switzerland

World Bank Group:

13. International Bank for Reconstruction and Development (IBRD). Established in 1945

14. International Development Association (IDA). Established in 1960

The IBRD and the IDA are often referred to jointly as the World Bank

15. International Finance Corporation (IFC). Established in 1956

16. Multilateral Investment Guarantee Agency (MIGA). Established in 1988 as the fourth body of the World Bank Group, MIGA is not formally a specialized agency

World Bank Group headquarters: 1818 H Street N.W., Washington, D.C. 20433, U.S.A.

17. World Health Organization (WHO). Established in 1948. Headquarters: 20, avenue Appia, CH-1211 Geneva 27, Switzerland

18. World Intellectual Property Organization (WIPO). Had its origins in the 1883 Paris Convention for the Protection of Industrial Property and the 1886 Berne Convention for the Protection of Literary and Artistic Works; established as WIPO in 1970; became a specialized agency in 1974. Headquarters: 34, chemin des Colombettes, CH-1211 Geneva 20, Switzerland

19. World Meteorological Organization (WMO). Had its origin in the International Meteorological Organization (which was established in 1878); established as WMO, a specialized agency, in 1950. Headquarters: 41, avenue Giuseppe-Motta, CH-1211 Geneva 20, Switzerland

(C) *Other Institutions in the United Nations System of Organizations*

20. General Agreement on Tariffs and Trade (GATT). In force since 1948; administered by a permanent secretariat. Headquarters: Centre William Rappard, 154, rue de Lausanne, CH-1211 Geneva 21, Switzerland

21. International Atomic Energy Agency (IAEA). Established in 1957. Headquarters: Vienna International Centre, A-1400 Vienna, Austria

VOLUME, SUBJECT MATTER AND PHYSICAL FORM OF THE DOCUMENTATION

Notable among prolific publishers and originators of documents are the UN and the major specialized agencies in the UN system -- Unesco, ILO, FAO, the World Bank and to a smaller extent, WHO and IMF. In 1979 -- the latest year for which comparative figures are available -- the New York and Geneva offices of the UN produced 907,650 pages of material in the organization's six official languages: English, French, Spanish, Russian, Chinese, and Arabic. (Most publications and documents appear in English, followed by French and Spanish; a much smaller number are produced in the other official languages of the UN.) The total number of page impressions for all copies of all UN editions was 930,734,945.[6] In 1985, the total number of page impressions for UN documents and publications was 812,061,203.[7] Small wonder that the UN system itself has been concerned with the enormous volume of its documents and publications. One of the more forceful statements on this subject was made in a report of the Joint Inspection Unit:

> An excessive volume of documentation is a hindrance. It tends to obscure issues by diverting attention from essentials, and it complicates the work of intergovernmental and other meetings. At the same time, it greatly overburdens available staff resources and can cause serious delays in processing and delivery of documents. The efficiency and cost-effectiveness of the United Nations system would greatly improve if its volume of documents could be reduced, their quality were improved and they were issued on time.[8]

The report adds that "intergovernmental bodies in almost all organizations have for decades called for a reduction of documentation, but with little effect."[9] A 1984 report of the Joint Inspection Unit shows that in 1981 the UN system of organizations produced 14,178,100 copies of 3,747 publications (no figures are given for documents).[10]

Brian Urquhart has made this comment on excessive UN documentation:

> The UN has a seemingly limitless capacity to produce often lengthy documents in six languages and in immense quantities. Efforts to eliminate the document usually provoke a group of governments to demand its continued existence, and other governments will probably support them in case they wish to exert a similar privilege in the future. These reams of battleship-grey prose are a heavy burden.[11]

The 1986 report of the UN Group of 18 -- formally called Group of High-level Intergovernmental Experts to Review the Efficiency of the Administrative and Financial Functioning of the United Nations -- observes that "the volume of documentation, both in relation to conferences and meetings as well as in more general terms, has increased considerably and has, to some extent, surpassed the limit of what can be studied and constructively used by Member States."[12] Notable among the Group's recommendations are Recommendation 7, aimed at the curtailment of documentation and Recommendation 8(3)(e) to reduce the number of reports and to avoid duplication of documentation.[13] The Group of 18 report and its recommendations were endorsed with some qualifications by the General Assembly in its resolution A/RES/41/213 of 19 December 1986.

In response, the UN has introduced some measures to curtail its publications program:

- There is less external printing than before; for example, the *Report on the World Social Situation* is now printed by the UN itself. On the other hand, the most recent (1985) edition of the major annual publication, *Yearbook of the United Nations*, was published for the UN by Nijhoff; the UN hopes that the resulting larger print run will generate additional income
- Publication of some issues of certain periodicals has been deferred
- The frequency of some periodicals has been reduced; for example, the *UN Chronicle* and *UNDOC* are now published four instead of eleven times a year
- The 1984 and subsequent annual cumulations of *UNDOC* are distributed in microfiche instead of paper copy
- Rented warehouse space in New York for UN publications and documents has been liquidated, resulting in reduced storage space, reduced print runs, and therefore, reduced stocks of back titles
- The length of meetings of certain UN bodies has been curtailed, presumably resulting in reduced documentation
- Certain UN organs are no longer entitled to verbatim records of their meetings and may issue summary records only; still other bodies have ceased to have published meeting records.[14]

Some savings have been achieved, but while many cutbacks have been salutary, others have proved to be false economies (for example, the temporary suspension of the summary records of subsidiary organs of the UN Economic and Social Council). Will continued financial difficulties and increased computerization achieve what all the proposals of the IGOs and their critics have failed to achieve: a substantial reduction of the volume of documents and publications?

Cutbacks notwithstanding, publications and documents of the UN system deal with a vast range of subjects, from atomic energy to psychotropic substances, from culture to public health, from international trade to weather reporting. In the various subject fields, IGO material includes basic documents, official records of meetings, regular activity reports, special reports and studies, conference proceedings, statistical publications, bibliographies, directories and other reference works, and public information material. As to physical form, IGO material includes printed and "near-print" items, microform, sound recordings, slides, films and video programs, and computerized information systems and their products.

DISTRIBUTION POLICIES AND PRACTICES OF ORGANIZATIONS OF THE UN SYSTEM

The UN classifies its material in the following major categories:

- *General* distribution documents (basic documents, final meeting records, resolutions, and other decisions of main organs, or studies and reports) receive the widest circulation

- *Limited* distribution documents (for example, draft reports and draft resolutions or papers relating to agenda items of meetings) are intended for governments and other recipients whom the UN considers to be interested in the work of the organ concerned. Actual interest in these documents is often wider. The contents of some limited distribution material eventually find their way into general distribution documents such as the final report of the body in which they were discussed. Another way, for libraries, of obtaining limited distribution documents is to subscribe to the Readex microfiche (from 1946 to 1981, microprint or microfiche) edition of *United Nations Documents and Publications*, which includes the *limited* category (it should be noted, however, that Secretariat documents of all distribution categories were excluded from the microprint edition, *Mimeographed and Printed Documents*). Limited distribution documents bear the letter *L* before the serial number in the document series symbol; for example, E/1984/C.4/L.1

- *Restricted* distribution is a designation usually given to documents and meeting records on the basis of confidentiality. The distribution of such documents and records is determined by the originating body. Having met certain conditions, such as the passage of time, many restricted distribution documents are subsequently declassified. Declassification is done routinely in the case of restricted documents of the UN Economic Commission for Europe. Derestricted project reports of the UN Development Programme (UNDP) were formerly listed regularly, but such lists are no longer issued. For other organs of the UN, declassification is less systematic and inadequately documented. The UN Library has a mandate to prepare an annual list of *restricted* series symbols of documents issued at least five years previously and held by the Library; these lists are then reviewed by the Executive Office of the Secretary-General, circulated to the originating office, and "in the absence of other instructions ... declassified by a specific date."[15] Derestricted documents are difficult to obtain because of small stocks, except for the declassified project reports of UNDP marketed by University Microfilms. Restricted distribution documents bear the letter *R* before the serial number in the document series symbol

- In addition to general, limited and restricted distribution categories, the UN employs some other designations: for example, *provisional* applies to meeting records issued first to participants of the meetings. For a number of years, the UN has offered for sale provisional meeting records of the General Assembly and the Security Council -- a useful step, because some meeting records may take several years to appear in final form

- Conference room papers and working papers "are not official documents but informal papers ... of concern primarily to the members of [a UN] organ." They bear the identifying letters *CRP* or *WP* before the serial number of the symbol[16]
- The UN, like many other organizations, holds some highly confidential material, often in its Archives. There is a general restriction period of twenty years for access to records in the Archives; some records, though, are subject to special rules and require approval by the office of the Secretary-General before access can be given.[17]

The UN maintains official distribution lists for its documents, meeting records, *Official Records*, and publications distributed free of charge. External distribution lists cover ministries, embassies, and other governmental bodies; NGOs which enjoy consultative status with the UN; specialized agencies and other IGOs; offices of the UN outside New York City; UN information centers; and depository libraries. Internal lists -- for distribution of material at UN headquarters in New York -- cover permanent missions of member states to the UN; permanent observers; the press; the UN Secretariat; offices servicing meetings and conferences; and the UN Sales Section.[18]

Other IGOs employ somewhat similar but often less clearly defined distribution categories. Several organizations in the UN system are more restrictive than the UN in making their source material available to outsiders. Unesco, for example, for many years made its publications but not its documents widely available; in 1983 it began making certain types of its documents more easily available on request, free of charge, while other documents are offered for purchase on microfiche. The World Bank makes a sharp distinction between its documents and publications for distribution purposes; its free and priced publications are easy to obtain, but its documents as a rule are inaccessible to most outsiders.

DEPOSITORY LIBRARIES

Several organizations of the UN family maintain a system of depository libraries throughout the world. The UN has designated over 300 depositories. These depositories (often national libraries and university or other large research libraries) receive publications and general distribution documents in the official language of their choice. Deposit may be partial or full; the latter includes mimeographed documents. Depository libraries "are expected to place the material received in the care of qualified library staff, to keep it in good order and to make it accessible to the public, free of charge, at reasonable hours."[19] In addition to serving users on library premises, many depositories lend material and some provide interlibrary loan service. Since 1 January 1975, most UN depositories have been required to pay an annual contribution, now amounting to U.S. $960 for full depositories and $600 for partial depositories in developed countries, and $300 for full depositories and $200 for partial depositories in developing countries. This expenditure is worthwhile in monetary terms alone because the cost of all sales items, including official records, would otherwise be U.S. $5,922 as of 1985.[20] Several categories of material are not included in the deposit: most publications of the International Court of Justice, UNICEF, the United Nations Institute for Training and Research, the United Nations Fund for Population Activities, the United Nations Environment Programme, the United Nations Institute of Disarmament Research, the United Nations International Training and Research Institute for Women, the United Nations University, and certain other types of documents and publications.[21] The International Court of Justice and the United Nations University have set up their own depository networks. The United Nations Industrial Development Organization, formerly a special body within the UN but since 1986 an autonomous specialized agency, still includes its documents and publications, at this writing, in the UN depository package. The most recent worldwide listing of UN depository libraries (and UN information centers) is the *List of Depository Libraries Receiving United Nations Material*, issued on 7 July 1987. Similar information may be found in *Disarmament Fact Sheet* no. 49, issued in December 1986 by the UN's Department for Disarmament Affairs.[22]

Unesco, too, maintains a worldwide system of depository libraries. It had 379 depositories in 1983. These fell into one of three categories: "Those that receive one or more copies of all publications (including periodicals) and certain types of documents; those that receive publications (including periodicals) but no documents; and those that receive periodicals only but have the right to select other free publications as announced by Unesco."[23] Among other organizations of the UN family that have worldwide systems of depositories are the Food and Agriculture Organization of the United Nations (which asks its depositories to maintain a permanent display of FAO publications), GATT, ICAO, WHO, and WIPO.

Some organizations have a more limited system of depository libraries. The World Bank maintained for many years a depository system in developing countries only.[24] Recently, the Bank extended the network by allowing one library in each member state to apply for depository status in order to provide free public access to its published information. The Bank requires each depository library to have a public reading room and adequate space to shelve and maintain some 300 new Bank publications issued each year; have on staff at least one trained librarian responsible for the collection of World Bank publications; place and maintain these publications under bibliographic control (including accessioning, cataloging, classifying, and shelving to ensure retrieval for library users); be open to the public during normal business hours and allow use of the collection without charge; show evidence of the types and number of clients served; and circulate accession or current-acquisition lists regularly to clients.[25] Other agencies -- for example, the IMF -- have not established depository systems.

Depository libraries constitute an important means whereby organizations in the UN system make their documents and publications widely available. These depositories have improved access to the literature in direct proportion to available staff and other resources, efficient organization of the material, and competent reference service.

BIBLIOGRAPHIC TOOLS

Bibliographic tools covering sources issued by the UN system of organizations are of various types. Sales catalogs, issued by most of the organizations to cover their own publications differ in scope, completeness, frequency, and timeliness, but they generally supply sufficient information for ordering purposes; in some cases, they are also a good source of brief information about the structure and major activities of the agencies concerned. The *United Nations Publications Catalogue*, the World Bank's *Index of Publications*, the *ILO Catalogue of Publications in Print*, and the Unesco *Publications Catalogue* are examples of this type of source. These mostly annual or biennial catalogs are in many cases kept up-to-date by monthly or occasional current-awareness bulletins or leaflets. Somewhat similar in nature are general and specialized listings issued by sales outlets for IGO material (for example, Kraus/UNIPUB in the United States and Renouf in Canada).

The primary purpose of bibliographies, indexes, and abstracts -- whether or not produced by the IGOs themselves -- is to facilitate bibliographic control and research rather than acquisition. Several professional and technical journals list or review IGO documents and publications. Kraus/UNIPUB's quarterly *International Bibliography: Publications of Intergovernmental Organizations* is a useful, though necessarily selective current-awareness service. *Government Publications Review* carries an annual listing of notable documents as well as an excellent current-awareness column, "International Organization News," by Robert W. Schaaf. *Documents to the People*, the quarterly newsletter of the Government Documents Round Table of the American Library Association, has a regular column entitled "International Documents Roundup." *United Nations Documentation News*, issued at irregular intervals by the Dag Hammarskjöld Library, is an informative source of current news and bibliographic notices about UN material. Other journals, such as *Government Information Quarterly* and *Serials Review*, carry articles, reviews, and bibliographic notices about IGO literature from time to time.

Periodicals published by the UN system, such as the *UN Chronicle*, ILO's *International Labour Review*, and the *WHO Chronicle*, regularly publish lists of recent material issued by the respective agencies. Many specialized journals published by professional associations or academic or commercial publishers also carry notices of important IGO publications in their subject fields. Informal direct contact with IGOs themselves or with professional organizations concerned with IGO activities is another useful source of information and acquisition.

All possible sources, whether or not primarily bibliographic in nature, should be considered as aids to bibliographic and physical access to IGO material. Ideally, IGOs themselves should "recognize that easy access, both physical and intellectual, to the information content of their documentation is as important as their original conception, preparation and publication".[26] It often remains, however, for the readers and researchers themselves, assisted by competent reference librarians, to gain the most important, intellectual access to IGO documents and publications.

CONCLUSIONS AND RECOMMENDATIONS

The programs of the UN system of organizations give rise to a vast corpus of documents and publications comprising an important source of research data and practical information. This literature reflects the complexity of the organizations that produce it. The types, quantity, and physical forms of the material pose a challenge to all of its users.

Equally essential for access are more responsive distribution policies and practices on the part of IGOs themselves. IGOs, quite legitimately, give preferential service to the primary users of their documents and publications -- the governments of their member states, officers of their own agencies and other IGOs, and a few other select groups. This is natural, for "the current records of an [international governmental] agency were created, received and maintained by the agency not primarily to facilitate research by non-staff members, but rather to conduct the business of the agency."[27] External constituencies are less well served, especially when it comes to access to documents as contrasted with publications. Part of the problem lies in the nature of accountability; even national governments seem at times far removed from the people to whom they are accountable. IGOs are accountable only to the governments of their member states, and are therefore still further removed from the public which is the end-user of their source material.[28]

Some promising recent developments, however, show increased IGO responsiveness to the needs of the public. One example of this is the current-awareness bulletin, *United Nations Documentation News*, referred to above and published by the UN since September 1981. Another example is the availability since 1983 of Unesco's nonrestricted documents and publications on microfiche from Unesco Microfiche Service through the Unesco Press.

The worldwide network of depositories has been extremely valuable for access to IGO literature, but some of its limitations must also be noted:

- Each IGO is responsible for the production and distribution of its own documents and publications, and decides autonomously whether or not to have a system of depositories. Some IGOs have established worldwide systems, while others have more limited systems and still others have no depository system at all. It would be desirable if at least all major IGOs had a worldwide system of depositories
- IGOs which have depository systems do not designate all their nonrestricted material for depository distribution; in fact, a good deal of the output is not sent to depositories. It is therefore desirable for depositories to obtain needed nondepository IGO items by purchase, gift, or exchange
- Most IGOs which have depository systems do not specify clearly the extent of the deposit. It would be useful if all such IGOs made clear to depositories the exact nature and extent of their entitlement
- As even the largest depository networks consist of no more than 300-400 libraries worldwide, it is clear that many nondepository libraries should acquire appropriate IGO material for the use of their clientele. This would complement the resources of depositories which are available to, and should be used by, a wider constituency than the institutions where the depositories are located.

Bibliographic control is an essential corollary of access to IGO material. It is indispensable both for the selection process and for the purposes of providing reference service using the documents and publications acquired. The scope, quality, and types of bibliographic tools vary greatly: they range from the general to the specific, from the inclusive to the limited, from sales catalogs to bibliographies and indexes, and from the IGOs' own products to items published commercially or academically. The fact that bibliographic control over IGO literature is uneven and often inadequate adversely affects access to such material.

In conclusion, a few recent trends of IGO publishing and documentation should be noted:
- External publishing and copublishing have been increasing, but may now be cut back, at least by the UN, due to budgetary pressures. Unesco and the World Bank are among the IGOs which use commercial publishers to an especially great extent. Jointly or externally published material is not always included in the IGOs' normal distribution packages or depository shipments; in such case, material must be bought separately on the commercial market
- IGOs increasingly produce their documents and publications in microform; other IGO material is produced and marketed in microform by commercial publishers. This type of material promotes access to IGO documents and publications because many libraries which do not have the resources to acquire large IGO collections in hard copy, or do not have the space to accommodate such collections may be able to acquire

microform sets. In addition to being a space-saver, microform can also be used to fill gaps in hard-copy holdings. But microform requires specialized handling and equipment. Microform may also present problems for some users

More and more IGOs are creating electronic databases. Most such databases are not yet available to the public, but an increasing number of them are -- online, or on magnetic tape, diskette or CD-ROM.

The challenges posed by the complexities of IGO documents and publications will be met successfully by researchers, librarians and other users of that material if they are aware of the context in which the documents and publications originate and of the issues involved in their distribution and acquisition.

NOTES

1. United Nations, Department of Conference Services, *United Nations Editorial Manual, Revised Text of Articles A to D* (New York: UN, 1985), 7. 5 March 1985; ST/DCS/5, part I.

2. *Ibid.*, 7-11.

3. *Ibid.*, 73.

4. J. J. Cherns, "Intergovernmental Organisations As Publishers," in *International Information: Documents, Publications, and Information Systems of International Governmental Organizations*, edited by Peter I. Hajnal (Englewood, Co.: Libraries Unlimited, 1988), 30.

5. *International Information: Documents, Publications and Information Systems of International Governmental Organizations*, edited by Peter I. Hajnal (Englewood, Co.: Libraries Unlimited, 1988), 81.

6. United Nations, Department of Conference Services, "United Nations Documentation," in *International Documents for the 80's: Their Role and Use*, edited by Theodore D. Dimitrov and Luciana Marulli-Koenig (Pleasantville, N.Y.: UNIFO Publishers, 1982), microfiche 3, p. 51.

7. Unpublished information from the UN Publications Board.

8. Joint Inspection Unit [of the United Nations System of Organizations], *Control and Limitation of Documentation in the United Nations System* (Geneva: JIU, December 1980), 1. JIU/REP/80/12.

9. *Ibid.*, 1-2.

10. Joint Inspection Unit [of the United Nations System of Organizations], *Publications Policy and Practice in the United Nations System* (Geneva: JIU, 1984; JIU/REP/84/5).

11. Brian Urquhart, *A Life in Peace and War* (New York: Harper & Row, 1987), 109.

12. United Nations, General Assembly, "Report of the Group of High-level Intergovernmental Experts to Review the Efficiency of the Administrative and Financial Functioning of the United Nations," *Official Records*, 41st sess., Supplement no. 49 (New York: UN, 1986), 1. A/41/49.

13. *Ibid.*, 6, 8.

14. United Nations, General Assembly, *Current Financial Crisis of the United Nations; Report of the Secretary-General* (New York: UN, 1986). 12 April 1986; A/40/1102 and *Corrigendum* (New York: UN, 1986). 17 April 1986; A/40/1102/Corr.2.

15. United Nations, Department of Conference Services, *United Nations Editorial Manual: A Compendium of Rules and Directives on United Nations Editorial Style, Publication Policies, Procedures and Practice* (New York: UN, 1983), 494. ST/DCS/2; S/N E.83.I.16.

16. *Ibid.*, 488.

17. Unesco, *Guide to the Archives*, 187; United Nations, Secretariat, *Administrative Instruction: The United Nations Archives* (New York: UN, 1984). 28 December 1984; ST/AI/326.

18. *United Nations Editorial Manual*, 489.

19. United Nations, Dag Hammarskjöld Library, *Instructions for Depository Libraries Receiving United Nations Material* (New York: UN, 1981), Annex I, 2. 9 January 1981; ST/LIB/13/Rev.4.

20. Unpublished information from the United Nations Sales Section, May 1986.

21. United Nations, *Instructions for Depository Libraries*, 3-4 and *Corrigendum 2* (New York: UN, 1986). 7 March 1986; ST/LIB/13/Rev.4 and ST/LIB/13/Rev.4/Corr.2.

22. United Nations, Secretariat, *List of Depository Libraries Receiving United Nations Material* (New York: UN, 1987). 7 July 1987. ST/LIB/12/Rev.7. United Nations, Department for Disarmament Affairs, "List of Libraries and Information Centres Receiving United Nations Publications," *Disarmament Fact Sheet*, 49 (December 1986): 19-53.

23. Peter I. Hajnal, *Guide to Unesco* (London/Rome/New York: Oceana, 1983), 206.

24. Marko Zlatich, "Publications and Documentation Systems of the World Bank, the International Development Association and the International Finance Corporation," *International Documents for the 80's: Their Role and Use*, microfiche 3 p. 75.

25. World Bank, Depository Library Program, *Directory of Libraries*, 2d ed. (Washington, D.C.: World Bank, 1990).

26. Michael Hopkins, "The Documentation of Intergovernmental Organizations: A Critical Survey of Supply-and-Demand Situations in the United Kingdom," *International Social Science Journal* 32, no. 2 (1980): 381.

27. F. B. Evans, "Access to Archives of United Nations Organizations," *International Documents for the 80's: Their Role and Use*, microfiche 2, p. 69.

28. Peter I. Hajnal, "IGO Documents and Publications: Volume, Distribution, Recent Developments, and Sources of Information," *Government Publications Review* 9 (March/April 1982): 124.

SUBJECTS

STRUCTURAL AND INSTITUTIONAL ISSUES

1. Administrative Committee on Co-ordination [of the United Nations System of Organizations]. *Inventory of Arrangements for Programme Co-ordination in the United Nations System.* Geneva?: ACC, 1987. 157 p. ACC/1987/INF/1.
    Covers ninety-four formal arrangements for program coordination among organizations of the UN system, indicating for each the establishing authority, mandate, main areas of collaboration, and participating organizations. In three sections: 1, established subsidiary bodies of the Administrative Committee on Co-ordination (ACC consists of the UN Secretary-General and the executive heads of the specialized agencies); 2, other inter-organizational coordinating mechanisms reporting to the ACC; and 3, other inter-organizational coordinating arrangements. Excludes ACC itself and ACC's Organizational Committee.

    Administrative Committee on Co-ordination [of the United Nations System of Organizations]. Secretariat. *United Nations System of Organizations and Directory of Senior Officials, 1989/1990.* See #361.

2. Aga Khan, Sadruddin, and Maurice F. Strong. "United Nations Financial Emergency: Crisis and Opportunity." New York, August 1986. Unpublished. iv, 65, 2, 5, 2, 3 p.
    Assesses the UN financial emergency, and recommends short-term remedies and longer-term measures aimed at program consolidation and rationalization, staff reductions, and the elimination of duplicated or ineffective UN programs. Although an independent effort, this study was seriously considered by the UN along with the report of the "Group of 18," formally known as the Group of High-level Intergovernmental Experts to Review the Efficiency of the Administrative and Financial Functioning of the United Nations (#87).

3. *Annual Review of United Nations Affairs.* 1949-. Dobbs Ferry, N.Y.: Oceana. ISSN 00664340.
    Running account of the major activities of the UN. Includes many references to UN documents and full texts of selected documents. Volumes covering 1949-1955/56 were published under the auspices of the New York University Graduate Program of Studies in the United Nations.

4. Bailey, Sydney Dawson. *The Procedure of the UN Security Council.* Oxford: Clarendon Press, 1975. xii, 424 p. ISBN 0198271999.
    Discusses the Council's institutional framework, meeting procedures, participation, decision-making process, the Council's relations with other bodies; the Council's structure; and the need for reform.

5. *La Charte des Nations Unies: commentaire, article par article.* Sous la direction de Jean-Pierre Cot, Alain Pellet et Paul Tavernier. Paris: Economica; Bruxelles: Bruylant; Montréal: Edition Y. Blais, 1985. xvi, 1553 p. ISBN 2717809430.
    Detailed commentary on each article of the Charter, contributed by a team of over eighty authors. An up-to-date counterpart, reflecting Francophone scholarship, of *Charter of the United Nations: Commentary and Documents* by Leland M. Goodrich, Edvard Hambro, and Anne Patricia Simons (#14). Includes a select general bibliography, special bibliographies on most chapters of the Charter, subject index, index of conventions and resolutions cited, and an index to the jurisprudence of the Permanent Court of International Justice and the International Court of Justice.

6. De Gara, John. *Administrative and Financial Reform of the United Nations: A Documentary Essay*. Reports and Papers, 1989-2. [s.l.:] Academic Council on the United Nations System, 1989. i, 23 p.

Selective annotated list of UN documents related to UN reform in general, and specific issues such as staff reduction, the planning and budget process, reform of the institutional mechanism and the UN's financial situation. Includes two appendices: an annotated list of documents and publications on other reform efforts, and a selected bibliography of non-UN titles on UN reform.

7. Finley, Blanche. *The Structure of the United Nations General Assembly: Its Committees, Commissions and Other Organisms, 1946-73*. Dobbs Ferry, N.Y.: Oceana, 1977. 3 vols. ISBN 0379102404.

Historical survey of ad hoc and standing committees and other subsidiary bodies set up by the GA. Excludes sessional bodies such as the main committees and some special bodies such as UNCTAD and UNDP. For each organ, identifies the establishing resolution, the organ's terms of reference, membership and activities, and refers to reports issued by the organs. There is a list of GA resolutions, selected reference sources on the GA, and a subject index. Updated by: Finley, Blanche. *The Structure of the United Nations General Assembly: An Organizational Approach to Its Work, 1974-1990s*. White Plains, N.Y.: UNIPUB/Kraus International Publications, 1988. 2 vols. ISBN 0527916188.

8. Fomerand, Jacques. *Strengthening the United Nations Economic and Social Programs: A Documentary Essay*. Reports and Papers, 1990-2. [s.l.:] Academic Council on the United Nations System, 1990. ii, 29 p.

Selective guide to (mostly 1985 and later) UN documents concerned with improving the UN's effectiveness in economic and social fields. Outlines the context of the subject, the 1986 recommendations of the Group of High-level Intergovernmental Experts to Review the Efficiency of the Administrative and Financial Functioning of the United Nations (popularly known as the Group of 18, *see* #87), the resulting ECOSOC activities, and the General Assembly's 1977 restructuring resolution (32/197). Annexes present annotated documentary references, references to resolutions, and a selected bibliography of non-UN titles.

9. Food and Agriculture Organization of the United Nations. *Basic Texts of the Food and Agriculture Organization of the United Nations*. Rome: FAO, 1989. 241 p. ISBN 9251028559.

Two volumes in one. Volume 1 contains the text of the FAO Constitution, general rules, financial regulations, and rules of procedure of the Council and the committees; volume 2 provides texts of other procedures and policies. Includes alphabetical index.

10. Food and Agriculture Organization of the United Nations. *FAO: Its Origins, Formation and Evolution, 1945-1981*. by Ralph W. Phillips. Rome: FAO, 1981. ix, 200 p.

Historical survey of FAO's origins, establishment, membership, structure and programs. Includes bibliography, and country and name indexes.

11. Food and Agriculture Organization of the United Nations. *Organization and Structure of FAO, Including Titles of Staff = Organisation et structure de la FAO, et titres des fonctionnaires*. Terminology Bulletin, No. 15/Rev.5. Rome: FAO, 1984. ix, 205 p. ISBN 9250021313.

Part 1 presents the structure of FAO, including its regional offices and the World Food Programme, in English, French, Spanish, Chinese, and Arabic. Part 2 lists FAO organizational units in English, French and Spanish, titles of staff, and FAO acronyms and abbreviations. Includes a list of documents issued by the FAO Terminology and Reference Section, 1966-1984.

General Agreement on Tariffs and Trade. *Basic Instruments and Selected Documents*. See #274.

Structural and Institutional Issues 3

12. General Agreement on Tariffs and Trade. *GATT Activities: An Annual Review of the Work of the GATT*. 1960-. Geneva: GATT. ISSN 0072-0615.

Reviews trade negotiations in progress, the work of the GATT Council, developments in the international trading system, and administrative and budgetary matters.

13. General Agreement on Tariffs and Trade. *General Agreement on Tariffs and Trade: Text of the General Agreement*. Geneva: GATT, 1986. vi, 96 p. Sales No. GATT/1986-4. ISBN 9287010226.

Complete text of the General Agreement on Tariffs and Trade, with amendments. Includes appendix providing a guide to legal sources of GATT provisions.

14. Goodrich, Leland M.; Hambro, Edvard; and Simons, Anne Patricia. *Charter of the United Nations: Commentary and Documents*. 3d, rev. ed. New York: Columbia University Press, 1969. xvii, 732 p.

Exhaustive, article-by-article commentary on the Charter, aiming to show how, through Charter interpretation, fundamental changes took place during the first twenty years of the UN. It has an index as well as an appendix containing the texts of the Charter, the League of Nations Covenant, and the Dumbarton Oaks proposals. *See also* a similar and more recent work, *La Charte des Nations Unies: commentaire, article par article* (#5).

15. *A Guide to Delegate Preparation: UNA-USA Model U.N. Survival Kit*. 1990-91 ed. Edited by James P. Muldoon, Jr. & John A. Diehl. New York: United Nations Association of the United States of America, 1990. viii, 184 p. ISBN 0934654859.

Latest edition of UNA/USA's annual guide to assist students and organizers in preparing for model UN conferences. In five sections: 1, methods for preparing for a model UN conference; 2, how nations interact; 3, sample GA resolutions and voting patterns; 4, annotated bibliography of UN issues; 5, list of permanent missions to the UN. Companion volume to *Issues before the United Nations* (#51).

16. Hajnal, Peter I. *Guide to Unesco*. London; Rome; New York: Oceana, 1983. xvii, 578 p. ISBN 0379206633.

Overview of Unesco's evolution, structure and work, with detailed discussion of programming, conferences, documentation and publishing, other information activities, and normative action. Includes an annotated bibliography of works by and about Unesco, a selection of basic texts, and index.

Hajnal, Peter I. *Guide to United Nations Organization, Documentation and Publishing for Students, Researchers, Librarians*. See #388.

Hill, Martin. *The United Nations System: Co-ordinating Its Economic and Social Work*. See #153.

17. Holborn, Louise W. *The International Refugee Organization, a Specialized Agency of the United Nations: Its History and Work, 1946-1952*. London: Oxford University Press, 1956. xiv, 805 p.

Based on IRO's records and archival files as well as on other documentary material. In three parts: 1, survey of IRO's creation, constitution, administration, personnel, finances, and relations with governments, voluntary organizations and the UN system; 2, origin and situation of refugees and displaced persons; 3, assistance to and protection of refugees and displaced persons, repatriation and resettlement. Appendices include texts of selected documents, chronology, bibliography, and index.

18. International Atomic Energy Agency. *The Annual Report*. 1957/1958-. Vienna: IAEA.

Provides an overview of the Agency's activities in the fields of technical co-operation, nuclear power, radioactive waste management, life sciences, safeguards, and other areas. Includes a section on administration and an organization chart.

19. International Atomic Energy Agency. *IAEA Yearbook.* 1989-. Vienna: IAEA.
    Includes a summary of the Agency's activities, as well as several sections previously issued as separate publications; for example, *Nuclear Power and Fuel Cycle: Status and Trends*, and *Nuclear Safety Review*. An appendix lists IAEA publications.

20. International Atomic Energy Agency. *International Atomic Energy Agency Bulletin.* Vol. 1-, 1959-. Vienna: IAEA.
    Contains brief articles on atomic energy, the Agency's activities, and notices of conferences and publications. Volume 1 preceded by a special issue dated September 1958. Title varies slightly.

21. International Atomic Energy Agency. *1957-1982: 25 Years -- International Atomic Energy Agency.* Vienna: IAEA, 1982. 40 p.
    Reproduces forty exhibit panels shown in the Hofburg, Vienna, on the twenty-fifth anniversary of the Agency. Contains illustrations, charts, statistical tables, and descriptive captions.

22. International Atomic Energy Agency. *Statute as Amended up to 28 December 1989.* Vienna: IAEA.
    The constitutional document of IAEA, incorporating three (1963, 1973 and 1989) amendments.

    International Bank for Reconstruction and Development. *See also* World Bank.

23. International Bank for Reconstruction and Development. *Articles of Agreement of the International Bank for Reconstruction and Development (As Amended Effective February 16, 1989).* Washington, D.C.: IBRD, 1989. 24 p. ISBN 0821312189.
    The constitutional document of the World Bank (formally known as International Bank for Reconstruction and Development). Includes index.

24. International Bank for Reconstruction and Development. *Convention Establishing the Multilateral Investment Guarantee Agency and Commentary on the Convention.* [Washington, D.C.:] IBRD, 1985. iii, 44, ii, 24 p.
    Provides for the establishment, operations, financing and other aspects of the Agency, which was formally constituted in April 1988 as the newest member of the World Bank Group.

25. International Bank for Reconstruction and Development. *Report of the Executive Directors on the Convention on the Settlement of Investment Disputes between States and Nationals of Other States.* Washington, D.C.: IBRD, 1965. 16, 26 p.
    Texts of the report and of the Convention of the International Centre for Settlement of Investment Disputes (ICSID).

26. International Bank for Reconstruction and Development. *Summary Proceedings of the Annual Meetings of the Boards of Governors [of the International Bank for Reconstruction and Development, International Finance Corporation, and International Development Association].* 1946-. Washington, D.C.: World Bank.
    The only publicly available record of Board meetings. Includes texts of addresses of the head of state or government of the host country, the World Bank president, the chairman of the Development Committee, as well as statements of governors and alternate governors, texts of resolutions, and other material.

27. International Centre for Settlement of Investment Disputes. *Annual Report.* 1966/1967-. Washington, D.C.: ICSID.
    Brief review of ICSID activities and financing. Includes abstracts of disputes before ICSID, texts of resolutions of the Administrative Council, and lists of publications.

28. International Centre for Settlement of Investment Disputes. *ICSID Basic Documents*. Washington, D.C.: ICSID, 1985. 107 p.

Contains the text of the Convention on the Settlement of Investment Disputes between States and Nationals of Other States, and texts of the following ICSID rules and regulations as revised in 1984: administrative and financial regulations; rules of procedure for the institution of conciliation and arbitration proceedings; rules of procedure for arbitration; rules of procedure for conciliation proceedings.

29. International Civil Aviation Organization. *Annual Report of the Council*. 1946-. ISSN 02512289. Montreal: ICAO.

Chapter 1 usually describes significant developments in civil aviation during the report year, and the rest of the report deals with ICAO's activities. Serves as documentation for each forthcoming ordinary session of the Assembly. Includes appendices. Former title (1946-19??): *Annual Report of the Council to the Assembly*.

30. International Civil Aviation Organization. *Convention on International Civil Aviation = Convention relative à l'aviation civile internationale = Convenio sobre Aviación Civil Internacional*. 6th ed. Montreal: ICAO, 1980. vi, 42 p. DOC. 7300/6.

English, French and Spanish text of the 1944 Convention (incorporating ICAO's constitutional document), with the Buenos Aires Protocol of 1968 and all amendments to the Convention that were in force on 30 November 1985.

31. International Development Association. *Articles of Agreement of the International Development Association (Effective September 24, 1960)*. Washington, D.C.: [s.n.], 1960. 15, 4 p.

The constitutional document of the IDA.

32. International Finance Corporation. *Annual Report*. 1956/1957-. Washington, D.C.: IFC. ISSN 02515385.

Reviews IFC's operations, finances, and regional and other activities. Includes statistical and other appendices.

33. International Finance Corporation. *Articles of Agreement*. Washington, D.C.: World Bank, 1986. 13 p.

IFC's constitution.

34. International Fund for Agricultural Development. *Agreement Establishing the International Fund for Agricultural Development*. Rome: IFAD, 1977. 43 p. IFAD/1.

IFAD's constitutional document was adopted by the United Nations Conference on the Establishment of the International Fund for Agricultural Development on 13 June 1976 and entered into force on 30 November 1977.

35. International Fund for Agricultural Development. *IFAD Annual Report*. 1979-. Rome: IFAD. ISSN 02510707.

Review of the agency's operations, projects, and technical assistance and other activities. Includes statistical annex.

36. International Fund for Agricultural Development. Governing Council. *Report*. 1st- session, 1977-. Rome: IFAD. GC/-.

Summary record of proceedings, and texts of Council decisions, statements and other documents. Annexes include list of documents, and program of work and budget.

37. International Labour Office. *Constitution of the International Labour Organisation and Standing Orders of the International Labour Conference = Constitution de l'Organisation internationale du Travail et Règlement de la Conférence internationale du Travail.* Geneva: ILO, 1989. 86, 87 p. ISBN 9220072017.

English and French text of the ILO Constitution, the ILC Standing Orders, and the Agreement between the UN and the ILO. Includes index.

38. International Maritime Organization. *Basic Documents.* 4th ed. London: IMO, 1985-1986. 2 vols.

Volume 1 (147 p.; Sales No. 001 86.17.E; ISBN 9280112139) contains texts of the IMO Convention, and rules and guidelines of IMO's subsidiary bodies; volume 2 (94 p.; Sales No. 007 85.09.E; ISBN 9280111868) provides texts of documents on the status, privileges and immunities of IMO, and agreements with other IGOs.

39. International Maritime Organization. *IMO News: The Magazine of the International Maritime Organization.* 1962-. London: IMO. ISSN 02538199.

Quarterly review of organizational and other news of maritime interest. Former titles: *IMCO Bulletin* (1962-1977), *IMCO News* (1977-1982).

40. International Monetary Fund. *Annual Report of the Executive Board.* 1946/1947-. Washington, D.C.: IMF. ISSN 02507498.

Provides an overview of the world economy, and a more detailed account of the Fund's operational and other activities. Appendices include statistical tables, texts of the Board's policy decisions, communiqués of the Interim Committee and the Development Committee, and administrative and financial information. Former title (1946/1947-1976/1977): *Annual Report of the Executive Directors.*

41. International Monetary Fund. *Articles of Agreement.* Washington, D.C.: IMF, reprinted 1988. viii, 132 p. ISBN 1557750386.

The constitutional document of the Fund, as adopted at the United Nations Monetary and Financial Conference at Bretton Woods, New Hampshire, July 22, 1944, and as amended in 1969 and 1978.

42. International Monetary Fund. *The IMF in a Changing World.* By Margaret Garritsen de Vries. Washington, D.C.: IMF, 1986. x, 226 p. ISBN 0939934655.

Collection of eighteen articles by the IMF Historian. In five parts: 1, "Attaining Initial Objectives" (1944-1965); 2, "Trying To Save the System" (1966-1971); 3, "Operating in a Troubled World Economy" (1972-1978); 4, "Responding to the Debt Crisis" (1979-1985); 5, "Looking Back at Forty Years". A more detailed history may be found in *The International Monetary Fund, 1945-1965: Twenty Years of International Monetary Cooperation* (#43); *The International Monetary Fund, 1966-71: The System under Stress* (#44); and *The International Monetary Fund, 1972-1978: Cooperation on Trial* (#45).

43. International Monetary Fund. *The International Monetary Fund, 1945-1965: Twenty Years of International Monetary Cooperation.* Washington, D.C.: IMF, 1969. 3 vols.

Volume 1, "Chronicle" (xviii, 663 p.), by J. Keith Horsefield, surveys the Fund's "prehistory," beginnings and activities through 1965 (with supplement through 1968). Includes appendices; indexes by subject, personal name, country, Articles of Agreement, Executive Board decisions; and bibliography. Volume 2, "Analysis" (xviii, 621 p.), by Margaret Garritsen de Vries and J. Keith Horsefield, discusses policy formation and objectives, exchange rates and gold markets, exchange restrictions, and IMF's resources and constitutional development. Also has indexes similar to those in Volume 1, and bibliography. Volume 3, "Documents" (vii, 549 p.), edited by J. Keith Horsefield, provides texts of selected major pre-Bretton Woods and IMF documents, and includes list of IMF publications.

44. International Monetary Fund. *The International Monetary Fund, 1966-71: The System under Stress*. By Margaret Garritsen de Vries. Washington, D.C.: IMF, 1976. 2 vols.

Volume 1, "Narrative" (xxii, 699 p.), describes the birth and use of SDRs, the use of gold and other resources, the 1967-71 exchange rate crisis, and the Fund as an institution. Includes appendices, index, and bibliography. Volume 2, "Documents" (xxii, 339 p.), includes selected major texts, and bibliography.

45. International Monetary Fund. *The International Monetary Fund, 1972-1978: Cooperation on Trial*. Edited by Margaret Garritsen de Vries. Washington, D.C.: IMF, 1985. 3 vols. ISBN 0939934434.

Volume 1, "Narrative and analysis" (pp. xxiii, 1-699), describes the end of the par-value system, reform efforts, the 1973 oil crisis, and the increased use of IMF resources. Volume 2, also titled "Narrative and analysis" (pp. x, 604-1152), gives an account of the resolution of the gold problem, the floating exchange rates, and further evolution of the Fund. Includes tables, appendices, and index to Volumes 1 and 2. Volume 3, "Documents" (xii, 657 p.), includes selected major texts.

46. International Monetary Fund. *The Role and Function of the International Monetary Fund*. Washington, D.C.: IMF, 1985. ix, 99 p.

Brief guide to the Fund's origin, evolution, organization, regulatory and assistance functions, the SDR (Special Drawing Rights) facility, and IMF publications. An appendix lists members, quotas and voting power.

47. International Monetary Fund. *Summary Proceedings of the Annual Meeting of the Board of Governors*. 1st-, 1946-. Washington, D.C.: IMF. ISSN 00747025.

The only publicly available record of Board's annual meetings. Gives the texts of opening and closing addresses of the Chairman of the Board, statements of Governors, committee reports and resolutions, presentation of the Managing Director's annual report, and other information.

International Organization and Integration: Annotated Basic Documents and Descriptive Directory of International Organizations and Arrangements. See #275.

48. International Telecommunication Union. *International Telecommunication Convention*. Nairobi: ITU, 1982. xviii, 364 p. ISBN 9261016510.

Contains the texts of the Convention, the Final Protocol, additional protocols, Optional Additional Protocol, and resolutions, recommendations and opinions, as adopted in Nairobi in 1982.

49. International Telecommunication Union. *Report on the Activities of the International Telecommunication Union*. 1949-. Geneva: ITU. ISSN 00852201.

Annual review of activities, meetings and conferences, regional activities, administration, finances, and publications.

50. International Trade Centre (UNCTAD/GATT). *The International Trade Centre, UNCTAD/GATT, 1964-1984.: An Historical Account of Twenty Years of Service to Developing Countries*. By Frederick J. Glover. Geneva: ITC, 1984. v, 80 p.

Review of the origins, activities, resources, policy-making and administration of the Centre, with an evaluation. Annexes include chronology, list of documentary sources, and organization charts.

51.   *Issues before the 45th General Assembly of the United Nations: An Annual Publication of the United Nations Association of the United States of America*. Edited by John Tessitore and Susan Woolfson. Lexington, Mass.; Toronto: Lexington Books, 1990. xiii, 273 p. ISBN 0669248134.

Latest edition of UNA/USA's overview of the year's activities of the UN system: dispute settlement and decolonization; arms control and disarmament; global resource management; human rights and social issues; legal issues; finance and administration. Includes index. Companion volume to *A Guide to Delegate Preparation: UNA-USA Model U.N. Survival Kit* (#15).

52.   Joint Inspection Unit [of the United Nations System of Organizations]. *Budgeting in the Organizations of the United Nations System*. Geneva: JIU, 1989. i, 32, 2,ii, 54 p. JIU/REP/89/9. Transmitted in United Nations, General Assembly, 45th sess., *Administrative and Budgetary Co-ordination of the United Nations with the Specialized Agencies and the International Atomic Energy Agency: Budgeting in the Organizations of the United Nations System*. New York: UN, 1989. A/45/130.

Examines budgetary policy and structure, preparation and submission procedures, definitions, budget increases and decreases, and the impact of currency fluctuations. Includes list of budget-related agreements, and, as "Volume 2," comparative tables. Document A/45/130/Add.1 contains comments on the report by the Secretary-General.

53.   Joint Inspection Unit [of the United Nations System of Organizations]. *Concluding Report on the Implementation of General Assembly Resolution 32/197 concerning the Restructuring of the Economic and Social Sectors of the United Nations System*. Geneva: JIU, 1989. ii, 28 p. JIU/REP/89/7. Transmitted in United Nations, General Assembly, 44th sess., *Concluding Report on the Implementation of General Assembly Resolution 32/197 concerning the Restructuring of the Economic and Social Sectors of the United Nations System*. New York: UN, 25 August 1989. A/44/486.

Discusses the functions of ECOSOC, the division of labor in the UN Secretariat, and the role of the Secretary-General. Document A/44/486/Add.1 contains comments on the report by the Secretary-General.

54.   Joint Inspection Unit [of the United Nations System of Organizations]. *Control and Limitation of Documentation in the United Nations System*. Geneva: JIU, December 1980. 34 p. JIU/REP/80/12. Transmitted in United Nations, General Assembly, 36th sess., *Control and Limitation of Documentation in the United Nations System*. New York: UN, 8 April 1981. A/36/167.

See also documents A/36/167/Add.1 and A/36/167/Add.2.

55.   Joint Inspection Unit [of the United Nations System of Organizations]. *Publications Policy and Practice in the United Nations System*. Geneva: JIU, 1984. 32 p. JIU/REP/84/5. Transmitted in United Nations, General Assembly, 39th sess., *Questions Relating to Information: Publications Policy and Practice in the United Nations System*. New York: UN, 14 May 1984. A/39/239.

Based on questionnaires and visits, it outlines the main features of publishing in the UN system, discusses policies and practices, distribution and sales, information management, and inter-agency co-operation. The Secretary-General's comments on this report may be found in document A/39/239/Add.1 and A/39/239/Corr.1; comments of the Administrative Committee on Co-ordination are in A/39/239/Add.2.

56.   Joint Inspection Unit [of the United Nations System of Organizations]. *Report on Autonomous Research Institutes of the United Nations*. Geneva: JIU, 1987. 25 p. JIU/REP/87/4 and JIU/REP/87/4/Add.1. Transmitted in United Nations, General Assembly, 42d sess., *Report on Autonomous Research Institutes of the United Nations*. New York: UN, 14 September 1987. A/42/540.

Describes the origins, mandates, governing bodies, and activities of UNITAR, CELADE, UNIDIR and other research institutes. Concentrates on funding, budgeting and administrative aspects. Includes recommendations. *See also* the Secretary-General's comments in document A/43/397 of 15 June 1988.

57. Joint Inspection Unit [of the United Nations System of Organizations]. *Reporting to the Economic and Social Council.* Prepared by Maurice Bertrand. Geneva: JIU, 1984. 32 p. JIU/REP/84/7. Transmitted in United Nations, General Assembly, 39th sess., *Reporting to the Economic and Social Council.* New York: UN, 31 May 1984. A/39/281.
See also documents A/39/281/Add.1, A/39/281/Add.2, A/39/281/Add.2/Corr.1 and A/40/284.

58. Joint Inspection Unit [of the United Nations System of Organizations]. *Review of United Nations Public Information Networks: United Nations Information Centres.* Geneva: JIU, 1989. 33 p. JIU/REP/89/6. Transmitted in United Nations, General Assembly, 44th sess., *Review of United Nations Public Information Networks: United Nations Information Centres.* New York: UN, 16 June 1989. A/44/329.
See also document A/44/329/Add.1.

59. Joint Inspection Unit [of the United Nations System of Organizations]. *Some Reflections on Reform of the United Nations.* Prepared by Maurice Bertrand. Geneva: JIU, 1985. 84 p. JIU/REP/85/9. Transmitted in United Nations, General Assembly, 40th sess., *Some Reflections on Reform of the United Nations; Note by the Secretary-General.* New York: UN, 1985. iv, 84 p. A/40/988.
The "Bertrand Report" reviews the nature, objectives, functions, and structure of the UN, and outlines major proposals for reform. The focus is on peace and security, negotiation of economic issues, and an integrated approach to economic and social development.

Manning, Raymond. "The Records of Conferences Resulting in the Foundation of Organizations." *See* #350.

60. Multilateral Investment Guarantee Agency. *Annual Report.* 1989-. Washington, D.C.: MIGA. ISSN 082131310X.
Highlights the programs and services of the newest member of the World Bank Group. Appendices include financial statements, list of signatory states, governors and directors, and budget.

61. Partan, Daniel G. *Documentary Study of the Politicization of Unesco.* [Boston]: American Academy of Arts and Sciences, 1975. vii, 174 p.
Based on an analysis of Unesco resolutions and other documents, it analyzes the organization's actions concerning Israel's archaeological excavations and participation in Unesco's regional activities. It has a briefer analysis of Unesco actions on southern Africa, Portugal, Taiwan and the Palestine Liberation Organization.

Peaslee, Amos Jenkins. *International Governmental Organizations: Constitutional Documents.* See #276.

Preparatory Commission of the United Nations. *Publications.* See #277.

Public Papers of the Secretaries-General of the United Nations. See #278.

62. *A Successor Vision: The United Nations of Tomorrow.* Edited by Peter J. Fromuth. New York: United Nations Association of the United Nations of America, 1988. xxxiv, 385 p. ISBN 0819169064.
A high-level 23-member international panel on the United Nations Association's UN management and decision-making project (1985-1987) considered the relationship between UN functions and structure; contemplated the strengthening of UN structure in the economic and social area including the establishment of a ministerial board; presented a two-step approach toward a more integrated UN system; and recommended the creation of a new development assistance board, the elimination of the General Assembly's Second and Third committees, the expansion of ECOSOC, and other structural changes, as well as the strengthening of peace and security activities and the improvement of the role of the Secretary-General. In addition to the panel's final report, this work includes research papers produced by the project staff.

63. Unesco. *A Chronology of Unesco, 1945-1987*. Paris: Unesco, 1987. xvi, 141 p. LAD.85/WS/4 Rev.
"Facts and events in Unesco's history with references to documentary sources in the Unesco Archives." In addition to the chronology, provides lists of member states, General Conference and Executive Board sessions and presiding officers, standard-setting instruments, and Directors-General, as well as information on the structure and staff of the Secretariat, the budget, and other matters. Includes bibliography, and subject and name indexes.

64. Unesco. *The Concept of International Organization*. Edited by Georges Abi-Saab. Paris: Unesco, 1981. 245 p. ISBN 923101742X.
Compendium of articles on historical and typological approaches, methodological and procedural aspects, and socialist, Western and Third-World perspectives on international organization.

Unesco. *Guide to the Archives of International Organizations, Part 1: The United Nations System*. See #353.

65. Unesco. *In the Minds of Men: Unesco, 1946 to 1971*. Paris: Unesco, 1972. 319 p.
Collection of essays to commemorate Unesco's twenty-fifth anniversary. In five parts: 1, Unesco's history; 2, international intellectual cooperation and communication; 3, Unesco's contribution to development; 4, normative action and peace activities; 5, the mind as a force in history.

66. Unesco. *Unesco News = Les nouvelles de l'Unesco*. 1-, 1979-. Paris: Unesco.
Provides information on Unesco organs and activities, news of national Unesco commissions, and notices of forthcoming meetings and recent publications. Continues *Unesco Chronicle* (1-26, 1955-1980; Paris: Unesco).

67. Unesco. *Unesco on the Eve of Its 40th Anniversary*. Prepared under the direction of Amadou-Mahtar M'Bow, Director-General of Unesco. Paris: Unesco, 1985. 216 p.
Overview of Unesco's history and activities in the fields of education, science and technology, social and human sciences, culture, information and communication. Annexes include the preamble to Unesco's Constitution, information on the medium-term plan, and statistical charts.

68. Unesco. *Unesco Sources*. No. 1-, February 1989-. ISSN 10146989. Paris: Unesco.
Illustrated monthly magazine on Unesco's activities.

69. Unesco. General Conference. *Records of the General Conference*. 1st- session, 1946-. Paris: Unesco.
The official records of Unesco's main policy-setting organ. For recent sessions, the *Records* include separate volumes for resolutions.

70. Unesco. General Conference. *Report of the Director-General on the Activities of the Organization*. 1947- . Paris: Unesco.
Biennial report, submitted to each regular session of the General Conference. Includes annexes that provide information on member states, administration and financing, publications, and statistical and other data.

71. United Nations. *Repertory of Practice of United Nations Organs*. New York, 1955. 5 vols. and index.
Comprehensive summary of UN decisions and other related material, arranged by Charter articles. Updated by periodic supplements (there is an index to supplements up to 1979.) *See also* United Nations, Department of Political and Security Council Affairs, *Repertoire of the Practice of the Security Council, 1946-1951* (#76).

United Nations Conference on International Organization, San Francisco, 1945. *Documents*. See #283.

72. United Nations Conference on Trade and Development. *The Changing Relationship between the World Bank and the International Monetary Fund: Report to the Group of Twenty-four*. By Richard E. Feinberg. UNDP/UNCTAD Studies on International Monetary and Financial Issues for the Developing Countries. Geneva: UNCTAD, 1987. i, 25 p. UNCTAD/MFD/TA/41.

Review of the origins of the Bretton Woods institutions and the evolving nature and problems of the relationship between the World Bank and the IMF. Includes bibliographic references.

73. United Nations Conference on Trade and Development. *Commemoration of the Twenty-fifth Anniversary of the United Nations Conference on Trade and Development*. New York: UN, 1989. vi, 72 p. UNCTAD/PSM/CAS/138.

Contains the text of the Trade and Development Board's declaration to commemorate the anniversary, and the texts of statements made, and written and videotaped messages received, during a special commemorative meeting of the Board on 5 October 1989.

74. United Nations Conference on Trade and Development. *The History of UNCTAD, 1964-1984*. New York: UN, 1985. ix, 294 p. UNCTAD/OSG/286; Sales No. E.85.II.D.6. ISBN 9211121892.

In four parts: 1, review of the evolution, philosophy and achievements of UNCTAD; 2, discussion of commodity policy, international monetary and financial issues, trade and industrialization policy, shipping, technology transfer, East-West trade relations, developing countries, and insurance issues; 3, other UNCTAD activities; 4, annexes containing organization chart, and selected lists of meetings and publications.

75. United Nations. Department of International Economic and Social Affairs. "Multilateralism and the United Nations." *Journal of Development Planning*, No. 17. Special issue. New York: UN, 1987. x, 325 p. ST/ESA/201; Sales No. E.87.II.A.22. ISBN 9211042178.

Compendium of twelve articles on UN reform, the global economy, peace and security, and other questions of multilateralism. Supplemented by brief opinion pieces and reports on current research.

76. United Nations. Department of Political and Security Council Affairs. *Repertoire of the Practice of the Security Council, 1946-1951*. New York: UN, 1954. ST/PSCA/1; Sales No. 54.VII.1.

Based on documents of the SC and other UN organs, this is a detailed compendium of SC's provisional rules of procedure, voting and other procedures, subsidiary organs, and other matters in the Council's purview. Updated by supplements of which the latest covers 1975-1980.

77. United Nations. Department of Public Information. *Basic Facts about the United Nations*. New York: UN, 1989. vii, 236 p. DPI/991; Sales No. E.90.I.2. ISBN 9211004209.

Latest edition of a concise guide published every few years. Outlines the history, structure and principal activities of the UN, with a briefer account of other organizations in the UN system.

78. United Nations. Department of Public Information. *Charter of the United Nations and Statute of the International Court of Justice*. New York: UN, 1989. 87 p. DPI/511.

The basic constitutional document of the UN. Sets out the organization's purposes and principles; rules of membership; composition, functions, powers and procedures of the principal organs; principles of dispute settlement, international economic cooperation, non-self-governing territories and other areas of international concern; procedures for amendment, signature and ratification. The Statute of the ICJ is considered an integral part of the Charter. The text of the Charter and the ICJ Statute may also be found in other sources, for example, *Everyone's United Nations* (#107).

United Nations. Department of Public Information. *UN Chronicle*. See #256.

79.   United Nations. Department of Public Information. *The United Nations at Forty: A Foundation To Build On*. New York: UN, 1985. vi, 202 p. DPI/865; Sales No. 85.I.24. ISBN 9211002850.
Describes the origins and functioning of the UN, and the major issues the organization has dealt with during its first forty years.

United Nations Development Programme. *Annual Report of the Administrator*. 1965-. New York: UNDP. See #181.

80.   United Nations Development Programme. *A Study of the Capacity of the United Nations Development System*. Geneva: UN, 1969. 2 vols. DP/5; Sales No. E.70.I.10.
Also known after its principal author, R. G. A. Jackson, as the "Jackson Report," it examines the organization, content, administration and financing of the development activities of the UN system, and recommends changes to improve the development system.

81.   United Nations. Economic and Social Commission for Asia and the Pacific. *ESCAP 1947-1987: Regional Co-operation for Development*. Bangkok: ESCAP, 1987. 84 p.
Provides an overview of the history of ESCAP and its predecessor, the Economic Commission for Asia and the Far East (ECAFE), and of the Commission's current activities. Annexes give ESCAP's terms of reference, program priorities, and a statement of functions and responsibilities.

82.   United Nations. Economic and Social Council. *Official Records*. 1st- sess., 1946-. New York: UN.
For 1946-1973, this major set of ECOSOC documents consisted of (a) summary meeting records; (b) supplements (these include *Resolutions Adopted by the Economic and Social Council*, usually issued as supplement 1; regular reports of subordinate or affiliated bodies, for example, those of the Commission on Human Rights and the Economic and Social Commission for Asia and the Pacific; as well as special reports); and (c) annexes (texts or checklists of documents relevant to specific agenda items). ECOSOC's annual reports appear as supplements (usually Supplement 3) to the *Official Records* of the General Assembly. For 1974 and subsequent years, annexes have been dispensed with, and the *Official Records* have comprised: summary records of plenary meetings and checklists of documents in sessional volumes; supplements; and sessional checklists and lists of delegates. ECOSOC *Official Records* are listed in *United Nations Official Records, 1948-1962: A Reference Catalogue* and its supplements for 1962-1981 and 1981-1984 (#492) as well as in "UNDI" (#468), *UNDEX* (#463), and *UNDOC* (#464) and *Index to Proceedings of the Economic and Social Council* (#455).

83.   United Nations. Economic and Social Council. *Rules of Procedure of the Economic and Social Council*. New York: UN, 1983. vi, 31 p. E/5715/Rev.1; Sales No. E.83.I.9.

84.   United Nations. Economic Commission for Europe. *ECE 1947-1987*. New York: UN, 1987. vi, 140 p. E/ECE/1132; Sales No. E.87.II.E.17. ISBN 9211163900.
Describes the development and programs of ECE, especially since 1977. Appendices include terms of reference, list of sessions held, and organization charts. A related publication, United Nations, Economic Commission for Europe, *Three Decades of the United Nations Economic Commission for Europe* (New York: UN, 1978; xi, 272 p.; E/ECE/962; Sales No. E.79.II.E.5) gives a more detailed account of ECE's first thirty years.

85.   United Nations. Economic Commission for Latin America and the Caribbean. *ECLAC: 40 Years (1948-1988)*. By José Cayuela. Santiago, Chile: ECLAC, 1988. 75 p.
Reviews ECLAC's history and activities. Includes lists of executive secretaries, member states, and sessions of the Commission.

United Nations. General Assembly. *Annotated Preliminary List of Items To Be Included in the Provisional Agenda of the 45th Regular Session of the General Assembly*. See #482.

Structural and Institutional Issues 13

86.   United Nations. General Assembly. *Official Records*. 1st- sess., 1946-. New York: UN.
    The three main components of this major set of GA documents are: (a) plenary and committee meeting records (verbatim for plenary and First Committee, summary records for the other six main committees); (b) supplements (these include the *Medium-Term Plan*, the biennial *Programme Budget*, the *Audited Accounts*, the *Report of the Secretary-General on the Work of the Organization* (usually the first supplement; #88), the *Resolutions and Decisions Adopted by the General Assembly* for each GA session (usually the last supplement; #288), the annual reports of the Security Council, the Economic and Social Council, the International Court of Justice, other subordinate or affiliated bodies and (until 1975) the Trusteeship Council, as well as other reports; and (c) annexes (texts or checklists of documents relevant to specific agenda items). GA *Official Records* are listed in *United Nations Official Records, 1948-1962: A Reference Catalogue* and its supplements for 1962-1981 and 1981-1984 (#492) as well as in "UNDI" (#468), *UNDEX* (#463) and *UNDOC* (#464), and *Index to Proceedings of the General Assembly* (#455).

87.   United Nations. General Assembly. "Report of the Group of High-level Intergovernmental Experts to Review the Efficiency of the Administrative and Financial Functioning of the United Nations." *Official Records*. 41st sess., Supplement No. 49. New York: UN, 1986. iii, 40 p. A/41/49.
    Presents the findings of the "Group of 18" and makes seventy-one recommendations aimed at coordination, consolidation, staff reduction, budgetary matters, simplification, and the avoidance of duplication. Submitted at about the same time as the informal report by Sadruddin Aga Khan and Maurice Strong, "United Nations Financial Emergency: Crisis and Opportunity" (#2). *See also* United Nations, General Assembly, *Review of the Efficiency of the Administrative and Financial Functioning of the United Nations: Progress Report of the Secretary-General on the Implementation of General Assembly Resolution 41/213* (#89).

88.   United Nations. General Assembly. *Report of the Secretary-General on the Work of the Organization*. 1946-. *Official Records* of the General Assembly, Supplement No. 1. New York: UN. ISSN 00828173.
    Contains personal observations of the incumbent Secretary-General on important issues facing the UN and the world community. For 1946-1976/77 the *Report* gave a detailed account of the year's activities and was, in effect, the annual report of the UN. For 1956-1976/77 the *Report* was accompanied by *Introduction to the Report of the Secretary-General on the Work of the Organization* (*Official Records* of the General Assembly, Supplement No. 1A). More precisely, for 1976/77 (32d Session) the *Report* is the equivalent to the previous *Introduction* and the *Addendum to the Report* is the equivalent to the previous *Report*. The current pattern begins with 1977/78 (33d GA session). The current *Report* is thus the successor to the earlier *Introduction*.

89.   United Nations. General Assembly. *Review of the Efficiency of the Administrative and Financial Functioning of the United Nations: Progress Report of the Secretary-General on the Implementation of General Assembly Resolution 41/213*. New York: UN, 1987. 39 p. A/42/234 and A/42/234/Corr.1.
    See also United Nations, General Assembly, *Review of the Efficiency of the Administrative and Financial Functioning of the United Nations: Second Progress Report of the Secretary-General on the Implementation of General Assembly Resolution 41/213* (New York: UN, 1988; 24 p.; A/43/286) and United Nations, General Assembly, *Review of the Efficiency of the Administrative and Financial Functioning of the United Nations; Establishment and Operation of a Reserve Fund: Report of the Secretary-General* (New York: UN, 1989; A/44/665.)

90.   United Nations. General Assembly. *Rules of Procedure of the General Assembly (Embodying Amendments and Additions Adopted by the General Assembly up to 31 December 1984)*. New York: UN, 1985. 86 p. A/520/Rev.15; Sales No. E.85.I.13.
    The GA's basic instrument. Gives rules for convening and conducting sessions; composition of delegations; election and terms of reference of officers and committees; other provisions. Includes index.

91.   United Nations. Group of Experts on the Structure of the United Nations System. *A New United Nations Structure for Global Economic Co-operation.* New York: UN, 1975. xvii, 112 p. E/AC.62/9; Sales No. E.75.II.A.7.

Known after its rapporteur as the "Gardner Report", this is an examination of the premises and goals of UN restructuring; analysis of issues and proposals; consideration of structures relating to trade, international monetary reform, development financing, food and agriculture, and industrialization; and a set of detailed recommendations.

92.   United Nations Industrial Development Organization. *Constitution of the United Nations Industrial Development Organization.* 24 p. Vienna: UNIDO, 1979.

The basic document of UNIDO was adopted on 8 April 1979 by the United Nations Conference on the Establishment of the United Nations Industrial Development Organization As a Specialized Agency. It came into force on January 1, 1986 when UNIDO, originally a special body of the UN, became an autonomous specialized agency.

93.   United Nations Industrial Development Organization. Industrial Development Board. *Annual Report of UNIDO.* 1967-. Vienna: UNIDO. ISSN 02588137.

Review of the activities, administration and funding of the organization. Includes statistical annex and appendices. Former title (1967-1984): *Annual Report of the Executive Director.*

94.   United Nations Institute for Training and Research. *Can the Common System Be Maintained? The Role of the International Civil Service Commission.* By John P. Renninger. Policy and Efficacy Studies, No. 10. New York: UN, 1986. 102 p. Sales No. E.86.XV.PE/10.

Survey of the international civil service from League of Nations days to the 1980s, and of the International Civil Service Commission.

95.   United Nations Institute for Training and Research. *Conference Diplomacy: An Introductory Analysis.* 2d, rev. ed.. By Johan Kaufmann. Dordrecht, Netherlands: Nijhoff, 1988. xxix, 208 p. Sales No. E.88.III.K.PS/11. ISBN 902473682X.

Overview of the organizational and human setting of conference diplomacy, decision-making, role of secretariats, presiding officers, delegations and groups, and conciliation and other tactics. Includes bibliography and index. Companion volume to the author's *Effective Negotiation: Case Studies in Conference Diplomacy* (#261).

96.   United Nations Institute for Training and Research. *ECOSOC: Options for Reform.* By John P. Renninger. Policy and Efficacy Studies, No. 4. New York: UN, 1981. 33 p. Sales No. E.81/XV.PE/4.

97.   United Nations Institute for Training and Research. *The Future Role of the United Nations in an Interdependent World.* Edited by John P. Renninger. Dordrecht; Boston; London: Nijhoff, 1989. xviii, 283 p. Sales No. E.89.III.K.CR/30. ISBN 0792305329.   Collection of papers of a roundtable discussion organized jointly by UNITAR and the USSR Association for the United Nations in September 1988 in Moscow. Themes include the changing international environment, political and military aspects of international security, world economic problems, North-South relations, and challenges facing the UN. Includes index.

98.   United Nations Institute for Training and Research. *Keeping Faith with the United Nations.* By B. G. Ramcharan. Dordrecht: Nijhoff and UNITAR, 1987. Sales No. E.87.III.K.RR/33. ISBN 9024735165.

Examines public perceptions, problems and prospects of the UN. Includes bibliography and index.

99. United Nations Institute for Training and Research. *Survey and Analysis of Evaluations of the United Nations Intergovernmental Structure and Functions in the Economic and Social Fields.* By John P. Renninger. Special Commission on the In-Depth Study of the United Nations Intergovernmental Structure and Functions in the Economic and Social Fields, Informal Paper, No. 15. New York: UN, 1987. 58 p.

100. United Nations Institute for Training and Research. *The Third Generation World Organization.* By Maurice Bertrand. Dordrecht; Boston; London: Nijhoff, 1989. xiii, 217 p. Sales No. E.89.III.K.FS/25. ISBN 0792303822.

Traces the world's progress toward peace, draws up a balance sheet of the UN system, outlines a theory of peace, describes the inadequacies of the present world organization, and advocates the establishment of a third generation of world organization.

101. United Nations Institute for Training and Research. *The United Nations: An Inside View.* By C. V. Narasimhan. New Delhi: UNITAR in association with Vikas Publishing House, 1988. xiv, 385 p. Sales No. E.88.III.K.ST/23. ISBN 0706941357.

Overview of political, economic, humanitarian, social, legal, peacekeeping and other activities of the UN system. Includes name and subject indexes.

United Nations Institute for Training and Research. *The World Court: What It Is and How It Works.* See #214.

102. United Nations. International Court of Justice. *Yearbook.* No. 1-, 1946-. The Hague: ICJ. ISSN 0074445X.

Provides information on the organization, jurisdiction, functioning, practice, and financing of the Court; a report on the work of the Court during the period covered (recently, two years); and a list of publications of and information on publishing by the Court and its predecessor, the Permanent Court of International Justice of the League of Nations.

103. United Nations. International Law Commission. *The Work of the International Law Commission.* 4th ed. New York: UN, 1988. x, 402 p. Sales No. E.88.V.1. ISBN 9211333032.

In three parts: 1, origin and background of the development and codification of international law; 2, organization, program and working methods of the ILC; 3, topics dealt with by the ILC. Annexes include the Commission's Statute, texts of selected multilateral conventions, and a select bibliography.

104. United Nations. International Law Commission. *Yearbook of the International Law Commission.* 1949-. New York: UN. A/CN.4/SER.A/-. ISSN 00828289.

Constitutes the Commission's official records. Two volumes per year, as of 1950: 1, summary records of the commission's annual session; 2, documents of the session.

105. United Nations Interregional Crime and Justice Research Institute. *Statute.* Rome: UNICRI, 1989. 7 p.

Sets out the objectives, functions, structure, financing, and other constitutional provisions of UNICRI, the successor of the United Nations Social Defence Research Institute.

106. United Nations Interregional Crime and Justice Research Institute. *UNICRI: United Nations Interregional Crime and Justice Research Institute.* Rome: UNICRI, 1989. 16 p.

Overview of the establishment, functions, activities and financing of UNICRI, with information on its place in the UN system. Includes a list of publications of UNICRI and of its predecessor, the United Nations Social Defence Research Institute.

16   United Nations Documentary and Archival Sources

United Nations. Library. *A Bibliography of the Charter of the United Nations.* See #489.

107.   United Nations. Office of Public Information. *Everyman's United Nations: A Complete Handbook of the Activities and Evolution of the United Nations during Its First Twenty Years, 1945-1965*. 8th ed. New York: UN, 1968. xii, 634 p. Sales No. E.67.I.5.

Guide to the structure and activities of the UN system of organizations. Each chapter gives a chronological account of activities in a particular subject area (political and security questions; economic and social questions; human rights; trust and non-self-governing territories; legal questions; administrative and budgetary questions). Includes appendices (texts of the Charter and the Universal Declaration of Human Rights, and a list of UN information centers and services) and an index. Updated but not superseded by United Nations, Department of Public Information, *Everyone's United Nations*, 9th ed. (New York: UN, 1979; xii, 477 p.; Sales No. E.79.I.5.) and United Nations, Department of Public Information, *Everyone's United Nations*, 10th ed. (New York: UN, 1986; 484 p.; Sales No. E.85.I.16; ISBN 9211002737.)

108.   United Nations Relief and Rehabilitation Administration. *UNRRA: The History of the United Nations Relief and Rehabilitation Administration.* Prepared by a special staff under the direction of George Woodbridge, Chief Historian of UNRRA. New York: Columbia University Press, 1950.

Although not a member of the UN system, UNRRA (formed in 1943 and dissolved in 1947/1948) fulfilled a number of functions later assumed by various bodies of the UN system. This work is a detailed survey with numerous documentary, bibliographic and archival references. In three volumes: volume 1 (xxxv, 518 p.) discusses UNRRA's structure, functions, administration and financing, and supply operations; volume 2 (xii, 601 p.) covers field operations and displaced person operations, and includes index to volumes 1 and 2; volume 3 (xiii, 520p.) consists of documentary and statistical appendices, and index.

United Nations. Secretariat. *List of Non-Governmental Organizations in Consultative Status with the Economic and Social Council.* See #499.

109.   United Nations. Security Council. *Official Records*. 1st- year, 1946-. New York: UN.

This major set of SC documents comprises verbatim meeting records, collected *Resolutions and Decisions* for each calendar year, supplements (now quarterly; texts or checklists of documents relevant to specific agenda items) and special supplements (these have included reports of the Trusteeship Council under Charter article 83 since 1975). SC *Official Records* are listed in *United Nations Official Records, 1948-1962: A Reference Catalogue* and its supplements for 1962-1981 and 1981-1984 (#492) as well as in "UNDI" (#468), *UNDEX* (#463) and *UNDOC* (#464), and *Index to Proceedings of the Security Council* (#455). The SC's annual reports appear as supplements (usually Supplement 2) of the *Official Records* of the General Assembly (#86).

110.   United Nations. Security Council. *Provisional Rules of Procedure of the Security Council.* New York: UN, 1983. 12 p. S/96/Rev.7; Sales No. E.83.I.4.

111.   United Nations Social Defence Research Institute. *UNSDRI at Twenty: 1968-1988.* Rome: UNSDRI, 1988. 45 p.

United Nations. Translation Division. German Section. *Trilingual Compendium of United Nations Terminology, English-French-German.* See #502.

Structural and Institutional Issues 17

112. United Nations. Trusteeship Council. *Official Records*. 1st- sess., 1947-. New York: UN.
   This set of major TC documents consists of verbatim meeting records; supplements (including *Resolutions and Decisions*, #263); special supplements; and selected documents in sessional fascicles. TC *Official Records* are listed in *United Nations Official Records, 1948-1962: A Reference Catalogue* and its supplements for 1962-1981 and 1981-1984 (#492) as well as in "UNDI" (#468), *UNDEX* (#463) and *UNDOC* (#464), and *Index to Proceedings of the Trusteeship Council* (#455). TC annual reports were issued until 1975 as supplements (usually Supplement 4) of the *Official Records* of the General Assembly; TC reports under Charter article 83 appear as special supplements to the *Official Records* of the Security Council (#109).

113. United Nations. Trusteeship Council. *Rules of Procedure of the Trusteeship Council (As Amended up to and during Its Twenty-ninth Session)*. New York: UN, 1962. iii, 19 p. T/1/Rev.6; Sales No. E.62.I.23.

114. United States. Congress. Senate. Committee on Foreign Relations. *Credentials Considerations in the United Nations General Assembly: The Process and Its Role*. Prepared by Marjorie A. Browne for the Foreign Affairs and National Defense Division, Congressional Research Service, Library of Congress. Washington, D.C.: Government Printing Office, 1983. 98th Cong., 1st sess., Committee Print S. Prt. 98-143. vii, 29 p.

115. United States. Department of State. *Report to Congress on Voting Practices in the United Nations*. 1984- . Washington, D.C.
   Comprises textual and tabular material. Initial table compares votes of the U.S. with those of other UN member states, and shows the number of identical votes, opposing or other types of differing votes, and percentage of coincidence with U.S. votes. Also gives votes of states within regional groups and other caucuses (for example, the non-aligned group), and votes on several issues (for example, Israel's credentials) considered important by the U.S. Latest issue (ix, 232 p.) is dated March 31, 1990.

116. United States. Department of State. *United States Contributions to International Organizations: Annual Report to the Congress*. 1st-, 1951/1952-. Washington, D.C.: Government Printing Office. Department of State Publication. ISSN 04991583.
   Issued 1952-19?? as House Document, 19??- as Department of State Publication.

117. United States. Department of State. *United States Participation in the UN; Report by the President to the Congress*. 1946-. Washington, D.C.: Government Printing Office.
   Former title (1947-1947): *The United States and the United Nations; Report by the President to the Congress*.

118. United States. Department of State. *Use of the Veto In Meetings of the Security Council of the United Nations*. Washington, D.C.: Dept. of State, 1990. [1], 43, [3] p. SD/SC/VETO/1/Rev.15.
   Chronological list of 191 cases in which the veto has been used. Identifies each case, with date, meeting number, draft resolution number and sponsors, voting record including permanent member casting a veto. Includes subject index. Latest issue of a semiannual publication.

119. United States. Library of Congress. Congressional Research Service. *United Nations Reform: Issues for Congress*. By Marjorie Ann Browne. Washington, D.C.: CRS, Library of Congress, 1988. 59 p.
   Reviews UN problems that led to U.S. congressional action to limit contributions to the UN, and surveys progress in three areas: the use of consensus in decision-making on UN budget issues; reduction of UN Secretariat staff; and reduction in the number of Soviet UN employees on fixed-term contract. Also examines proposals on restructuring and administrative reform. Includes tables, charts, and bibliography.

18   United Nations Documentary and Archival Sources

120.   Universal Postal Union. *Annual Report on the Work of the Union.* 1964?-. Bern: UPU. ISSN 05032466.
Provides information on UPU and other postal activities, including financing, technical cooperation, and meetings held during the report year. Title varies slightly.

World Bank. *See also* International Bank for Reconstruction and Development.

121.   World Bank. *Annual Report.* 1st- , 1945/1946- . Washington, D.C.: World Bank. ISSN 02522942.
Reports on the activities, policies, projects, finances of the World Bank and the World Bank Group. Includes administrative and statistical appendices.

122.   World Bank. *Convention Establishing the Multilateral Investment Guarantee Agency and Commentary on the Convention.* [Washington, D.C]: World Bank, 1985. iii, 44, ii, 24 p.

123.   World Bank. *The Evolving Role of IDA.* Washington, D.C.: World Bank, 1989. ix, 53 p. ISBN 0821312014.
Overview of the evolution of the role, activities and programs of the International Development Association, the soft-loan affiliate of the World Bank. Includes statistical appendix.

124.   World Bank. *IDA in Retrospect: The First Two Decades of the International Development Association.* New York: Oxford University Press for the World Bank, 1982. xvi, 142 p. ISBN 0195204085.

125.   World Bank. *The World Bank and the International Finance Corporation.* Washington, D.C.: World Bank, 1983. 65 p. ISBN 0821301780.
Brief guide to the activities, projects and finances of the World Bank (including the International Development Association) and its soft-loan affiliate, the IFC. Includes organization charts.

126.   World Bank. *World Bank Operations: Sectoral Programs and Policies.* Baltimore, Md.; London: Johns Hopkins University Press for the World Bank, 1972. xiii, 513 p. ISBN 0801814480.

127.   World Health Organization. *Four Decades of Achievement: Highlights of the Work of the World Health Organization.* Geneva: WHO, 1988. v, 39 p. ISBN 9241542349.
Overview of the main activities, changing strategies, and future challenges of the WHO.

128.   World Health Organization. *The Work of WHO: Biennial Report of the Director-General to the World Health Assembly and to the United Nations.* 1948-. Geneva: WHO. ISSN 05092558.

129.   World Intellectual Property Organization. *Convention Establishing the World Intellectual Property Organization, Signed at Stockholm on July 14, 1967 and As Amended on October 2, 1979.* Geneva: WIPO, 1985. 24 p.

130.   World Intellectual Property Organization. *WIPO: General Information.* Geneva: WIPO, 1990. 83 p. WIPO Publication No. 400. ISBN 9280502387.
Describes WIPO's history, activities, and structure. Includes selected list of publications.

131.   World Meteorological Organization. *Annual Report of the World Meteorological Organization.* 1951-. Geneva: WMO. ISSN 00841994.
Includes list of WMO publications issued during the report year.

World Meteorological Organization. *Basic Documents. See* #294.

132. World Meteorological Organization. *Composition of the World Meteorological Organization = Composition de l'OMM*. 19??-. WMO Publication No. 5. Geneva: WMO. ISSN 02509288.
    Provides information on the membership, structure, regional associations, technical commissions, secretariat and other institutional matters of the WMO.

133. World Meteorological Organization. *One Hundred Years of International Co-operation in Meteorology (1873-1973): A Historical Review*. Geneva: WMO, 1973. v, 53, [4] p. WMO-No. 345.
    Outlines the history of the WMO and its predecessor, the International Meteorological Organization. Annexes include lists of presidents and other officers of the two organizations, and a chronology.

PEACE AND SECURITY, DISARMAMENT AND ARMS CONTROL

Bailey, Sydney Dawson. *The Procedure of the UN Security Council.* See #4.

134. *Basic Documents on United Nations and Related Peace-keeping Forces.* 2d, enl. ed. Compiled and edited by Robert C. R. Siekmann. Dordrecht, The Netherlands: Nijhoff, 1989.
xxi, 415 p. ISBN 902473701X.

Compendium of documents relating to the establishment and functioning of the UN Emergency Force, the UN Operation in the Congo, the UN Peace-keeping Force in Cyprus, and other UN peacekeeping forces as well as the non-UN Multinational Force and Observers set up following the 1979 Egypt-Israel peace treaty, and the 1982-1984 Multinational Force in Lebanon. Includes appendix on UN military observer missions, bibliography, and index. Updates the documentary portion of Rosalyn Higgins, *United Nations Peacekeeping, 1946-1967: Documents and Commentary* (#135).

Deardorff, John. *United Nations Security Council Index, 1946-1964.* See #376.

135. Higgins, Rosalyn. *United Nations Peacekeeping, 1946-1967: Documents and Commentary.* London: Oxford University Press under the Auspices of the Royal Institute of International Affairs, 1969-1981. 4 vols.

Compendium and analysis of full or partial texts of documents on constitutional, administrative, financial and other aspects of UN peacekeeping operations, with factual commentaries. Volume 1 (1969; xiv, 674 p.) covers the Middle East; Volume 2 (1970; xviii, 486 p.), Asia; Volume 3 (1980; xiii, 472 p.), Africa; and Volume 4 (1981; xii, 419 p.), Europe. Includes bibliographies and indexes. Its documentary portion is updated by *Basic Documents on United Nations and Related Peace-keeping Forces* (#134).

136. Independent Commission on Disarmament and Security Issues.
Common Security: A Blueprint for Survival. New York: Simon and Schuster, 1982. xvii, 202 p. ISBN 0671458795.

This Commission, chaired by Prime Minister Olof Palme of Sweden, consisted of seventeen prominent members from East and West as well as North and South. The "Palme Report" discusses arms control, disarmament and security issues and makes recommendations, including a call for the strengthening of the UN's role in these fields. Indexed, along with the Brandt Memorandum (#154), the Brandt Report (#155), and the Brundtland Report (#237) in *Common Index and Glossary to the Brandt, Palme and Brundtland Reports of the Independent Commissions on International Development, Disarmament and Security, and Environment and Development* (London: Commonwealth Secretariat, 1990; #374).

International Atomic Energy Agency. *International Treaties Relating to Nuclear Control and Disarmament.* See #202.

137. *The Laws of Armed Conflicts: A Collection of Conventions, Resolutions and Other Decisions.* Edited by Dietrich Schindler and Jiří Toman. Dordrecht, The Netherlands: Nijhoff; Geneva: Henry Dumont Institute, 1988. xxxiv, 1033 p.

Compendium of texts of eighty-seven multilateral conventions, resolutions or other decisions on the law of armed conflicts (*jus in bello*) adopted since the 1856 Paris Declaration. Includes lists of signatures, ratifications and accessions, texts of reservations, and index.

Resolutions and Statements of the United Nations Security Council, 1946-1989: A Thematic Guide. See #279.

138.	Unesco. *Unesco Yearbook on Peace and Conflict Studies.* 1-, 1980-. Paris: Unesco.
	Concentrates on research and teaching in the fields of arms control, disarmament and peace. Includes information on Unesco activities, meetings and research programs.

139.	Unesco. *World Directory of Peace Research and Training Institutions = Répertoire mondial des institutions de recherche et de formation sur la paix = Repertorio Mundial de Instituciones de Investigación y de Formación sobre la Paz.* 6th ed. World Social Science Information Directories. Deddington, Oxford: Berg; Paris: Unesco, 1988. xvi, 271 p. ISBN 9231024868.
	Lists over 300 international, regional and national institutions in forty-six countries, indicating name, acronym, address, date of establishment, activities, publications and recent research projects. Includes subject, geographical, senior staff and course indexes.

140.	United Nations. Department for Disarmament Affairs. *Disarmament: A Periodic Review.* Vol. 1-, May 1978-. New York: UN. ISSN 02519518.
	Quarterly magazine on UN and other international activities in the field of arms limitation and disarmament. Includes texts of selected documents, and book reviews.

141.	United Nations. Department for Disarmament Affairs. *Multilateral Aspects of the Disarmament Debate.* New York: Taylor & Francis for and on behalf of the United Nations, 1989. vi, 204 p. ISBN 0844816167.
	Collection of papers of two meetings of experts held in 1987 and 1988. Topics include conventional and nuclear weapons, international security and outer space, and verification.

142.	United Nations. Department for Disarmament Affairs. *The United Nations and Disarmament: A Short History.* New York: UN, 1988. xv, 112 p.
	Overview of UN activities in the field of disarmament in general, nuclear non-proliferation, conventional, chemical and biological weapons, peaceful uses of outer space, and the economic and social consequences of the arms race.

143.	United Nations. Department for Disarmament Affairs. *The United Nations Disarmament Yearbook.* Vol. 1-, 1976-. New York: UN. ISSN 02525607.
	Timely annual survey of comprehensive approaches to disarmament, nuclear disarmament (including peaceful uses of nuclear energy), chemical, bacteriological and other weapons of mass destruction, conventional armaments, confidence-building measures, and other related issues. Includes information on disarmament activities of the UN system, and on legal instruments in the field of arms regulation and disarmament.

	United Nations. Department of Political and Security Council Affairs. *Repertoire of the Practice of the Security Council, 1946-1951.* See #76.

144.	United Nations. Department of Public Information. *The Blue Helmets: A Review of United Nations Peace-keeping.* New York: UN, 1985. vi, 350, [11] p. Sales No. E.85.I.18. ISBN 9211002753.
	Provides detailed description of: UN peacekeeping operations in connection with the Arab-Israeli conflict; India-Pakistan observation activities; observation activities in Lebanon, Yemen, and the Dominican Republic; the Congo operation; the Cyprus operation; and activities in West Irian. Appendices include information on the composition and organization of UN peacekeeping operations, statistical and other facts, and maps.

145.	United Nations Institute for Disarmament Research. *UNIDIR Repertory of Disarmament Research, 1990*. Compiled and edited by Chantal de Jonge Oudraat and Péricles Gasparini Alves. New York: UN, 1990. xiii, 402 p. UNIDIR/90/60; Sales No. GV.0.90.0.10.

In two parts: part 1 describes 730 research institutes in 121 countries; part 2 is a subject list of publications of the institutes. Includes institute name, research project, personal name, publications title, and author indexes. Updated and revised version of *Repertory of Disarmament Research* issued in 1982.

United Nations. Security Council. *Official Records.* See #109.

United Nations. Security Council. *Provisional Rules of Procedure of the Security Council.* See #110.

United Nations. Security Council. *Resolutions and Decisions of the Security Council.* See #292.

ECONOMIC AND SOCIAL ISSUES

Advisory Committee for the Co-ordination of Information Systems [of the United Nations System of Organizations]. *Register of Development Activities of the United Nations System.* See #367.

146. Commission on International Development. *Partners in Development: Report.* New York: Praeger, 1969. xvi, 400 p.
Established on the initiative of the World Bank and chaired by former Canadian Prime Minister Lester B. Pearson, the Commission on International Development surveyed the situation of developing countries in the 1950s and 1960s, examined private and official development assistance, discussed the role of international organizations, and presented recommendations, including a proposed ODA target of 0.7% of donor countries' GNP.

Deardorff, John. *United Nations Economic and Social Council Index, 1946-1965.* See #376.

Fomerand, Jacques. *Strengthening the United Nations Economic and Social Programs: A Documentary Essay.* See #8.

Food and Agriculture Organization of the United Nations. *FAO Production Yearbook.* See #295.

Food and Agriculture Organization of the United Nations. *FAO Trade Yearbook.* See #296.

147. Food and Agriculture Organization of the United Nations. *Food and Nutrition.* Vol. 1-, 1975-. Rome: FAO. ISSN 03048942.
Semiannual journal of articles on all aspects of food and nutrition, developments concerning the *Codex Alimentarius* (#417), and book reviews. Each issue emphasizes a special theme. Not to be confused with *Food and Nutrition Bulletin* issued by UNU.

Food and Agriculture Organization of the United Nations. *World Crop and Livestock Statistics: Area, Yield and Production of Crops; Production of Livestock Products.* See #297.

148. Food and Agriculture Organization of the United Nations. *World Food Survey.* 1st-, 1946-. Rome: FAO.
These surveys, published so far in 1946, 1952, 1963, 1977 and 1987, examine the state of food supplies and aspects of malnutrition, and set out policy implications for food demand, production and distribution.

General Agreement on Tariffs and Trade. *GATT Activities: An Annual Review of the Work of the GATT.* See #12.

149. General Agreement on Tariffs and Trade. *GATT Focus.* 1-, February/March 1981-. Geneva: GATT. ISSN 02560119.
Published ten times a year, this newsletter reports on the work of GATT and related activities in GATT contracting party states.

150.   General Agreement on Tariffs and Trade. *International Trade*. 1952-. Geneva: GATT. ISSN 0072064x.
Annual statistics and overview of the world economy, with special emphasis on world trade. Beginning with 1987/88, in two volumes, with statistical tables and charts comprising volume 2.

151.   General Agreement on Tariffs and Trade. *Review of Developments in the Trading System*. [1-12,] January/August 1983?-September 1988/February 1989. Geneva: GATT. ISSN 10119205.
Semiannual summary of trade policies and measures: sectoral and regional developments, tariffs, generalized system of preferences, non-tariff restrictions, anti-dumping and other government measures, trade policy trends, other trade-related activities, and exchange rates.

152.   General Agreement on Tariffs and Trade. *The Texts of the Tokyo Round Agreements*. Geneva: GATT, 1986. vii, 208 p. Sales No. GATT/1986-5. ISBN 9287010234.
Contains texts of the codes of the 1973-1979 Tokyo Round of multilateral trade negotiations ("standards code," "subsidies code," "customs valuation code," "anti-dumping code") as well as other agreements and decisions of the Tokyo Round.

153.   Hill, Martin. *The United Nations System: Co-ordinating Its Economic and Social Work*. New York: Cambridge University Press, 1978. xv, 252 p. ISBN 0521216745.
Examines problems and types of coordination among the UN system of organizations, with a set of conclusions and recommendations. Appendices include documents, charts and other material. Based on an earlier version prepared under the auspices of the United Nations Institute for Training and Research (E/5491).

Holborn, Louise W. *The International Refugee Organization, a Specialized Agency of the United Nations: Its History and Work, 1946-1952. See* #17.

154.   Independent Commission on International Development Issues. *Common Crisis North-South: Co-operation for World Recovery; Memorandum of the Independent Commission on International Development Issues*. London; Sydney: Pan Books, 1983. 174 p. ISBN 0330281305.
Published three years after the Brandt Report and noting lack of progress in North-South economic cooperation, this "Brandt Memorandum" presents a more up-to-date version of the Independent Commission's original emergency program. It deals with international cooperation in finance, trade, food and energy, as well as with the North-South negotiating process, and makes a number of new proposals in these areas. Indexed in *Common Index and Glossary to the Brandt, Palme and Brundtland Reports of the Independent Commissions on International Development, Disarmament and Security, and Environment and Development* (#374).

155.   Independent Commission on International Development Issues. *North-South: A Programme for Survival; Report of the Independent Commission on International Development Issues*. Cambridge, Mass.: MIT Press, 1980. 304 p. ISBN 0262520591.
This Commission, proposed by World Bank president Robert McNamara and chaired by Willy Brandt, consisted of a group of prominent international figures from developing and developed countries. The "Brandt Report" deals with "global issues arising from the economic and social disparities of the world community". Topics discussed include mutual interests of North and South, problems of the poorest countries, hunger and food, population and environment, disarmament, energy, and world trade. Proposes an international program of priorities, and discusses the role of the UN system. Indexed, along with the "Brandt Memorandum" (#154), the "Palme Report" (#136), and the "Brundtland Report" (#237) in *Common Index and Glossary to the Brandt, Palme and Brundtland Reports of the Independent Commissions on International Development, Disarmament and Security, and Environment and Development* (#374).

Economic and Social Issues 25

International Bank for Reconstruction and Development. *Summary Proceedings of the Annual Meetings of the Boards of Governors [of the International Bank for Reconstruction and Development, International Finance Corporation, and International Development Association].* See #47.

International Finance Corporation. *Annual Report.* See #32.

156. International Finance Corporation. *Emerging Stock Markets Factbook.* 1988?-. Washington, D.C.: IFC. ISSN 10128115.
Designed primarily for institutional investors, investment bankers, academics, economists and journalists, it provides data on leading stock markets, mostly in developing countries: market capitalization, number of listed domestic companies, value traded, US dollar currency exchange rates, and various other stock market indices and equity market profiles. The latest (1990) edition covers thirty markets, including newly opened exchanges in Hungary and Yugoslavia.

International Fund for Agricultural Development. *IFAD Annual Report.* See #35.

International Labour Office. *The Cost of Social Security.* See #300.

157. International Labour Office. *The ILO and the World of Work.* 1984. 74 p. ISBN 9221031500.
Outlines ILO's objectives, structure, working methods, and activities in the fields of working conditions, employment, human resources development, social institutions, and sectors and occupations.

158. International Labour Office. *International Labour Review.* Vol. 1-, 1921-. Geneva: ILO. ISSN 00207780.
Bimonthly journal on economic and social aspects of labor. Includes book reviews.

159. International Labour Office. *Official Bulletin.* 1919-. Geneva: ILO.
Series A (ISSN 03785882) provides International Labour Conference and other ILO documents; Series B (ISSN 03785890) gives reports of the Governing Body's Committee on Freedom of Association. Series C (ISSN 03785874) was published 1919-1978.

International Labour Office. *Year Book of Labour Statistics.* See #302.

International Monetary Fund. *Annual Report of the Executive Board.* See #40.

International Monetary Fund. *Direction of Trade Statistics.* See #303.

International Monetary Fund. *Finance & Development.* See World Bank. *Finance & Development,* #194.

International Monetary Fund. *The IMF in a Changing World.* See #42.

160. International Monetary Fund. *IMF Survey.* Vol. 1-, 1972-. Washington, D.C.: IMF. ISSN 0047083X.
Biweekly publication of IMF news and other topics of monetary and financial interest. Has an annual "Supplement on the Fund."

International Monetary Fund. *International Financial Statistics.* See #304.

International Monetary Fund. *The International Monetary Fund, 1945-1965: Twenty Years of International Monetary Cooperation.* See #43.

International Monetary Fund. *The International Monetary Fund, 1966-71: The System under Stress.* See #44.

International Monetary Fund. *The International Monetary Fund, 1972-1978: Cooperation on Trial.* See #45.

International Monetary Fund. *The Role and Function of the International Monetary Fund.* See #46.

161. International Monetary Fund. *Selected Decisions of the International Monetary Fund and Selected Documents of the International Monetary Fund.* 1st- issue, 1962-. Washington, D.C.: IMF. ISSN 00941735.
Provides texts of decisions, interpretations and resolutions of the Executive Board and the Board of Governors, as well as other important documents. Former title (1962-197?): *Selected Decisions of the Executive Directors and Selected Documents.*

162. International Monetary Fund. *Staff Papers.* Vol. 1-, February 1950-. Washington, D.C.: IMF. ISSN 00208027.
Quarterly journal providing selected studies by Fund staff on balance of payments, debt, exchange rates, international liquidity, and various other monetary and fiscal questions. Also publishes comments by external contributors. There is a cumulative index for volumes 1-27 (1950-1980.)

International Monetary Fund. *Summary Proceedings of the Annual Meeting of the Board of Governors.* See #47.

163. International Monetary Fund. *World Economic Outlook: A Survey by the Staff of the International Monetary Fund.* 1980-. World Economic and Financial Surveys. Washington, D.C.: IMF. ISSN 02566877.
Reviews the current economic situation in industrial and developing countries, and presents policy issues and short- and medium-term prospects of the world economy. From 1984, issued twice a year, in April and October; the October edition gives revised projections. Includes statistical appendix.

164. International Trade Centre (UNCTAD/GATT). *Annual Report on the Activities of the International Trade Centre, UNCTAD/GATT.* 1980?-. Geneva: ITC.
Covers developments of markets and trade promotion. Annexes deal with sources of financing, distribution of experts, training, trust fund contributions and expenditures.

Joint FAO/WHO Food Standards Programme. *Codex Alimentarius.* See #417.

Joint Inspection Unit [of the United Nations System of Organizations]. *Concluding Report on the Implementation of General Assembly Resolution 32/197 concerning the Restructuring of the Economic and Social Sectors of the United Nations System.* See #53.

Multilateral Investment Guarantee Agency. *Annual Report.* See #60.

Unesco. *International Directory of Youth Bodies.* See #435.

165. Unesco. *International Social Science Journal.* Vol. 1-, 1949-. Paris: Unesco. ISSN 00208701.
Interdisciplinary quarterly, with each issue featuring a special topic. Includes calendars of conferences and book reviews.

166.   Unesco. *Reports and Papers in the Social Sciences*. 1-, 1955-. Paris: Unesco.
Describes Unesco's social science programs and provides bibliographies, directories and repertories in the social sciences. Published at irregular intervals.

167.   Unesco. ***World Directory of Social Science Institutions: Research, Advanced Training, Professional Bodies** = Répertoire mondial des institutions de sciences sociales: recherche, formation supérieure, organismes professionnels = Repertorio Mundial de Instituciones de Ciencias Sociales: Investigación, Capacitación Superior, Organismos Profesionales*. 5th ed. World Social Science Information Directories. Paris: Unesco, 1990. xv, 1211 p. ISBN 9230025526.
Covers 2,088 national and international institutions in 199 countries. For each, indicates name, address, geographic and subject scope, activities, staff size, and publications. Does not cover peace research and human rights research institutions, for which *see* Unesco, *World Directory of Peace Research and Training Institutions* (#139) and Unesco, *World Directory of Human Rights Teaching and Research Institutions* (#223). Includes subject and institutional name and institutional head indexes.

168.   United Nations. *Global Outlook 2000: An Economic, Social, and Environmental Perspective*. New York: UN, 1990. xi, 340 p. ST/ESA/215/Rev.1; Sales No. E.90.II.C.3. ISBN 9211091187.
Based on a study prepared for the General Assembly, it covers long-term (1960-1990) trends in production, resource allocation, structural adjustment and international trade, and provides socio-economic perspectives for the environment, energy, agriculture, technology, production and trade, demographic and labor-force issues, human settlements, education, health, and social policy. Includes bibliographical references and statistical tables. Lacks index.

169.   United Nations. Centre for Human Settlements (Habitat). *Global Report on Human Settlements*. Oxford; New York: Oxford University Press for the United Nations Centre for Human Settlements, 1987. xv, 229, [109] p. ISBN 0198286023.
Discusses human settlement strategy (including issues of the urban poor), global conditions and trends, and policy areas in settlement development. A copious statistical annex contains tables on population characteristics such as urban and rural distribution, and housing and health conditions.

United Nations Centre on Transnational Corporations. *Transnational Corporations: A Selective Bibliography, 1983-1987*. *See* #447.

170.   United Nations Centre on Transnational Corporations. *Transnational Corporations in World Development: Trends and Prospects*. New York: UN, 1988. xxi, 623 p. ST/CTC/89. Sales No. E.88.II.A.7. ISBN 9211042917.
Overview and analysis of the activities of transnational corporations and their impact on the world economy. Discusses developmental, socio-economic, environmental, trade, policy and other aspects. Includes statistical annex and index. This is the fourth survey of TNCs, continuing *Multinational Corporations in World Development* (New York: UN, 1973; Sales No. E.73.II.A.11); *Transnational Corporations in World Development: A Re-examination* (New York: UN, 1978; Sales No. E.78.II.A.5); and *Transnational Corporations in World Development: The Third Survey* (New York: UN, 1983; Sales No. E.83.II.A.14.)

171.   United Nations Children's Fund. *Assignment Children = Les carnets de l'enfance*. No. 1-, 1963-. Geneva; New York: UNICEF. ISSN 00045128.
"A multidisciplinary journal concerned with major social development issues, with particular reference to children, women, and youth." Each issue is devoted to a special theme; for example: universal child immunization; literacy, health, nutrition and income; basic services in regional development. Recent issues have appeared in a monographic series with the same title.

172. United Nations Children's Fund. *Children and Development in the 1990s: A UNICEF Sourcebook.* New York: UNICEF, 1990. viii, 256 p.

Issued on the occasion of the September 1990 World Summit for Children, it discusses maternal and child health; nutrition; water and sanitation; education; the situation of children in armed conflicts and of street children, girls and urban children; and the economic base for assistance to children. Includes statistical tables and suggested further readings.

173. United Nations Children's Fund. *The Children and the Nations: The Story of UNICEF.* By Maggie Black. Sydney: P.I.C. Pty. Ltd. for UNICEF, 1986. x, 502 p. ISBN 9211003024.

Comprehensive, readable history of UNICEF from its origins to the 1980s. Includes statistics and index.

174. United Nations Children's Fund. *Compilation of Economic and Social Council and General Assembly Resolutions on UNICEF and the International Year of the Child, 1946-1977.* New York: UNICEF, 197?. E/ICEF/Misc.175/Rev.2.

Updated by supplements for 1978-1979 (E/ICEF/Misc.175/Rev.2/Add.1) and 1980-1982 (E/ICEF/Misc.175/Rev.2/Add.2).

175. United Nations Children's Fund. *The State of the World's Children.* 1980-. Oxford; New York: Oxford University Press for UNICEF. ISSN 0265718X.

Annual report on issues of children's health, education, welfare, problems and opportunities. Includes economic and social statistics.

United Nations Children's Fund. *Statistics on Children in UNICEF Assisted Countries.* See #308.

United Nations Conference on Trade and Development. *Atlas of the Least Developed Countries.* See #450.

United Nations Conference on Trade and Development. *Handbook of International Trade and Development Statistics.* See #309.

United Nations Conference on Trade and Development. *UNCTAD Commodity Yearbook.* See #310.

176. United Nations Conference on Trade and Development. *Uruguay Round: Papers on Selected Issues.* New York: UN, 1989. xxv, 382 p. UNCTAD/ITP/10.

A series of studies on important issues of the Round, prepared by UNCTAD to help developing countries in their negotiatiating objectives. Discusses proposals for a review of GATT Article XVIII; safeguards; trade in services; intellectual property rights; trade-related investment; agriculture; and other issues. Complemented by *Uruguay Round: Further Papers on Selected Issues* (New York: UN, 1990; xxi, 316 p.; UNCTAD/ITP/42.) which deals with proposals on GATT rules and disciplines on agriculture; trade-related investment measures; intellectual property rights; anti-competitive practices in the services sector; banking services; EC anti-dumping legislation and practices; and the Canada-U.S. free trade agreement.

177. United Nations. Department of International Economic and Social Affairs. *Elements of an International Development Strategy for the 1990s: Views and Recommendations of the Committee for Development Planning.* New York: UN, 1989. viii, 90 p. ST/ESA/214; Sales No. E.89.IV.3. ISBN 9211301319.

Analysis and recommendations of the Committee in the areas of economic growth, human development, reduction of poverty, and the environment.

178. United Nations. Department of International Economic and Social Affairs. *Human Resources Development: A Neglected Dimension of Development Strategy; Views and Recommendations of the Committee for Development Planning.* New York: UN, 1988. ix, 45 p. ST/ESA/208; Sales No. E.88.II.A.11. ISBN 9211042933.

The Committee for Development Planning, whose mandate is to assess world development trends and make recommendations on development and international economic cooperation, reviews in this report the state of the world economy and trends of human resources development, and sets out future tasks in the areas of trade, debt, finance, water resources management, and international development strategies. Includes statistical tables and annexes.

179. United Nations. Department of International Economic and Social Affairs. *Report on the World Social Situation.* 1952-. New York: UN. ISSN 00828068.

Quadrennial survey of the family, advancement of women, food consumption and supply, poverty and inequality, the social impact of new technologies, the situation of migrants and refugees, and other topics of social development. Includes statistical tables and charts. Supplements accompany some issues.

180. United Nations. Department of International Economic and Social Affairs. *World Economic Survey: Current Trends and Policies in the World Economy.* 1945/1947-. New York: UN. ISSN 00841714.

Annual review and analysis of the state of the world economy. Discusses global economic trends and prospects, international trade, finance and debt, energy, interest rates, and other economic topics. Includes statistical annex. Supplements accompany some issues. *See also* regional surveys: *Economic and Social Survey of Asia and the Pacific* (#183); *Economic Survey of Europe* (#186); *Economic Survey of Latin America and the Caribbean*; and *Survey of Economic and Social Conditions in Africa*.

United Nations. Department of International Economic and Social Affairs. Information Systems Unit. *Development Information Abstracts.* See #473.

181. United Nations Development Programme. *Annual Report of the Administrator.* 1965-. New York: UNDP.

182. United Nations Development Programme. *Human Development Report 1990.* New York: Oxford University Press for the UNDP, 1990. x, 189 p. ISBN 019506481X.

First issue of an annual report on the human dimension of development. Analyzes life expectancy, literacy, access to health services and to safe water, GNP and real GDP per capita, deprivation and other aspects of human development in fourteen countries over the last three decades. Includes tables of human development indicators, and bibliography.

United Nations Development Programme. *A Study of the Capacity of the United Nations Development System.* See #80.

183. United Nations. Economic and Social Commission for Asia and the Pacific. *Economic and Social Survey of Asia and the Pacific.* 1947-. Bangkok: ESCAP, UN. ISSN 02525704.

Former title (1947-1974): *Economic Survey of Asia and the Far East*.

United Nations. Economic and Social Commission for Asia and the Pacific. *ESCAP 1947-1987: Regional Co-operation for Development.* See #81.

United Nations. Economic and Social Commission for Asia and the Pacific. *Statistical Yearbook for Asia and the Pacific.* See #311.

United Nations. Economic and Social Council. *Official Records.* See #82.

184.	United Nations. Economic and Social Council. *Resolutions Adopted by the Economic and Social Council.* Economic and Social Council. *Official Records.* 1st- sess., 1946-. New York: UN.
Annual edition of ECOSOC resolutions. Usually issued as Supplement 1 to the ECOSOC *Official Records.*

United Nations. Economic Commission for Africa. *Compendium of Resolutions Adopted by the United Nations Economic Commission for Africa from the First to the Eighth Sessions, 1958-1967.* See #284.

United Nations. Economic Commission for Europe. *Compendium of Resolutions and Decisions of the Economic Commission for Europe, 1947-1972.* See #285.

United Nations. Economic Commission for Europe. *ECE 1947-1987.* See #84.

185.	United Nations. Economic Commission for Europe. *Economic Bulletin for Europe.* Vol. 1-, 1949-. New York: UN. ISSN 0041638X.
Another edition is issued in Geneva and Oxford by Pergamon with the UN. Similar periodicals for other regions are: *Economic Bulletin for Asia and the Pacific* and *CEPAL Review* (formerly *Economic Bulletin for Latin America*).

186.	United Nations. Economic Commission for Europe. *Economic Survey of Europe.* [1947]- . New York: UN. ISSN 00708712.
Former title (1947): *A Survey of the Economic Situation and Prospects of Europe.*

187.	United Nations. Economic Commission for Europe. *Overall Economic Perspective to the Year 2000.* New York: UN, 1988. x, 224 p. ECE/EC.AD/32; Sales No. E.88.II.E.4.
Review of global economic prospects, human resources, environment, science and technology, energy, and policy issues in Europe and North America. Includes statistical appendices and bibliography.

United Nations. Economic Commission for Latin America. *Collected Resolutions on the International Development Strategy and the New International Economic Order Adopted by the United Nations General Assembly and Economic and Social Council, the Economic Commission for Latin America and the Caribbean Development and Co-operation Committee.* See #286.

United Nations. Economic Commission for Latin America. *Resolutions Adopted by the Economic Commission for Latin America, the Committee of the Whole and the Trade Committee, 1948-1973.* See #287.

United Nations. Economic Commission for Latin America and the Caribbean. *ECLAC: 40 Years (1948-1988).* See #85.

United Nations Fund for Population Activities. *See* United Nations Population Fund (the new name was approved in December 1986 but the acronym UNFPA has been kept.)

United Nations Industrial Development Organization. *Handbook of Industrial Statistics.* See #313.

United Nations Industrial Development Organization. *Industrial Development Abstracts.* See #484.

United Nations Industrial Development Organization. Industrial Development Board. *Annual Report of UNIDO.* See #93.

188. United Nations Industrial Development Organization. *Industry and Development: Global Report.* 1985-. Vienna: UNIDO. ISSN 02593033.
Annual review and perspectives of the industrial economy of the world. Includes statistical annex.

United Nations Institute for Training and Research. *ECOSOC: Options for Reform.* See #96.

United Nations Institute for Training and Research. *A New International Economic Order: Selected Documents, 1945-1975.* See #290.

United Nations Institute for Training and Research. *Survey and Analysis of Evaluations of the United Nations Intergovernmental Structure and Functions in the Economic and Social Fields.* See #99.

United Nations. Office of the United Nations High Commissioner for Refugees. *Refugee Abstracts.* See #495.

United Nations. Office of the United Nations High Commissioner for Refugees. *United Nations Resolutions and Decisions Relating to the Office of the United Nations High Commissioner for Refugees.* See #291.

189. United Nations Population Fund. *Inventory of Population Projects in Developing Countries around the World.* 1973/1974-. New York: UNFPA.
Annual guide to sources of funding and other assistance in population matters by multilateral, regional, bilateral, non-governmental and other agencies.

190. United Nations Population Fund. *Population Policy Compendium.* New York: UNFPA, 19??-. Looseleaf.
Compendium of population policies of countries around the world. Issued jointly with the UN's Department of International Economic and Social Affairs.

191. United Nations Population Fund. *Populi: A Journal of the United Nations Population Fund.* 1973?-. New York: UNFPA. ISSN 02516861.

United Nations Population Fund. *UNFPA Publications and Audiovisual Guide.* See #496.

United Nations Relief and Rehabilitation Administration. *UNRRA: The History of the United Nations Relief and Rehabilitation Administration.* See #108.

United Nations Social Defence Research Institute. *UNSDRI at Twenty: 1968-1988.* See #111.

United Nations. Statistical Office. *Commodity Trade Statistics.* See #314.

United Nations. Statistical Office. *Compendium of Human Settlement Statistics, 1983.* See #315.

United Nations. Statistical Office. *Compendium of Statistics and Indicators on the Situation of Women, 1986.* See #316.

United Nations. Statistical Office. *Construction Statistics Yearbook.* See #317.

United Nations. Statistical Office. *Demographic Yearbook.* See #318.

United Nations. Statistical Office. *Energy Statistics Yearbook.* See #320.

United Nations. Statistical Office. *Handbook on Social Indicators.* See #321.

United Nations. Statistical Office. *Industrial Statistics Yearbook.* See #323.

United Nations. Statistical Office. *International Standard Industrial Classification of All Economic Activities.* See #324.

United Nations. Statistical Office. *International Trade Statistics Yearbook.* See #325.

United Nations. Statistical Office. *National Accounts Statistics.* See #327.

United Nations. Statistical Office. *Population and Vital Statistics Report.* See #328.

United Nations. Statistical Office. *World Trade Annual.* See #332.

192. World Bank. *Accelerated Development in Sub-Saharan Africa: An Agenda for Action.* Washington, D.C.: World Bank, 1981. viii, 198 p.
See also World Bank, *Sub-Saharan Africa: A Long-term Perspective Study* (Washington, D.C.: World Bank, 1989; xiv, 300 p.; ISBN 0821313495.)

World Bank. *African Economic and Financial Data.* See #333.

193. World Bank. *Annual Review of Project Performance Results.* 1975-. Washington, D.C.: World Bank. ISSN 02515261.
Variant title: *Annual Review of Project Performance Audit Results.*

World Bank. *The Development Data Book: A Guide to Social and Economic Statistics.* See #334.

World Bank. *The Evolving Role of IDA.* See #123.

194. World Bank. *Finance & Development.* Vol. 1-, June 1964-. Washington, D.C.: World Bank; International Monetary Fund. ISSN 01451707.
Quarterly journal, intended for the general public and issued jointly by the two Bretton Woods institutions. Covers a full range of financial and monetary subjects relating to development. Includes book reviews.

World Bank. *IDA in Retrospect: The First Two Decades of the International Development Association.* See #124.

World Bank. *Social Indicators of Development.* See #335.

World Bank. *Trends in Developing Economies.* See #336.

195. World Bank. *The Uruguay Round: A Handbook on the Multilateral Trade Negotiations.* Edited by J. Michael Finger and Andrzej Olechowski. Washington, D.C.: World Bank, 1987. 269 p. ISBN 0821309757.

World Bank. *The World Bank and the International Finance Corporation.* See #125.

World Bank. *World Bank Atlas.* See #337.

196. World Bank. *The World Bank Economic Review.* 1986-. Washington, D.C.: World Bank. ISSN 02586770.
   Directed primarily to professional economists, it disseminates results of research supported by the World Bank and emphasizing application and policy rather than economic theory. Published three times a year, with the occasional extra issue devoted to a specific theme.

   World Bank. *World Bank Operations: Sectoral Programs and Policies.* See #126.

197. World Bank. *The World Bank Research News.* Vol. 1-, 1980-. Washington, D.C.: World Bank. ISSN 02533928.

198. World Bank. *The World Bank Research Observer.* 1986-. Washington, D.C.: World Bank. ISSN 02573032.
   Semiannual journal for non-specialist readers about current research in development economics carried out at the World Bank.

   World Bank. *The World Bank Research Program: Abstracts of Current Studies.* See #514.

   World Bank. *World Debt Tables: External Debt of Developing Countries.* See #338.

199. World Bank. *World Development Report.* 1978- . New York: Oxford University Press for the World Bank. ISSN 01635085.
   Annual assessment of major development issues, with each report providing a detailed treatment of a special topic. The theme of the 1990 report is poverty. Includes World Development Indicators (selected social and economic data for over 100 countries.)

   World Bank. *World Tables.* See #339.

   World Commission on Environment and Development. *Our Common Future.* See #237.

INTERNATIONAL LAW

Bossuyt, Marc J. *Guide to the "Travaux préparatoires" of the International Covenant on Civil and Political Rights.* See #219.

La Charte des Nations Unies: commentaire, article par article. See #5.

Documents on the International Court of Justice. See #273.

200. General Agreement on Tariffs and Trade. *Status of Legal Instruments.* Geneva: Contracting Parties to the General Agreement on Tariffs and Trade. 1980-. Looseleaf. GATT/LEG/1.
Periodically updated tables of accessions, ratifications and other government action related to multilateral GATT agreements, declarations and other instruments.

201. International Atomic Energy Agency. *Agreements Registered with the International Atomic Energy Agency.* 10th ed. Legal Series, No. 3. Vienna: IAEA, 1989. 243 p. STI/PUB/831. ISBN 9201760892.
Lists agreements registered up to 31 December 1988. In three parts: 1, chronological list; 2, major multilateral agreements deposited with the IAEA; 3, country and organization index. Parts 1 and 2 give IAEA registration numbers, the subject of each agreement, names of parties, dates of signature and entry into force, and publications where the text may be found.

202. International Atomic Energy Agency. *International Treaties Relating to Nuclear Control and Disarmament.* Legal Series, No. 9. Vienna: IAEA, 1975. 78 p. ISBN 9201760752.
Presents the official English texts of eight important treaties relating to nuclear arms control and disarmament, including the 1959 Antarctic Treaty and the 1968 Nuclear Non-proliferation Treaty.

203. International Civil Aviation Organization. *Aeronautical Agreements and Arrangements: Tables of Agreements and Arrangements Registered with the Organization, 1 January 1946-31 December 1985.* 14th ed. Montreal: ICAO, 1986. 380 p. DOC. 9460; LGB/382.
Provides information on the status of multilateral and bilateral agreements and arrangements. Kept up to date by annual supplements.

International Court of Justice. *See* United Nations. International Court of Justice.

204. International Labour Conference. *List of Ratifications of Conventions.* 1919-. Geneva: ILO.
Biennial list of ratifications, arranged chronologically by date of adoption of international labor conventions. Issued as Report 3, part 5 of the respective sessions of the International Labour Conference.

205. International Labour Office. *Labour Law Documents: Treaties and Legislation on Labour and Social Security*. 1919-. Geneva: ILO. ISSN 00207764.
Published three times a year. Each issue consists of an international and a national section, and provides reprints and translations of labor and social security legislation of many countries as well as international instruments, regulations and directives. Another feature is bibliographic information including indexes of cases handled by ILO supervisory bodies and lists of legislation extracted from the LABORLEX database. There is a *Consolidated Index* (compiled by Mina Pease; UNIFO Publishers, 1975; ISBN 0891110003), a *Chronological Index, 1919-84* (Geneva: ILO; ISBN 9221050661) and a *General Subject Index, 1919-88* (Geneva: ILO; ISBN 9221064050). Former title (1919-1989): *Legislative Series*.

206. International Labour Organisation. *International Labour Conventions and Recommendations, 1919-1981, Arranged by Subject-matter*. Geneva: International Labour Office, 1982. xxxiv, 1167 p. ISBN
Contains the texts of 146 conventions in force and 102 recommendations still applicable, out of the total of 156 conventions and 165 recommendations adopted by the International Labour Conference between 1919 and 1981. Subjects covered are: basic human rights, employment, social policy, labor administration, labor relations, conditions of work, social security, women, children and young persons, older workers, migrant workers, indigenous and tribal populations, and specific occupational sectors. Lacks index but has detailed table of contents. Texts of international labor conventions may also be found in the *Record of Proceedings* of the International Labour Conference and the ILO *Official Bulletin* (#159).

207. *International Legal Materials*. Vol. 1- , August 1962- . Washington, D.C.: American Society of International Law. ISSN 00207829.
Bimonthly journal. Good source of current information on, and texts of, international treaties, agreements and other international legal instruments, including some not yet in force.

208. International Maritime Organization. *Status of Multilateral Conventions and Instruments in Respect of which the International Maritime Organization or Its Secretary-General Performs Depositary or Other Functions*. 19??-. London: IMO.
Successively cumulating annual statement of signatures, ratifications and other action related to the status of multilateral instruments in IMO's purview. Title varies.

The Laws of Armed Conflicts: A Collection of Conventions, Resolutions and Other Decisions. See #137.

Osmańczyk, Edmund Jan. *The Encyclopedia of the United Nations and International Relations*. See #422.

Unesco. *No Distant Millennium: The International Law of Human Rights*. See #222.

209. Unesco. *Unesco's Standard-setting Instruments*. Paris: Unesco, 1981-. Loose-leaf. ISBN 9231018388.
Arranged by topic: Unesco's Constitution; education; natural sciences; social sciences; culture and communication; miscellaneous. Within each subject chapter, subarranged by type of instrument: conventions and agreements; recommendations; declarations and charters. Includes tables of ratifications and accessions, and country index. Updated by supplements issued in 1982 and 1987.

210. Unesco. *World Directory of Teaching and Research Institutions in International Law = Répertoire mondial des institutions de formation et de recherche en droit international = Repertorio Mundial de Instituciones de Formación y de Investigación en Derecho Internacional.* 2d ed. World Social Science Information Directories. Paris: Unesco, 1990. 387 p. ISBN 9230026441.

Identifies courses offered by 421 national and international institutions, entrance formalities, contents and structure of teaching programs, and continuing education. Includes institutional name, personal name and subject indexes, and a list of periodicals concerned with international law.

211. United Nations. *Treaty Series: Treaties and International Agreements Registered or Filed and Recorded with the Secretariat of the United Nations.* Vol. 1-, 1946/1947-. New York: UN. ISSN 03798267.

Collection of authentic texts of treaties, with English and French translation where applicable, published in accordance with Article 102 of the UN Charter. Contains agreements concluded by states at least one of which is a UN member, and general international agreements, as well as subsequent action affecting the agreements. Excludes financial, commercial and certain other types of agreements. Continues the League of Nations *Treaty Series*. There is a *Cumulative Index* (No. 1-, 1956-; New York: UN; ISSN 02525321), each issue of which covers fifty or a hundred volumes of the *Treaty Series*. *See also Multilateral Treaties Deposited with the Secretary-General* (a much more timely and less cumbersome index for locating multilateral instruments; #215) and *Cumulative Index to the General International Agreements in the United Nations Treaty Series* (Riyadh, Saudi Arabia: Library and Documents Center, Institute of Public Administration, 1984; vi, 127 p.)

United Nations. Centre for Human Rights. *Human Rights: A Compilation of International Instruments.* See #225.

United Nations. Centre for Human Rights. *Human Rights: Status of International Instruments.* See #226.

United Nations. Centre for Social Development and Humanitarian Affairs. *Compendium of International Conventions concerning the Status of Women.* See #229.

212. United Nations Commission on International Trade Law. *UNCITRAL: The United Nations Commission on International Trade Law.* New York: UN, 1986. x, 199 p. Sales No. E.86.V.8. ISBN 9211332842.

In two parts: 1, introduction to UNCITRAL and its work toward the harmonization and unification of international trade law; 2, topics dealt with by UNCITRAL. Appendices list UNCITRAL chairmen and other officials.

United Nations Environment Programme. *Register of International Treaties and Other Agreements in the Field of the Environment.* See #234.

213. United Nations Institute for Training and Research. *A Diplomat's Handbook of International Law and Practice.* 3d, rev. ed. By B. Sen. Dordrecht, The Netherlands: Nijhoff, 1988. xli, 606 p. Sales No. E.88.III.K.ST/22. ISBN 9024736471.

In three parts: 1, diplomatic relations, functions and privileges; 2, consular functions, immunities and privileges; 3, selected topics of international law, including treaty-making. Includes bibliography, lists of diplomatic and consular treaties and laws, and index.

214.   United Nations Institute for Training and Research. *The World Court: What It Is and How It Works*. 4th rev. ed.. By Shabtai Rosenne. Legal Aspects of International Organization, 10. Dordrecht; Boston; London: Nijhoff; UNITAR, 1989. xix, 320 p. Sales No. E.88.III.K.ST/24. ISBN 9024737729.

Guide and introduction to the World Court for politicians, diplomats, those engaged in the study of international law and international relations, and others. Provides a historical overview, a description of the Court and its judges, of jurisdictional questions, of how a case is tried, and an account of the work of the Court. Includes appendices and indexes.

United Nations. International Court of Justice. *Bibliography of the International Court of Justice*. See #486.

United Nations. International Court of Justice. *Publications of the International Court of Justice; Catalogue*. See #487.

United Nations. International Court of Justice. *Yearbook*. See #102.

United Nations. International Law Commission. *International Law Commission: A Guide to the Documents, 1949-1969*. See #488.

United Nations. International Law Commission. *The Work of the International Law Commission*. See #103.

United Nations. International Law Commission. *Yearbook of the International Law Commission*. See #104.

United Nations Interregional Crime and Justice Research Institute. *Statute*. See #105.

United Nations Interregional Crime and Justice Research Institute. *UNICRI: United Nations Interregional Crime and Justice Research Institute*. See #106.

215.   United Nations. Office of Legal Affairs. *Multilateral Treaties Deposited with the Secretary-General*. 1967-. New York: UN. ST/LEG/SER.E/-. ISSN 0255724X.

Successively cumulated annual list of signatures, ratifications, accessions, reservations and other action related to the status of multilateral UN and League of Nations treaties deposited with the UN Secretary-General. Also provides information about the date of adoption, entry into force, and location of the text of each treaty. Former title (1967-1980): *Multilateral Treaties in Respect of which the Secretary-General Performs Depositary Functions*.

United Nations. Office of Legal Affairs. *Statement of Treaties and International Agreements Registered or Filed and Recorded with the Secretariat*. See #494.

216.   United Nations. Office of Legal Affairs. *United Nations Juridical Yearbook*. 1964-. New York: UN. ST/LEG/SER.C/-. ISSN 00828297.

Gives legislative texts and treaty provisions related to the UN system of organizations, a review of legal activities of the UN system, texts of treaties concerning international law, and texts of decisions of administrative tribunals of the UN system. Includes bibliography. Published with a long delay (the 1983 issue appeared in 1990).

217. United Nations. Office of Legal Affairs. *United Nations Legislative Series = Série législative des Nations unies*. Vol. 1-, 1951-. New York: UN. ST/LEG/SER.B/-. ISSN 00828300.

Compendium of texts of international treaties and agreements, and other legislative material. Topics covered include the law of the sea, nationality laws, diplomatic privileges and immunities, succession of states.

Vambery, Joseph T. *Cumulative List and Index of Treaties and International Agreements Filed or Recorded with the Secretariat of the United Nations, December 1969-1974*. See #508.

218. World Health Organization. *International Digest of Health Legislation*. Vol. 1-, 1948-. Geneva: WHO. ISSN 00206563.

Quarterly compendium of national and international legislation on health protection and medical care.

HUMAN RIGHTS

219. Bossuyt, Marc J. *Guide to the "Travaux préparatoires" of the International Covenant on Civil and Political Rights*. Dordrecht; Boston: Nijhoff, 1987. xxvi, 851 p. ISBN 9024734673.

Traces the legislative history of all the articles of the International Covenant on Civil and Political Rights, and its Optional Protocol. Reproduces the pertinent portions of summary records and other documents of the Commission on Human Rights, the GA's Third Committee and other bodies active in the preparation of the Covenant and the Optional Protocol. There is a paragraph-by-paragraph comparison of the articles of these international instruments with the relevant "travaux préparatoires." Includes bibliography, chronological list of documents, and voting records.

220. International Covenant on Civil and Political Rights. *Yearbook of the Human Rights Committee*. 1977/1978-. New York: UN. CCPR/-. ISSN 02569639.

In two volumes for each biennial edition: 1, summary records of the Committee's meetings; 2, documents of the Committee's sessions, including its reports to the GA. Issued in this form with considerable time-lag; volumes for 1981-1982 appeared in 1989. More recent documents are available in mimeographed version with series symbol CCPR/C/-; the Committee's reports to the GA are also issued as Supplement No. 40 of the *Official Records* of the GA (#86); summary records of meetings appear first in mimeographed form with series symbol CCPR/C/SR.-

221. Unesco. *Human Rights Teaching*. Vol. 1-, 1980-. Paris: Unesco.

Covers various aspects of human rights and provides information on governmental, NGO and international human rights activities. Includes bibliographies.

222. Unesco. *No Distant Millennium: The International Law of Human Rights*. By John Humphrey. Paris: Unesco, 1989. 204 p. ISBN 9231026151.

Published on the occasion of the fortieth anniversary of the Universal Declaration of Human Rights, it traces the evolution of international human rights law from the earliest times, and discusses the role of the League of Nations, the UN system, and NGOs in this field, with special chapters devoted to the Universal Declaration, the UN Covenants, and other conventions, declarations, and institutions.

223. Unesco. *World Directory of Human Rights Teaching and Research Institutions = Répertoire mondial des institutions de recherche et de formation sur les droits de l'homme = Repertorio Mundial de Instituciones de Investigación y de Formación en Materia de Derechos Humanos*. World Social Science Information Directories. Deddington, Oxford: Berg; Paris: Unesco, 1988. xxiv, 216 p. ISBN 923102504X..

Lists 331 international, regional and national educational institutions and human rights organizations worldwide. Provides details of teaching, research and documentation activities of each. Includes indexes by institutional name and acronym, research subject, teaching subject and course, and an index of institutions providing scholarships.

224. United Nations. *Yearbook on Human Rights*. 1946-. New York: UN. ISSN 02516519.
   Compendium of national and international provisions concerning human rights. In three parts since 1979: 1, selected material on legislative, administrative, judicial and other measures of governments reporting to the UN under international human rights instruments; and information on developments in Trust and Non-Self-Governing Territories; 2, extracts from reports and decisions of human rights "supervisory bodies" (for example, the Human Rights Committee and the Committee on the Elimination of Racial Discrimination); and 3, a brief account of human rights activities of the UN system. Published with a long time-lag; 1985 volume issued in 1989 (Sales No. E.88.XIV.4).

225. United Nations. Centre for Human Rights. *Human Rights: A Compilation of International Instruments*. New York: UN, 1988. viii, 416 p. ST/HR/1/Rev.3; Sales No. E.88.XIV.1; ISBN 9211540666.
   Presents the texts of sixty-seven human rights conventions, declarations, proclamations, rules and other international instruments originating with the UN, Unesco and ILO. Indicates where and when adopted, and date of entry into force when applicable.

226. United Nations. Centre for Human Rights. *Human Rights: Status of International Instruments*. New York: UN, 1987. vi, 336 p. ST/HR/5; Sales No. E.87.XIV.2; ISBN 9211540631.
   Gives lists of signatures and ratifications or accessions, and texts of declarations and reservations applicable to twenty-two international human rights conventions, covenants and protocols. Indicates when and where adopted, and shows entry into force. Updated annually by ratification charts.

227. United Nations. Centre for Human Rights. *Study Series*. 1-. New York: UN, 1989-.
   Reproduces reports and studies on human rights issues, initiated by the Commission on Human Rights, its Sub-Commission on Prevention of Discrimination and Protection of Minorities, and other human rights bodies. No. 1: *Right to Adequate Food As a Human Right* (New York: UN, 1989; Sales No. E.89.XIV.2; ISBN 9211540755).

228. United Nations. Centre for Human Rights. *United Nations Action in the Field of Human Rights*. New York: UN, 1988. xviii, 359 p. ST/HR/2/Rev.3; Sales No. E.88.XIV.2; ISBN 9211540674.
   Reviews forty years of UN human rights activity. In two parts: 1, descriptions of human rights functions and procedures of the principal organs of the UN, treaty-monitoring bodies and specialized agencies and NGOs, and a survey of human rights concerns and instruments; 2, survey of standard-setting and implementing operations and procedure.

229. United Nations. Centre for Social Development and Humanitarian Affairs. *Compendium of International Conventions concerning the Status of Women*. New York: UN, 1988. iv, 186 p. ST/CSDHA/3; Sales No. E.88.IV.3. ISBN 9211301289.

230. United Nations. Centre for Social Development and Humanitarian Affairs. *The Work of CEDAW: Reports of the Committee on the Elimination of Discrimination against Women*. Vol. 1-, 1982/1985-. New York: UN. ST/CSDHA/-.
   Contains texts of reports and summary records of the Committee's sessions.

231. United Nations. Commission on Human Rights. *Report on the ... Session*. 1st-, 1947-. Economic and Social Council. *Official Records: Supplement*. New York: UN. ISSN 02519623.
   Annual report on the work of the Commission, including texts of resolutions and decisions, draft resolutions and decisions, summary records of meetings, voting results, and other information. In recent years, the Commission's report has appeared as Supplement 2 of the ECOSOC *Official Records*.

232. United Nations. Human Rights Committee. *Report*. 1977-. General Assembly. *Official Records: Supplement No. 40*. New York: UN. ISSN 02552353.

The text of the *Report* may also be found in International Covenant on Civil and Political Rights, *Yearbook of the Human Rights Committee* (#220).

United Nations. World Conference to Combat Racism and Racial Discrimination, 2d, Geneva, 1-12 August 1983. *Compilation of United Nations Resolutions and Decisions Relevant to the Struggle against Racism, Racial Discrimination and Apartheid. See* #293.

ENVIRONMENT

Commonwealth Secretariat. *Common Index and Glossary to the Brandt, Palme and Brundtland Reports of the Independent Commissions on International Development, Disarmament and Security, and Environment and Development.* See #374.

United Nations. *Global Outlook 2000: An Economic, Social, and Environmental Perspective.* See #168.

United Nations. Economic Commission for Europe, and United Nations, Statistical Commission. *Environment Statistics in Europe and North America: An Experimental Compendium.* See #312.

United Nations Environment Programme. *Environment in Print: 1990/91 Publications Catalogue.* See #480.

233. United Nations Environment Programme. *Environmental Data Report.* 1st- ed., 1987-. Oxford: Blackwell. ISSN 09569324.
Compiled by GEMS (UNEP's Global Environment Monitoring System) in co-operation with the World Resources Institute and the United Kingdom Department of the Environment, this biennial work provides data on aspects of environmental pollution, natural resources, population, settlements, human health, energy, transport, waste disposal and recovery, and natural disasters. It alternates with the biennial *World Resources: A Report* (#236).

United Nations Environment Programme. *An Index to the Decisions and Resolutions of the Governing Council of the United Nations Environment Programme.* See #481.

234. United Nations Environment Programme. *Register of International Treaties and Other Agreements in the Field of the Environment.* Nairobi: UNEP, 1989. xii, 250 p. UNEP/GC.15/Inf.2.
Lists 140 environmental conventions, agreements, protocols and other instruments, and provides information about the objectives, provisions, date of adoption, entry into force of each. Lacks index.

235. United Nations Environment Programme. *The State of the Environment.* 1974-. Nairobi, Kenya: UNEP. ISSN 02523310.
Annual survey of a broad spectrum of environmental concerns. The edition covering 1972-1982 is a comprehensive report. Recent reports give, in alternating years, data and results of assessments obtained through the Global Environment Monitoring System, and selected economic and social issues of the environment. The 1990 report, *Children and the Environment*, was issued jointly by UNEP and UNICEF. Variant title: *The State of the World Environment*.

236. United Nations Environment Programme. *World Resources: A Report by the World Resources Institute and the International Institute for Environment and Development, in Collaboration with the United Nations Environment Programme.* 1986- . New York: Basic Books.
Review of population, health, human settlements, food and agriculture, forests and rangelands, wildlife, energy, water, climate, and other resources. Now alternates with the biennial *Environmental Data Report* (#233). Includes statistical tables and index.

237. World Commission on Environment and Development. *Our Common Future*. New York: Oxford University Press, 1987. xv, 383 p. ISBN 019282080X.

Established by the UN General Assembly but independent of control by the UN system and by governments, the World Commission on Environment and Development consisted of twenty-two prominent figures from East and West as well as North and South, and was chaired by Prime Minister Gro Harlem Brundtland of Norway. The "Brundtland Commission Report" deals with mankind's common concerns, common challenges and common action needed to achieve environmentally sustainable development. Some of the Report's recommendations are aimed at strengthening the leadership role of the UN system by such means as "organizational reform, ... greater economy and efficiency ... [and] building sustainable development objectives and criteria into the mandates, programmes, and budget of each agency" of the UN family. Indexed, along with the Brandt Report (#155), the Brandt Memorandum (#154), and the Palme Report (#136), in *Common Index and Glossary to the Brandt, Palme and Brundtland Reports of the Independent Commissions on International Development, Disarmament and Security, and Environment and Development* (#374).

World Meteorological Organization. *Annual Report of the World Meteorological Organization*. See #131.

World Meteorological Organization. *Catalogue of Publications, 1951-1977: Meteorology and Related Fields Such As Hydrology, Marine Sciences and Human Environment*. See #522.

World Meteorological Organization. *WMO Bulletin*. See #270.

OTHER TOPICS AND GENERAL INFORMATION

Food and Agriculture Organization of the United Nations. *Food and Nutrition*. See #147.

238. *History of Mankind: Cultural and Scientific Development*. London: Allen & Unwin, 1963-1976. 6 vols.

Produced by some 1,000 author-editors and other contributors under the aegis of the International Commission for a History of the Scientific and Cultural Development of Mankind (which was created by Unesco in 1950), this is one of Unesco's most ambitious cultural undertakings. Emphasizes cultural and scientific development rather than political, economic and military factors. Volume 1, *Prehistory and the Beginnings of Civilization*, by Jacquetta Hawkes and Leonard Woolley (xlviii, 873 p.); volume 2, *The Ancient World, 1200 BC to 500 AD*, by Luigi Pareti (in three parts; xxvi, xvi, xv, 1048 p.); volume 3, *The Great Medieval Civilizations*, by Gaston Wiet and others (in three parts; xx, xvi, xix, 1082, 108 p.); volume 4, *The Foundations of the Modern World*, by Louis Gottschalk and others (in two parts; xxiii, 1133, 108 p.); volume 5, *The Nineteenth Century*, edited by Charles Morazé (in four parts; xxx, xii, xii, 1394, 72 p.); volume 6, *The Twentieth Century*, by Carolyne F. Ware and others (in four parts; xlviii, xv, 1387 p.) In 1978, Unesco decided (20th General Conference resolution 4/1.2/6) to revise the *History*.

239. International Atomic Energy Agency. *Atomic Energy Review = Revue d'énergie atomique = Obzory po Atomnoi Energii = Revista de Energia Atomica*. 1963-1983. Vienna: IAEA. ISSN 00047112.

Contains articles on all aspects of atomic energy, as well as brief reports on conferences and symposia. Comprises seventy-two issues in eighteen regular volumes, three supplements, a commemorative issue, and nine special issues. Includes cumulative index for 1963-1983 (214 p.; ISBN 9201791836.)

International Atomic Energy Agency. *IAEA Yearbook*. See #19.

International Atomic Energy Agency. *International Atomic Energy Agency Bulletin*. See #20.

240. International Atomic Energy Agency. *Resolutions and Other Decisions of the General Conference*. 1957-. Vienna: IAEA. GC ([session])/RESOLUTIONS.

Issued separately for each regular session. Indexed in *Index to Resolutions and Decisions of the General Conference* (#392).

International Civil Aviation Organization. *Annual Report of the Council*. See #29.

International Civil Aviation Organization. *Convention on International Civil Aviation*. See #30.

241. International Civil Aviation Organization. *ICAO Journal*. Vol. 1-, 1946-. Montreal: ICAO. ISSN 00188778.

Monthly review of ICAO activities and other aeronautical information. Former titles: *ICAO Monthly Bulletin* (1946-1952); *ICAO Bulletin: Official Magazine of International Civil Aviation* (1953-1989).

International Development Research Centre. *International Cooperative Information Systems*. See #400.

242. International Telecommunication Union. *Centenary of the Telephone*. Booklet No. 20. Geneva: ITU, 1976.
Collection of articles on the history and development of the telephone, and on the future prospects of telecommunications.

243. International Telecommunication Union. *From Semaphore to Satellite*. By Anthony R. Michaelis. Geneva: ITU, 1965. 343 p.
Published on the occasion of ITU's centenary, this illustrated volume traces the history of the telegraph and the telephone from 1793 to 1932 and radio from 1888 to 1947, and gives an overview of ITU during the years 1947 through 1965. Includes bibliography.

244. International Telecommunication Union. *Telecommunication Journal*. Vol. 29-, 1962-. Geneva: ITU. ISSN 0497137X.
Provides information on developments in telecommunications through reports on recent meetings and accounts of the work of ITU organs and regional units. Includes notices of forthcoming meetings and on publications issued and planned. Continues the volume numbering of *Journal UIT*.

International Telecommunication Union. *Yearbook of Public Telecommunication Statistics. See* #305.

245. Unesco. *Communication Policy Studies*. Paris: Unesco, 1974-.
A series of country studies on public, professional and institutional communication policies. Last published in 1980?

246. Unesco. *Cultures: Dialogue between the Peoples of the World*. No. 1-36, 1973-1985; Special Number, 1986. Paris: Unesco. ISSN 0304078X.
Journal of cultural studies, theories, methodology and institutions. Many issues were devoted to specific themes. Included news notes and abstracts of publications. Continues *Journal of World History* (1953-1972).

247. Unesco. *International Yearbook of Education*. 10-, 1948-. Paris: Unesco; Geneva: International Bureau of Education.
Beginning with 1980, issues give profiles of national education systems and comparative worldwide studies of educational trends. Each recent issue emphasizes a special theme. Continues the volume numbering of *Annuaire international de l'éducation et de l'enseignement* (published by the International Bureau of Education). Publication suspended between 1970 and 1979. An experimental issue titled *International Guide to Education Systems* appeared in 1979 prior to resumption of regular publication.

248. Unesco. *Many Voices, One World: Report by the International Commission for the Study of Communication Problems*. London: Kogan Page; New York: UNIPUB; Paris: Unesco, 1980. xx, 312 p. ISBN 0 9231018027.
Known popularly as the "MacBride Report" (from the Commission's chairman, Sean MacBride), this is an examination of the mass media and of the historical, political, socioeconomic and cultural dimensions of communication. Recommends a "new world information and communication order". Includes index.

249. Unesco. *Reports and Papers in Mass Communication*. 1-, 1952-. Paris: Unesco.
A series of papers on various aspects of mass communication and the media. Title varies.

250. Unesco. *Science Policy Studies and Documents*. 1-, 1965-. Paris: Unesco. NS/SPS/1-.
Includes national science policy studies, studies of science and technology policy planning and administration, and reports of international meetings on science policy convened by Unesco.

46 United Nations Documentary and Archival Sources

251.   Unesco. *Studies and Documents on Cultural Policies*. Paris: Unesco, 1969-.
A series of country studies on cultural policies, needs and structures, and on international cultural cooperation.

252.   Unesco. *The Unesco Courier: A Window Open on the World*. 1948-. Paris: Unesco. ISSN 00415278
Illustrated monthly magazine on educational, scientific, cultural and communication subjects. Each issue features a special theme.

253.   Unesco. *World Communication Report*. Paris: Unesco, 1989. xix, 551 p. ISBN 9231026283.
Initiated by Unesco's Intergovernmental Programme for the Development of Communication (IPDC), it presents statistical data and other information about the news media, telecommunications, and information technology, with emphasis on developing countries. Describes national, regional and international activities. Includes bibliography and index.

254.   United Nations. Centre for Science and Technology for Development. *ATAS Bulletin*. 1984-. New York: UN. ISSN 02575973.
Launched in 1984 with the objective of alerting developing countries to potential implications of new technologies, ATAS (Advance Technology Alert System) comprises a technology assessment network, assistance to member states, and the *ATAS Bulletin*. The *Bulletin* relates specific new technologies to development.

255.   United Nations. Department of Conference Services. *A Guide to Writing for the United Nations*. New York: UN, 1984. vii, 71 p. ST/DCS/3; Sales No. E.83.I.22.
Written by W. H. Hindle, former chief of the Editorial Control Section of the Department of Conference Services, this witty and sensible treatise discusses planning, style, accuracy and consistency, and cites positive and negative examples. Includes bibliography.

United Nations. Department of Public Information. *Basic Facts about the United Nations*. See #77.

United Nations. Department of Public Information. *Everyone's United Nations*. See #107.

256.   United Nations. Department of Public Information. *UN Chronicle*. 1965- . New York: UN. ISSN 02517329.
Summarizes major UN activities. Regular features include "The 38th Floor" (excerpts from statements of the Secretary-General), "BookWatch" (concise reviews of selected publications of the UN system), "A Look Back" (highlights of important past events), brief news items, and "Coming Up" (announcement of important forthcoming UN conferences and events). A noteworthy annual feature (usually in the March issue) is a roundup of the general debate of the General Assembly's latest session. Former titles: *United Nations Bulletin* (January 1950-June 1954), *United Nations Review* (July 1954-December 1964), *UN Monthly Chronicle* (1980-19??).

257.   United Nations. Department of Public Information. *United Nations Focus: Notes for Speakers*. New York: UN, 1990. 90 p. DPI/1082.
Presents concise information for those who speak or teach about the UN system, describing activities and programs in peace-making and peacekeeping, disarmament, human rights, decolonization, African recovery, drug control, the environment, literacy, population, refugees, status of women, and economic development. Includes a brief guide to information sources.

258. United Nations. Department of Public Information. *World Concerns and the United Nations: Model Teaching Units for Primary, Secondary and Teacher Education.* Rev. ed. New York: UN, 1986. 235 p. Sales No. E.86.I.8.

Based on the work of the UN Fellowship Programme for Educators (1975-1981) and the Unesco Associated Schools Project, this collection of twenty-six teaching units aims to facilitate teaching about major world developments and the activities of the UN system related to those developments. Includes appendices, and subject and country indexes.

259. United Nations. Department of Public Information. *Yearbook of the United Nations.* 1946/1947- . New York: UN. ISSN 00828521.

Perhaps the most important reference work issued by the UN, the *Yearbook* is a comprehensive annual record of the organization's activities, proceedings and decisions. Arranged by broad subject, it covers all political, economic, legal and other issues of concern to the UN. Includes many documentary references in the text, complete texts of resolutions, and appendices providing the texts of the Charter and other major documents. Gives a brief account of activities of other organizations in the UN system. The first edition includes a review of the origin of the UN. Issued with considerable time-lag; 1985, published for the first time by Nijhoff in Dordrecht, Boston and London, appeared in late 1989.

260. United Nations. Division of Narcotic Drugs. *Bulletin on Narcotics.* Vol. 1-, October 1949-. New York: UN. ISSN 0007523X.

United Nations. General Assembly. *Report of the Secretary-General on the Work of the Organization.* See #88.

United Nations Institute for Training and Research. *Conference Diplomacy: An Introductory Analysis.* See #95.

United Nations Institute for Training and Research. *Directory of European Training Institutions in the Fields of Bilateral and Multilateral Diplomacy, Public Administration and Management, Economic and Social Development.* See #485.

261. United Nations Institute for Training and Research. *Effective Negotiation: Case Studies in Conference Diplomacy.* Edited by Johan Kaufmann. Dordrecht, Netherlands: Nijhoff, 1989. xxxiv, 316 p. Sales No. E.89.III.K.PS/12. ISBN 9024737176.

Companion volume to Kaufmann's *Conference Diplomacy: An Introductory Analysis* (#95). Presents sixteen case studies: the 1963 General Assembly special session on peacekeeping finance; the UN Convention Against Torture; the UN Code of Conduct on Transnational Corporations; the Law of the Sea Conference; the launching of the Uruguay Round of multilateral trade negotiations; the 1986 GA special session on the economic crisis in Africa; the 1960s' Tanzania aid project; two post-Chernobyl conventions on nuclear accidents; summit diplomacy; European policy-making; the second Review Conference of the 1972 Biological Weapons Convention; the Common Fund for Commodities; the eleventh special session of the GA; the third Review Conference of the Non-Proliferation Treaty; the evolution of 'soft financing' in the UN's early years; and the 1980-83 Madrid Conference on Security and Co-operation in Europe.

262. United Nations Institute for Training and Research. *Handbook of Foreign Policy Analysis: Methods for Practical Application in Foreign Policy Planning, Strategic Planning and Business Risk Assessment.* By Daniel Frei and Dieter Ruloff. Dordrecht; Boston; London: Nijhoff, 1989. x, 392 p. Sales No. E.89.III.K.ST/25. ISBN 0792301080.
Describes tasks, methods and procedures, including situation assessment, explanation, forecast, decision preparation, decisionmaking, and the use of computers for foreign policy analysis. Includes technical appendix, and bibliography.

United Nations. Office of Public Information. *Everyman's United Nations.* See #107.

United Nations. Trusteeship Council. *Official Records.* See #112.

263. United Nations. Trusteeship Council. *Resolutions and Decisions = Résolutions et décisions.* 1st- sess., 1947-. New York: UN.
Issued as supplement (usually Supplement 1) to the *Official Records* of the Trusteeship Council (#112). Title varies slightly.

264. United Nations University. *Annual Report.* 19??-. Tokyo: UNU.
Reviews the University's program activities, institutional development and financing. Current programs cover eight areas: peace, culture and governance; the global economy and development; global life-support systems; alternative rural-urban configurations; science, technology and society; food, nutrition and biotechnology; human and social development; and global learning and informatics.

Universal Postal Union. *Annual Report on the Work of the Union.* See #120.

265. Universal Postal Union. *Three-Yearly Report on the Development of the Postal Services, 1982-1984 and World Postal Activity in 1986.* Bern: UPU, 1988. ISSN 10107665.
Latest issue of a publication providing data and narrative reporting on national and international postal trends and developments. Covers such topics as domestic and international service, the world's postal network, and automatic letter-sorting. Also includes a one-year projection of world postal activity, and special sections, for example, a study of parcel-post traffic. Title varies.

266. World Health Organization. *Bulletin of the World Health Organization: The Scientific Journal of the WHO = Bulletin de l'Organisation mondiale de la santé: la revue scientifique de l'OMS.* Vol. 1-, 1948-. Geneva: WHO. ISSN 00429686.

World Health Organization. *Four Decades of Achievement: Highlights of the Work of the World Health Organization.* See #127.

World Health Organization. *International Digest of Health Legislation.* See #218.

267. World Health Organization. *WHO Chronicle.* Vol. 1-, 1947-. Geneva: WHO. ISSN 00429694.
Latest issue: Volume 40, No. 6 (1986); publication was suspended due to financial difficulties. Former title (1947-1958): *Chronicle of the World Health Organization.*

World Health Organization. *The Work of WHO.* See #128.

268. World Intellectual Property Organization. *Copyright: Monthly Review of the World Intellectual Property Organization.* Vol. 1-, 1965-. Geneva: WIPO. ISSN 00108626.

World Meteorological Organization. *One Hundred Years of International Co-operation in Meteorology (1873-1973)*. See #133.

269. World Meteorological Organization. *Weather Reporting*. Geneva: WMO.
In four volumes: A, Observing Stations (1952-; ISSN 02509393); B, Data Processing (1984-; ISSN 02509407); C, Transmissions (1952-; ISSN 02509415); D, Information for Shipping (1952-; ISSN 02509423).

270. World Meteorological Organization. *WMO Bulletin*. Vol. 1-, 1952-. Geneva: WMO. ISSN 00429767. Official quarterly journal of the WMO.

RESEARCH RESOURCES

COLLECTIONS OF DOCUMENTS

Basic Documents on United Nations and Related Peace-keeping Forces. See #134.

271. *A Comprehensive Handbook of the United Nations: A Documentary Presentation.* Compiled and edited by Min-chuan Ku. New York: Monarch Press, 1978. 2 vols. ISBN 0671187740.

Collection of constitutional documents, rules of procedure and other texts of the UN system and non-UN IGOs, with additional reference material such as a chart of member states of organizations of the UN system, basic statistical data, and organization charts of the Secretariat. In eight parts: 1, background material, including the Covenant of the League of Nations and other pre-UN documents; 2, "Formation and Operation of the UN", including the Charter and headquarters agreements; 3, rules of procedure of the principal UN organs; 4, constitutional documents of the UN system, and agreements between the UN and the specialized agencies; 5, lists of NGOs in consultative status with ECOSOC and with other bodies of the UN system; 6, trusteeship agreements; 7, regional arrangements, including the North Atlantic Treaty and the OAS Charter; 8, a selection of GA resolutions. Includes a brief bibliography and separate indexes for each volume.

272. Cyprus. Press and Information Office. *Resolutions Adopted by the United Nations on the Cyprus Problem, 1964-1988.* [Nicosia]: Press and Information Office, Ministry of Interior, 1988. 125, [3] p.

Compendium of texts of General Assembly and Security Council resolutions.

273. *Documents on the International Court of Justice.* 2d ed. Compiled and edited by Shabtai Rosenne. Alphen aan den Rijn: Sijthoff & Nordhoff, 1979. xii, 497 p. ISBN 9028603794.

Reproduces the UN Charter, rules of the Court, GA resolutions pertinent to the Court, judicial statistics and other basic texts and source material.

274. General Agreement on Tariffs and Trade. *Basic Instruments and Selected Documents.* Vols. 1-2, 1952; 1st- supplement, 1953-. Geneva: Contracting Parties to the General Agreement on Tariffs and Trade. ISSN 00720623.

Volume 1, text of the Agreement and other instruments and procedures (revised edition, 1955); volume 2, decisions, declarations, resolutions, rulings and reports. Annual supplements contain texts of decisions, protocols, conclusions and reports.

International Atomic Energy Agency. *International Treaties Relating to Nuclear Control and Disarmament.* See #202.

International Labour Organisation. *International Labour Conventions and Recommendations, 1919-1981.* See #206.

International Maritime Organization. *Basic Documents.* See #38.

Collections of Documents   51

275.   *International Organization and Integration: Annotated Basic Documents and Descriptive Directory of International Organizations and Arrangements.* 2d., rev. ed. Edited by P. J. G. Kapteyn and others. The Hague; Boston; London: Nijhoff, 1981-1984. ISBN 902472578X.

Compendium of constitutional documents, rules of procedure, international agreements, resolutions and other documents related to international organization and integration. Volumes 1A and 1B cover the UN system; volumes 2A, 2B-2J (in one) and 2K cover other major IGOs. In addition to texts of documents, each volume has a "Directory" section providing information on the background, structure, membership, functions, financing and activities of each organization covered. Includes bibliographies and indexes.

The Laws of Armed Conflicts: A Collection of Conventions, Resolutions and Other Decisions. See #137.

Osmańczyk, Edmund Jan. *The Encyclopedia of the United Nations and International Relations.* See #422.

276.   Peaslee, Amos Jenkins. *International Governmental Organizations: Constitutional Documents.* 3d, rev. ed. Prepared by Dorothy Peaslee Xidis. The Hague: Nijhoff, 1974-1979. 5 parts.

In addition to texts of constitutional documents, this compendium of 225 entries includes brief background information on each organization covered, as well as bibliographies and indexes. Part 1, in two volumes (Volume 1, xvii, pp. 1-800; Volume 2, xv, pp. 801-1479; ISBN 9024716012), covers general and regional political, economic, social, legal, and defense organizations. Part 2 (xi, 663 p.; ISBN 902471687X) covers organizations in the fields of agriculture, commodities, fisheries, food and plants. Parts 3 and 4 (xi, 616 p.; ISBN 9024720877) cover education, culture, copyright, science, and health. Part 5 (xi, 686 p.; ISBN 9024718260) covers transport and communications.

277.   Preparatory Commission of the United Nations. *Publications.* London, 1945.

The Commission held its first session in San Francisco on 27 June 1945, and its second in London from 24 November to 24 December 1945. The following four documents were issued:
Report of the Preparatory Commission of the United Nations. 182 p. PC/20.
Report of the Executive Committee of the Preparatory Commission of the United Nations. 144 p. PC/EX/113/Rev.1.
Handbook: A Delegation and Secretariat Directory. Rev. ed. 48 p.
Journal of the Preparatory Commission, with eight supplements containing the summary records of each of the Commission's committees.

278.   *Public Papers of the Secretaries-General of the United Nations.* Selected and edited by Andrew W. Cordier, Wilder Foote, and Max Harrelson. New York: Columbia University Press, 1969-1977. 8 vols.

A substantial selection, with commentaries, of official documents as well as addresses given outside the UN, transcripts of press conferences, radio and television broadcasts. Volume 1 (xiv, 535 p.): Trygve Lie, 1946-1953; Volume 2 (xiv, 716 p.; ISBN 0231036337): Dag Hammarskjöld, 1953-1956; Volume 3 (xv, 729 p.; ISBN 023103735X): Dag Hammarskjöld, 1956-1957; Volume 4 (xiv, 659 p.): Dag Hammarskjöld, 1958-1960; Volume 5 (xv, 592 p.): Dag Hammarskjöld, 1960-1961; Volume 6 (xviii, 708 p.; ISBN 0231039662): U Thant, 1961-1964; Volume 7 (xvii, 633 p.; ISBN 0231040989): U Thant, 1965-1967; Volume 8 (xv, 709 p.; ISBN 0231042329): U Thant, 1968-1971. Each volume has an introduction and an index. For more information on public, official and private papers of Secretaries-General, *see* Unesco, *Guide to the Archives of International Organizations, Part 1: The United Nations System* (#353) and Unesco, *Guide to the Archives of International Organizations, Part 2: Archives of International Organizations and Their Former Officials in the Custody of National and Other Archival Manuscript Repositories* (#354).

279. ***Resolutions and Statements of the United Nations Security Council, 1946-1989: A Thematic Guide.*** By T. M. C. Asser Instituut. Edited by Karel C. Wellens. Dordrecht; Boston; London: Nijhoff, 1990. xxxiv, 691 p. ISBN 0792307968.

Compilation of Security Council resolutions and decisions, and statements of Council presidents on substantive issues. Arranged, for questions considered by the Council under its responsibility for international peace and security, in the following geographic/thematic classes: general; Western Europe and other states; Eastern Europe; Africa; Asia; Latin America; the Palestine question; and the Middle East. Also includes material on other matters before the Council. Annexes include a chronological list of resolutions, the composition of the Council (1946-1989), and a list of matters of which the Council was seized as of June 15, 1989.

280. United Nations. *Mimeographed and Printed Documents.* 1946-1981. New York: Readex Microprint Corp.

A nearly comprehensive collection, in microprint, of the official records of the GA and the three councils, and other documents including those in the "limited distribution" category. Excludes most documents issued by the Secretariat and some conference proceedings. Also available on microfiche. Continued by: *United Nations Documents and Publications* (#282).

281. ***United Nations Resolutions on Palestine and the Arab-Israeli Conflict.*** Washington, D.C.: Institute for Palestine Studies, 1975-1988. 3 vols.

Compendium of texts of resolutions of the General Assembly, Security Council, and Economic and Social Council, as well as of several other organizations in the UN system. Volume 1 (edited by George J. Tomeh; xxiii, 294 p.; ISBN 0887281613) covers 1947-1974; Volume 2 (edited by Regina S. Sharif; xxi, 304, [xxix] p.; ISBN 0887281621) covers 1975-1981; and Volume 3 (edited by Michael Simpson; ISBN 088728163X) covers 1982-1986. Includes subject guides to resolutions, voting charts and other related information.

United Nations. *Treaty Series. See* #211.

282. United Nations. *United Nations Documents and Publications* [on microfiche]. 1982-. New York: Readex Microprint Corp.

A nearly comprehensive collection, in microfiche, of the official records of the GA and the three councils, and other documents including those in the "limited distribution" category. Continues United Nations, *Mimeographed and Printed Documents* (#280). Unlike the 1946-1981 *Mimeographed and Printed Documents* set, this microfiche collection also includes UN Secretariat documents. Readex has begun producing and offering a CD-ROM index to the set.

United Nations. Centre for Social Development and Humanitarian Affairs. *Compendium of International Conventions Concerning the Status of Women. See* #229.

United Nations Children's Fund. *Compilation of Economic and Social Council and General Assembly Resolutions on UNICEF and the International Year of the Child, 1946-1977. See* #174.

283. United Nations Conference on International Organization, San Francisco, 1945. *Documents.* New York: UN, 1945-1955. 22 vols.

The first fifteen volumes contain the English and French texts of the major documents of the UN's founding conference. These were published with an index (volume 16) jointly by the United Nations Information Organizations and the U.S. Library of Congress. Volumes 17-20 (documents of the Co-ordination Committee and the Advisory Committee of Jurists) were published by the UN. An exhaustive English and French general index (volumes 21-22) complete the set.

United Nations. Economic and Social Commission for Asia and the Pacific. *Index to Resolutions of the Economic and Social Commission for Asia and the Pacific, 1947-1978*. See #456.

United Nations. Economic and Social Council. *Official Records*. See #82.

284. United Nations. Economic Commission for Africa. *Compendium of Resolutions Adopted by the United Nations Economic Commission for Africa from the First to the Eighth Sessions, 1958-1967*. [s.l.:] ECA, UN, 1967. 14 p. E/CN.14/DOC/2/Rev.1/Add.12.

285. United Nations. Economic Commission for Europe. *Compendium of Resolutions and Decisions of the Economic Commission for Europe, 1947-1972*. Geneva: UN, 1973. xl, 260 p. E/ECE/836.
   Brought up to date by United Nations, Economic Commission for Europe, *Compendium of Resolutions and Decisions of the Economic Commission for Europe, 1973-1989* (New York: UN, 1990; xli, 207 p.; ECE/836/Add.1.)

286. United Nations. Economic Commission for Latin America. *Collected Resolutions on the International Development Strategy and the New International Economic Order Adopted by the United Nations General Assembly and Economic and Social Council, the Economic Commission for Latin America and the Caribbean Development and Co-operation Committee*. Santiago, Chile: ECLA, UN, 1981. E/CEPAL/G.1157.
   Compendium of texts.

287. United Nations. Economic Commission for Latin America. *Resolutions Adopted by the Economic Commission for Latin America, the Committee of the Whole and the Trade Committee, 1948-1973*. Santiago, Chile: ECLA, UN, 1973. 2 vols. E/CN.12/LIB/4.
   Compendium of texts of the resolutions. Volume 1: lvii, 267 p.; Volume 2: pp. 268-531.

United Nations. General Assembly. *Official Records*. See #86.

288. United Nations. General Assembly. *Resolutions and Decisions Adopted by the General Assembly*. 1st-sess., 1946-. *Official Records* of the General Assembly, [last] Supplement. New York: UN.
   Resolutions are issued first in provisional form with the symbol A/RES/[session No.]/ and are later republished in this collected edition for each GA session as the last supplement of the GA *Official Records* (#86). Another form in which GA resolutions are available is an annual preliminary compilation of texts, with voting records and index: United Nations, Department of Public Information, *Resolutions and Decisions Adopted by the General Assembly during the ... Session* (Press Release GA/-; New York: UN.) There is also a commercially published version: *United Nations Resolutions, Series 1: Resolutions Adopted by the General Assembly*; Volume 1-, 1946-1948--; compiled by Dusan J. Djonovich; Dobbs Ferry, N.Y.: Oceana Publications, 1973-) which, in addition to the texts of resolutions, provides voting records and successively cumulating indexes by subject; composition of UN organs; and conventions, declarations and other instruments.

289. United Nations Institute for Namibia. *United Nations Resolutions on Namibia, 1946-1978*. Compiled by A. O. Evborokhai. Lusaka, Zambia: United Nations Institute for Namibia, 1980. 2 vols.
   Compendium of texts of GA, Security Council and ECOSOC resolutions. *See also Compendium of Major Resolutions, Decisions and Other Documents Relating to Namibia*. New York: UN, 1984. A/AC.131/1984/CRP.17.

290. United Nations Institute for Training and Research. *A New International Economic Order: Selected Documents, 1945-1975*. Compiled by Alfred George Moss and Harry N. M. Winton. UNITAR Document Service, No. 1. New York: UNITAR, 1976. 2 vols.
   Reproduces selected resolutions, declarations and joint programs of action of the UN, and related documents issued outside the UN system. Includes subject index.

United Nations. Office of Legal Affairs. *United Nations Legislative Series.* See #217.

291. United Nations. Office of the United Nations High Commissioner for Refugees. *United Nations Resolutions and Decisions Relating to the Office of the United Nations High Commissioner for Refugees.* Geneva: UNHCR, 1989-. Looseleaf. HCR/INF/49.

Compendium of texts of GA and ECOSOC resolutions from 1949 on. Includes bibliographical references. To be updated by supplements; index to be published.

United Nations. Security Council. *Official Records.* See #109.

292. United Nations. Security Council. *Resolutions and Decisions of the Security Council.* 1946-. *Official Records* of the Security Council. New York: UN. S/INF/-.

SC resolutions are issued first in provisional form with the symbol S/RES/-; republished in a collected annual version as part of the SC *Official Records* (#109). There is also a commercially published version: *United Nations Resolutions, Series 2: Resolutions and Decisions of the Security Council, 1946-1947--*, compiled by Dusan J. Djonovich (Dobbs Ferry, N.Y.: Oceana Publications, 1988-) which, in addition to the texts of resolutions and, selectively, decisions, also provides voting records, successively cumulating topical index, and texts of documents related to the subjects of the resolutions. Another useful source is *Resolutions and Statements of the United Nations Security Council, 1946-1989: A Thematic Guide*, edited by Karel C. Wellens (#279).

United Nations. Trusteeship Council. *Official Records.* See #112.

293. United Nations. World Conference to Combat Racism and Racial Discrimination, 2d, Geneva, 1-12 August 1983. *Compilation of United Nations Resolutions and Decisions Relevant to the Struggle against Racism, Racial Discrimination and Apartheid.* Geneva: UN, 1983. A/CONF.119/15.

In five parts: 1, Security Council, 1960-1980 (42 p.); 2, General Assembly, 1946-1978 (200 p.); 3, General Assembly, 1979-1982 (196 p.); 4, Economic and Social Council, 1946-1982 (71 p.); and 5, Commission on Human Rights, 196?-1982 (113 p.) Lacks index.

294. World Meteorological Organization. *Basic Documents.* 1987 ed. Basic Documents, No. 1. Geneva: WMO. 169 p. WMO-No. 15. ISBN 9263110158.

STATISTICS

295. Food and Agriculture Organization of the United Nations. *FAO Production Yearbook = Annuaire FAO de la production = Anuario FAO de Producción*. Vol. 1- , 1948- . FAO Statistics Series. Rome: FAO. ISSN 00717118.

Presents worldwide data on land, population, crops, livestock, food supply, means of production, and prices, as well as FAO indexes of agricultural production. Continues Food and Agriculture Organization of the United Nations, *Yearbook of Food and Agricultural Statistics, 1947* (Washington, D.C., 1947). Former title (1948-1957): *Production Yearbook*.

296. Food and Agriculture Organization of the United Nations. *FAO Trade Yearbook*. Vol. 1- , 1948- . FAO Statistics Series. Rome: FAO. ISSN 00717126.

Provides worldwide export and import statistics of trade in agricultural and related products by commodity, agricultural trade values by country, and FAO volume and value indices. Continues Food and Agriculture Organization of the United Nations, *Yearbook of Food and Agricultural Statistics, 1947* (Washington, D.C., 1947). Other slight variations in title.

297. Food and Agriculture Organization of the United Nations. *World Crop and Livestock Statistics: Area, Yield and Production of Crops; Production of Livestock Products = Statistiques mondiales des cultures et de l'élévage = Estadísticas Agropecuarias Mundiales*. FAO Processed Statistics Series, 1. Rome: FAO, 1987. v, 760 p. ISBN 9250025300.

Presents data on the production of 237 agricultural commodities of 170 countries.

General Agreement on Tariffs and Trade. *International Trade. See* #150.

298. *Index to International Statistics*. Vol. 1-, 1983-. Bethesda, Md.: Congressional Information Service. ISSN 07374461.

Index and abstract of statistical publications of IGOs and other IGO material with substantial statistical content. In two main parts: indexes (subject, name and other indexes); and abstracts. Most of the publications and documents covered are obtainable on microfiche from the Congressional Information Service. Monthly, with quarterly and annual cumulations and, for the subject index only, a cumulation for 1983-1987. Along with two other series issued by CIS, *American Statistics Index* and *Statistical Reference Index*, available also on CD-ROM under the title *Statistical Masterfile*.

299. International Civil Aviation Organization. *Civil Aviation Statistics: ICAO Statistical Yearbook*. 1st- ed., 1975-. Montreal: ICAO. ICAO.DOC/9180.

Presents worldwide data on the number of aircraft, pilot licences, aviation safety, air traffic, finance, airports, and other aviation statistics. ICAO also publishes several series of detailed statistics on specific subjects, for example, *Traffic, Commercial Air Carriers* (1947-; Digest of Statistics, Series T; ISSN 10140077.)

300. International Labour Office. *The Cost of Social Security = Le coût de la sécurité social = El Costo de la Seguridad Social.* 2d- international inquiry, 1949/1951- . Geneva: ILO. ISSN 05388295.

Provides worldwide data on receipts and expenditures of social insurance, family allowance, public health services and other social security schemes. Each "inquiry", starting with the eighth (1967-1971), is published in two volumes: comparative tables, and basic tables. Results of the first "inquiry" appeared in *International Labour Review* 65 (June 1952): 726-91 and *International Labour Review* 67 (March 1953): 292-303 (#158).

301. International Labour Office. *Developments in International Labour Statistics.* Edited by Ralph Turvey. London; New York: Pinter Publishers for the International Labour Office, 1990. xvii, 446 p. ISBN 0861878183.

Compendium of papers on labor accounting, measuring the labor force, standard classifications, labor cost, and other topics of labor statistics. Includes bibliographic references, but lacks index.

302. International Labour Office. *Year Book of Labour Statistics = Annuaire des statistiques du travail = Anuario de Estadísticas del Trabajo.* 1st- issue, 1935/1936- . Geneva: ILO. ISSN 00843857.

Annual compilation of country data on employment, unemployment, wages, hours of work, consumer price indexes, strikes and other industrial disputes, and occupational injuries. Supplemented by *Year Book of Labour Statistics: Retrospective Edition on Population Censuses, 1945-89* (Geneva: ILO, 1990; xxxix, 1059 p.; ISBN 9220064286). Updated by *Bulletin of Labour Statistics* (1965-; Geneva: ILO; ISSN 00074950).

303. International Monetary Fund. *Direction of Trade Statistics.* 1-, 1964- . Washington, D.C.: IMF. ISSN 0252306X.

Monthly. Presents data on the value, in U.S. dollars and by trading partner, of exports and imports of 135 countries. A companion serial, *Direction of Trade Statistics Yearbook* (ISSN 02523019) provides seven-year time series for 161 countries. The data are available also on magnetic tape from the IMF.

304. International Monetary Fund. *International Financial Statistics.* Vol. 1-, 1948-. Washington, D.C.: IMF. ISSN 00206725.

This monthly, the "flagship" statistical publication of IMF, is a standard source of data on exchange rates, money and banking, international liquidity, prices and production, interest rates, national accounts, and other aspects of finance. Provides statistics for 144 countries as well as world aggregates. A companion serial, IMF's *International Financial Statistics Yearbook*, gives annual statistics beginning with 1960. The data are available also on magnetic tape from the IMF. Related publications, with data similarly available on magnetic tape, are IMF's *Balance of Payments Statistics* (Volume 1-, 1938/1947-); *Direction of Trade Statistics* (#303); and *Government Finance Statistics Yearbook* (Volume 1-, 1977.)

305. International Telecommunication Union. *Yearbook of Public Telecommunication Statistics = Annuaire statistique des télécommunications du secteur public = Anuario estadístico de las telecomunicaciones del sector público.* 1st- ed., 1963/1972?- . Geneva: ITU.

Provides country-by-country data on telephone, telegram, telex and data transmission services, as well as demographic statistics related to telecommunications. Each edition gives a ten-year time series. Previous title (1963/1972?-1978/1987: *Yearbook of Common Carrier Telecommunication Statistics.*

306. Unesco. *Compendium of Statistics on Illiteracy = Compendium des statistiques relatives à l'analphabétisme = Compendio de Estadísticas Relativas al Analfabetismo.* Statistical Reports and Studies, No. 31. Paris: Unesco, 1990. 103 p. ISBN 923002709X.

Presents estimates and projections of illiteracy, and country-by-country data on illiteracy since 1960. Latest edition of a compendium issued at irregular intervals.

Unesco. *International Yearbook of Education.* See #247.

307. Unesco. *Statistical Yearbook = Annuaire statistique = Anuario Estadístico.* 1963- . Paris: Unesco. ISSN 00827541.
Provides statistics of education, science and technology, culture and communication, including literacy, book production, media, expenditures and structures, and other indicators. Continues Unesco, *Basic Facts and Figures* (1952-1959/1961) which contained similar statistics.

United Nations Children's Fund. *Children and Development in the 1990s: A UNICEF Sourcebook.* See #172.

United Nations Children's Fund. *The State of the World's Children.* See #175.

308. United Nations Children's Fund. *Statistics on Children in UNICEF Assisted Countries.* New York: UNICEF, 1990. 319 p.
Covers key indicators of child survival and development, and nutrition, health, educational and economic indicators. Provides data for 137 countries and territories. Includes definitions, list of sources of data, and introductions in French and Spanish.

309. United Nations Conference on Trade and Development. *Handbook of International Trade and Development Statistics*, and *Supplement.* 1964-. New York: UN. E/CONF.46/12/Add.1 and TD/STAT/-. ISSN 02519461.
Annual compilation of data on development and world trade, with special emphasis on developing countries.

310. United Nations Conference on Trade and Development. *UNCTAD Commodity Yearbook.* 1984- . New York: UN. ISSN 10120793.
Presents disaggregated data for commodity trade and consumption at world, regional and country levels. Former title (1984-1985): *Yearbook of International Commodity Statistics.*

United Nations. Department of Public Information. *World Media Handbook: Selected Country Profiles.* See #476.

United Nations Development Programme. *Human Development Report 1990.* See #182.

311. United Nations. Economic and Social Commission for Asia and the Pacific. *Statistical Yearbook for Asia and the Pacific = Annuaire statistique pour l'Asie et le Pacifique.* 1968-. Bangkok: ESCAP, UN. ISSN 02523655.
Former title (1968-1972): *Statistical Yearbook for Asia and the Far East.*

United Nations. Economic Commission for Europe. *Overall Economic Perspective to the Year 2000.* See #187.

312. United Nations. Economic Commission for Europe, and United Nations, Statistical Commission. *Environment Statistics in Europe and North America: An Experimental Compendium.* Conference of European Statisticians, Statistical Standards and Studies, No. 39. New York: UN, 1987. 100, 87 p. Sales No. E.87.II.E.28.
In two parts: 1, time series data and indicators on environmental resources, waste generation and treatment, concentration of pollutants, topical issues, climate and other background information; 2, statistical monograph on resources and ecosystem of the Baltic Sea environment. Includes bibliography.

United Nations Environment Programme. *Environmental Data Report.* See #233.

United Nations Environment Programme. *World Resources: A Report by the World Resources Institute and the International Institute for Environment and Development, in Collaboration with the United Nations Environment Programme.* See #236.

313. United Nations Industrial Development Organization. *Handbook of Industrial Statistics = Manuel de statistiques industrielles.* 1982-. Vienna: UNIDO. ID/-.
Biennnial compendium of data on manufacturing and manufactures.

United Nations Industrial Development Organization. *Industry and Development: Global Report.* See #188.

314. United Nations. Statistical Office. *Commodity Trade Statistics.* Vol. 1- , 1949- . Statistical Papers, Series D. New York: UN. ST/ESA/SER.D/-.
Detailed import and export statistics by commodity and trading partner. Cumulated annually in United Nations, Statistical Office, *World Trade Annual* (#331). Former title (1949-1950): *Summary of World Trade Statistics.*

315. United Nations. Statistical Office. *Compendium of Human Settlement Statistics, 1983 = Recueil des statistiques des établissements humains, 1983.* New York: UN, 1985. xxxv, 541 p. ST/ESA/STAT/SER.N/4; Sales No. E/F.84.XVII.5.
Continues United Nations, Statistical Office, *Compendium of Housing Statistics* (1974-1980; New York: UN; ISSN 02509865.)

316. United Nations. Statistical Office. *Compendium of Statistics and Indicators on the Situation of Women, 1986 = Recueil de statistiques et d'indicateurs sur la situation des femmes, 1986.* Social Statistics and Indicators, Series K, No. 5. New York: UN, 1989. xi, 592 p. ST/ESA/STAT/SER.K/5; Sales No. E/F.88.XVII.6. ISBN 9210611306.

317. United Nations. Statistical Office. *Construction Statistics Yearbook.* 1963/1972- . New York: UN. ST/ESA/STAT/SER.U/-. ISSN 02579073.
Former title (1963/1972-1974/1981): *Yearbook of Construction Statistics.*

318. United Nations. Statistical Office. *Demographic Yearbook = Annuaire démographique.* 1st- issue; 1948-. New York: UN. ST/ESA/STAT/SER.R/-. ISSN 00828041.
Compendium of population, birth, death, marriage and divorce, and migration statistics covering some 220 countries or areas of the world. Each issue also features intensive treatment of particular field of demographic statistics. 1963 and subsequent issues include cumulative subject indexes. *See also Population and Vital Statistics Report* (#327).

319. United Nations. Statistical Office. *Directory of International Statistics, Vol. 1.* Statistical Papers, Ser. M, No. 56, Rev.1. New York: UN, 1982. vii, 274 p. ST/ESA/STAT/SER.M/56/Rev.1. Sales No. E.81.XVII.6.
Detailed guide to statistical series compiled by the UN system and several other IGOs, and to databases of economic and social statistics. Volume 2, in preparation, will provide information on the organization and responsibilities of statistical services of the UN system and of other IGOs. It will also have information on international standards, definitions, concepts and classifications.

320. United Nations. Statistical Office. *Energy Statistics Yearbook = Annuaire des statistiques de l'énergie.* 1-, 1929/1950-. New York: UN. ST/ESA/STAT/SER.J/-. ISSN 02566400.
Former titles: *World Energy Supplies* (1929/1950-1978); *Yearbook of World Energy Statistics* (1979-1981).

Statistics   59

321.　United Nations. Statistical Office. *Handbook on Social Indicators*. Studies in Methods, Ser. F, No. 49. New York: UN, 1989. vii, 154 p. ST/ESA/STAT/SER.F/49; Sales No. E.89.XVII.6. ISBN 9211613043.

322.　United Nations. Statistical Office. *Industrial Statistics Yearbook*. 1938/1961-. New York: UN. ST/ESA/STAT/SER.P/-. ISSN 02577208.
　　　Former titles: *The Growth of World Industry* (1938/1961-1973); *Yearbook of Industrial Statistics* (1974-1981).

323.　United Nations. Statistical Office. *International Standard Industrial Classification of All Economic Activities*. 3d rev. Statistical Papers, Series M, No. 4, Rev.3. New York: UN, 1990. x, 189 p. ST/ESA/STAT/SER.M/4/Rev.3.; Sales No. E.90.XVII.11. ISBN 9211613190
　　　Provides statistical classification of activities in agriculture, mining, manufacturing, construction, service industries, public administration, health, and other sectors of the economy. Includes copious methodological explanations.

324.　United Nations. Statistical Office. *International Trade Statistics Yearbook = Annuaire statistique du commerce international*. 1950- . New York: UN. ST/ESA/STAT/SER.G/-. ISSN 1010447X.
　　　Former title (1950-1982): *Yearbook of International Trade Statistics*.

325.　United Nations. Statistical Office. *Monthly Bulletin of Statistics = Bulletin mensuel de statistique*. Vol. 1-, January 1947-. New York: UN. ST/ESA/STAT/SER.Q/-. ISSN 00417432.
　　　Provides demographic, economic, agricultural, industrial, trade, transport, national accounts and other data. Keeps the UN *Statistical Yearbook* (#329) up-to-date, and gives monthly as well as quarterly and annual time series. Each issue also features one or more special topics.

326.　United Nations. Statistical Office. *National Accounts Statistics*. 1957-. New York: UN. ST/ESA/STAT/SER.X/-.
　　　Former title (1957-1981): *Yearbook of National Accounts Statistics*.

327.　United Nations. Statistical Office. *Population and Vital Statistics Report*. Vol. 1- , 1949-. Statistical Papers, Series A. New York: UN. ST/ESA/STAT/SER.A/-.
　　　See also *Demographic Yearbook* (#318).

328.　United Nations. Statistical Office. *Standard International Trade Classification*. Revision 3. Statistical Papers, Series M, No. 34/Rev.3. New York: UN, 1986. xvii, 106, 31, 25 p. ST/ESA/STAT/SER.M/34/Rev.3. Sales No. E.86.XVII.12.
　　　Five-digit classification for commodities for export-import purposes. Also serves as a guide to various international trade statistics series. Appendices include headings of the Harmonized Commodity Description and Coding System, and headings of SITC revision 2 in terms of SITC revision 3.

329.　United Nations. Statistical Office. *Statistical Yearbook = Annuaire statistique*. 1st- issue, 1948-. New York: UN. ST/ESA/STAT/SER.S/-. ISSN 00828459.
　　　Provides demographic, economic, agricultural, industrial, trade, transport, national accounts and other data on an annual basis, with multi-year time series. Part of an interrelated set of statistical publications. Other titles in the set, also issued by the UN Statistical Office, include, among others: *Demographic Yearbook* (#318); *Energy Statistics Yearbook* (#320); *Commodity Trade Statistics* (#314); *Monthly Bulletin of Statistics* (#325); *International Trade Statistics Yearbook* (#324); *National Accounts Statistics* (#326); *Population and Vital Statistics Report* (#327); and *World Statistics in Brief* (#330). Also co-ordinated with the products of the UN Statistical Office are statistical compilations issued by specialized agencies and other organizations in the UN system; for example: WHO's *World Health Statistics Annual* (#340); and ILO's *Year Book of Labour Statistics* (#302).

330. United Nations. Statistical Office. *World Statistics in Brief: United Nations Statistical Pocketbook*. No. 1-, 1976-. Statistical Papers, Series V. New York: UN. ST/ESA/STAT/SER.V/-. ISSN 02519747.
   Annual compilation of basic demographic, labor, trade, agricultural, industrial, health, and other statistics. Provides data for 159 countries.

331. United Nations. Statistical Office. *World Trade Annual*. 1963-. New York: Walker.
   Provides export and import statistics for the principal developed countries, except for Eastern Europe. Arranged by commodity in several volumes each year, it shows trade value and volume. The *Supplement* (1965-; also issued in several volumes each year), provides statistics for exports and imports between the principal developed countries and Eastern Europe and the Third World. The two sets together cumulate data first published in *Commodity Trade Statistics* (#314).

332. Universal Postal Union. *Statistique des services postaux*. 1875-. Bern: International Bureau, UPU. ISSN 02523752.
   Since 1974 issued annually in looseleaf form.

333. World Bank. *African Economic and Financial Data*. Washington, D.C.: World Bank; New York: United Nations Development Programme, 1989. xiii, 204 p. ISBN 0821312510.
   Presents a set of data on national economic indicators, balance of payments, prices, commodity trade, debt and debt servicing, government finance, agriculture, public enterprises, and aid flows. Includes bibliography. The data are also available on computer diskettes from the World Bank.

   World Bank. *Annual Report*. See #121.

334. World Bank. *The Development Data Book: A Guide to Social and Economic Statistics*. 2d ed. Washington, D.C.: World Bank, 1989. [1], 16, [1] p. ISBN 0821311182.
   Provides economic and social data for countries with populations of over one million. Includes definitions.

335. World Bank. *Social Indicators of Development*. 1987-. Baltimore; London: Johns Hopkins University Press for the World Bank. ISSN 10128026.
   Summarizes data collected by the World Bank, the WHO, UNICEF, Unesco and other international organizations on population, labor force, health, income, education, nutrition, and other social characteristics. Covers three broad time spans: '25-30 years ago', '15-20 years ago', and 'most recent estimates'. The data are also available on computer diskettes from the World Bank.

336. World Bank. *Trends in Developing Economies, 1989*. Washington, D.C.: World Bank, 1989. vii, 530 p. ISBN 0821313584.
   First edition of an annual publication. Provides brief analyses of recent economic performance and trends, with economic and social data of developing countries that are borrowers from the World Bank.

337. World Bank. *World Bank Atlas*. 1st- ed., 1966- . Washington, D.C.: World Bank. ISSN 00858293.
   Brief summary of GNP, population, life expectancy, literacy, and other current economic and social indicators of many countries.

338. World Bank. *World Debt Tables: External Debt of Developing Countries*. 1973/1979-. Washington, D.C.: World Bank. ISSN 02532859.
   Annual compilation of data, in two volumes: 1, analysis and summary tables; 2, country tables. Also available on computer diskettes from the World Bank.

World Bank. *World Development Report.* See #199.

339. World Bank. *World Tables.* 1968?-. Baltimore; London: Johns Hopkins University Press for the World Bank. ISSN 10435573.

Annual compilation of GNP per capita, foreign trade, balance of payments, external debt, origin and use of resources, and other core socio-economic indicators. The 1988/1989 edition covers 138 countries. The data are also available on computer diskettes and magnetic tape from the World Bank.

340. World Health Organization. *World Health Statistics Annual = Annuaire de statistiques sanitaires mondiales.* 1947-. Geneva. ISSN 02503794.

Former title (1947-1965): *Annual Epidemiological and Vital Statistics.*

341. World Intellectual Property Organization. *Industrial Property Statistics = Statistiques de propriété industrielle.* 1975?-. Geneva: WIPO. IP/STAT/[year]/B. ISSN 03770044.

Annual compilation of data on applications and registrations for patents, trademarks, service marks and industrial designs. Also includes data for patents and marks by type of product or service. In two parts since 1985: 1, patents; 2, trademarks and service marks. Preceded each year by a briefer advance edition, *Industrial Property Statistics* (IP/STAT/[year]/A.) Former title (1975?-1984): *Industrial Property Statistics in the Form of Summary Tables = Statistiques de propriété industrielle sous la forme de tableaux résumés.*

342. World Intellectual Property Organization. *100 Years of Industrial Property Statistics: Synoptic Tables on Patents, Trademarks, Designs, Utility Models and Plant Varieties, 1883-1982 = 100 ans de statistiques de propriété industrielle: tableaux synoptiques pour les brevets, les marques, les dessins et modèles industriels, les modèles d'utilités et les obtentions végétales, 1883-1982.* Geneva: WIPO, 1983. ii, 245 p. WIPO Publication No. 876. ISBN 9280501046.

ARCHIVAL RESOURCES

343. Erlandsson, Alf M. E. "Archives of the United Nations." *Archivaria* No. 7 (Winter 1978): 5-15.
Describes the origin, evolution and component record groups of the UN Archives, as well as the relationship of the Archives with the creators and users of the records.

344. Erlandsson, Alf M. E. "The Relations between Archives and Libraries within the UN Family." In ***International Documents for the 80's: Their Role and Use*** (#401): mf 2/43-53.
Highlights the differences between libraries and archives, and advocates separation between the two.

345. Evans, F. B. "Access to Archives of United Nations Organizations." In ***International Documents for the 80's: Their Role and Use*** (#401): mf 2/65-72.
Reviews the divergent access policies and procedures of organizations in the UN system.

346. Evans, Luther H. "UNESCO." In *The New Guide to the Diplomatic Archives of Western Europe*, edited by Daniel H. Thomas (Philadelphia: University of Pennsylvania Press, 1975; ISBN 0812276973): 399-408.
Provides a historical sketch of Unesco and a description of the organization, classification and regulation of Unesco's archives.

347. Ghebali, Victor-Yves. "Les archives des organisations internationales: le point de vue du chercheur." In ***International Documents for the 80's: Their Role and Use*** (#401): mf 2/84-90.
Reviews difficulties facing academic researchers in the use of archives of international organizations.

348. Herzstein, Robert Edwin. "The Recently Opened United Nations War Crimes Archives: A Researcher's Comment." *American Archivist* 52 (Spring 1989): 208-13.
Describes the United Nations War Crimes Commission records in the UN Archives, discusses critically the UN's access rules, and points out the pitfalls of confining oneself to records found in a single repository.

349. Järvinen, Markku. "Archival Finding Aids in International Organizations." In ***International Documents for the 80's: Their Role and Use*** (#401): mf 2/30-35.
Drawing on Unesco's experience, this paper summarizes various types of finding aids to the contents of archives.

350. Manning, Raymond. "The Records of Conferences Resulting in the Foundation of Organizations." In ***International Documents for the 80's: Their Role and Use*** (#401): mf 2/55-58.
Points out that documents of founding conferences are often placed in national archives or other institutions rather than in the archives of the organization to which they relate.

351. Pavesković, N. "Registry and Archives." In ***International Documents for the 80's: Their Role and Use*** (#401): mf 2/74-82.
Discusses the respective roles of archives and registry units, as well as questions of records management in international organizations.

352.	Pérotin, Gilberte. "Archives et documentation." In *International Documents for the 80's: Their Role and Use* (#401): mf 2/60-63.
Reviews definitions and presents differences between archives and documentation centers.

353.	Unesco. *Guide to the Archives of International Organizations, Part 1: The United Nations System.* Documentation, Libraries and Archives: Bibliographic and Reference Works, 8. Paris: Unesco, 1984. 279 p. ISBN 9231020900.
An overview of the archival resources of the UN, FAO, GATT, IMCO, IAEA, ICAO, ILO, IMF, ITU, Unesco, UNIDO, UPU, the World Bank Group, WHO, WIPO, and WMO (with separate entries for special UN bodies such as UNICEF, UNDP and UNEP, and principal organs and other subsidiary bodies such as the International Court of Justice and the Pan American Health Organization). Covers archival records in manuscript, print, multi-copied form, microform, maps, magnetic tape, sound recordings and other media. In addition to describing archive groups, includes brief administrative histories, and bibliographies.

354.	Unesco. *Guide to the Archives of International Organizations, Part 2: Archives of International Organizations and Their Former Officials in the Custody of National and Other Archival Manuscript Repositories.* Compiled by Peter Walne. Paris: Unesco, 1985. 132 p. PGI.85/WS/18.
Covers archival material held in Finland, France, West Germany, the Netherlands, Poland, Sweden, Switzerland, the United Kingdom, and the United States. Describes holdings as well as rules of access. Especially interesting are detailed inventories of Dag Hammarskjöld's papers held in the Swedish Royal Library and Andrew Cordier's papers at Columbia University in New York. Includes bibliographies and index.

355.	Unesco. *Guide to the Archives of International Organizations, Part 3: Archives of Other International Inter-governmental Organizations and Non-governmental Organizations.* Compiled by A. W. Mabbs. Paris: Unesco, 1985. 40 p. PGI.85/WS/19.
Brief description of the archives of sixty-four IGOs and NGOs, indicating conditions of access and availability of research facilities. Includes index.

356.	Unesco. General Information Programme and UNISIST. *Access to the Archives of United Nations Agencies: A RAMP Study with Guidelines.* Prepared by Bodil Ulate Segura. Paris: Unesco, 1987. ii, 103, [v] p. PGI-86/WS/24.
Using deliberations of the International Council on Archives as a point of departure, this study discusses the problem of access to archives in general and UN system archives in particular. The author presents findings of a 1985-86 survey of archives of thirty-four organizations in the UN system, to which fourteen responded: FAO, GATT, IMF, PAHO, UN, UNDP, UNDRO, ECA, Unesco, UNHCR, UNICEF, UNIDO, UNOG and WHO. The survey reveals that archival regulations and procedures vary greatly and that there are many inadequacies in satisfying the public's right to information. Includes appendices and bibliography.

Unesco. *Inventory of General Conference Documents, 1946-1989.* See #436.

United Nations. Archives Section. *Index to Microfilm of United Nations Documents in English, 1946-1961.* See #446.

357.	United Nations. Secretariat. *Administrative Instruction: The United Nations Archives.* New York: UN, 28 December 1984. 6 p. ST/AI/326.
Sets out the responsibilities of the UN Archives Section (including conditions of access, and disposal of records), of other Secretariat units (for transfer, retention and disposal of records) and of members of the Secretariat. Includes archival guidance to other UN organs, explanation of archival terms, and guidelines concerning classification and declassification of records of Secretaries-General.

358. Welander, Sven. "Archives of International Organizations: Introductory Report for Panel IV." In *International Documents for the 80's: Their Role and Use* (#401): mf 2/2-10.

Discusses definitions, archives access and control, the contents of archives, and the place of archives within the secretariats of international organizations. Includes recommendations.

359. Welander, Sven. "The 'Guide to the Archives of International Organizations'." In *International Documents for the 80's: Their Role and Use* (#401): mf 2/12-19.

Describes the evolution of Unesco's *Guide to the Archives of International Organizations*.

360. Zarb, M. "Archives et droit d'auteur." In *International Documents for the 80's: Their Role and Use* (#401): mf 2/21-29.

This working paper of the World Intellectual Property Organization discusses the principles of copyright and applications of those principles by international organizations.

CATALOGS, INDEXES, GUIDES, AND OTHER BIBLIOGRAPHIC TOOLS

Administrative Committee on Co-ordination [of the United Nations System of Organizations]. *Inventory of Arrangements for Programme Co-ordination in the United Nations System.* See #1.

361. Administrative Committee on Co-ordination [of the United Nations System of Organizations]. Secretariat. *United Nations System of Organizations and Directory of Senior Officials, 1989/1990.* New York: UN, 1989. 139 p.

Under each organ, lists main organizational subdivisions with addresses, telephone and fax numbers, and names of senior officials. Includes a table showing member states of each organization of the UN system, a list of UNDP and "operational activities for development" resident representatives, directors of UN information centers, and an alphabetical index of UN system organs. On title page: *United Nations System of Organizations : Members of the United Nations, the Specialized Agencies and the International Atomic Energy Agency, and Contracting Parties to the General Agreement on Tariffs and Trade, and Directory of Senior Officials.* Latest issue of an annual publication.

362. Advisory Committee for the Co-ordination of Information Systems [of the United Nations System of Organizations]. *ACCIS Newsletter.* Vol. 1- , May 1983- . Geneva. ISSN 02543133.

Bimonthly news of documentation, archives and information (including electronic information) activities, with special emphasis on the UN system. Includes announcements of recent and forthcoming meetings, publications and projects.

363. Advisory Committee for the Co-ordination of Information Systems [of the United Nations System of Organizations]. *Directory of Selected Collections of United Nations System Publications.* New York: UN, 1991. xii, 126 p. ISBN 9211003512. Sales No. E.GV.90.0.4.

Lists libraries and documentation centers of the UN system, and depository libraries and information services that maintain collections of material issued by the UN system. Covers 170 countries and areas.

364. Advisory Committee for the Co-ordination of Information Systems [of the United Nations System of Organizations]. *Directory of United Nations Databases and Information Services.* 4th ed. New York: UN, 1990. x, 484 p. Sales No. GV.E.90.0.1. ISBN 9211003490.

Guide to 872 databases, and information systems and services of thirty-nine organizations in the UN system. In three sections: 1, description of the functions and structure of the thirty-nine organizations, with lists of databases and information services; 2, description of the information services; 3, description of the databases. Sections 2 and 3 indicate the name, type, status, subject scope, availability, indexing and classification tools, and other characteristics of each database, information service or system. Includes name/acronym index, and subject indexes in English, French and Spanish. ACCIS has also published guides in specific subject areas, for example: *ACCIS Guide to United Nations Information Sources on International Trade and Development Finance* (New York: UN, 1990; xiv, 193 p.; Sales No. GV.E.88.0.2) and *Information Sources of Food and Agriculture* (ACCIS Guides to United Nations Information Sources, No. 1; Rome: Food and Agriculture Organization of the United Nations, 1987; iii, 124 p.)

365. Advisory Committee for the Co-ordination of Information Systems [of the United Nations System of Organizations]. *Directory of United Nations Serial Publications, 1988*. New York: UN, 1988. x, 500 p. ISBN 9211003377.
    Covers some 4,000 serial publications, including annual reports, published by thirty-eight UN organizations. The main listing is by key title, with each entry giving publisher, place, dates and frequency, subject descriptors and other bibliographic information, and indicating other language versions when available. Includes indexes by organization, subject and ISSN, and a list of UN system publication offices and libraries.

366. Advisory Committee for the Co-ordination of Information Systems [of the United Nations System of Organizations]. *Providing Access to United Nations Databases: A Guide for United Nations Database Producers*. Geneva: ACCIS, 1988. 90 p. ISBN 9211003423.
    Revised version of the 1987 *Final Report of the [ACCIS] Technical Panel on Database Access*. Part 1 identifies issues relevant to UN database producers, and UN units serving as hosts, in developing access policies. Part 2 is a compendium of existing database access policies of thirty-one bodies within the UN system. Databases are classified as bibliographic, directory, full text, referral, statistical/numerical, and thesaurus/terminology. Entries indicate restrictions on access, availability of products, and other information. Appendices include lists of online hosts, bibliography, and glossary.

367. Advisory Committee for the Co-ordination of Information Systems [of the United Nations System of Organizations]. *Register of Development Activities of the United Nations System, 1988*. New York: UN, 1988. xliii, 752 p. ISBN 9211003415.
    Provides descriptive and financial information on economic and social development activities of thirty-three organizations and bodies of the UN system. Covers concrete aid projects as well as research and information projects and programs; and technical cooperation projects funded by the UNDP, development activities funded from regular budgets, and capital assistance provided by the World Bank Group and by IFAD. In five sections (each subdivided by sectors): development activities in individual countries or areas; regional activities; interregional activities; global activities; summaries. Includes annexes.

368. Atherton, Alexine L. *International Organizations: A Guide to Information Sources*. International Relations Information Guide Series, Vol. 1. Detroit: Gale, 1976. xxviii, 350 p. ISBN 0810313243.
    Bibliography (partly annotated) of about 1,500 books, periodicals, pamphlets and documents by and about IGOs, including the UN system. In two parts: 1, sources of information; 2, bibliography. Includes author, title, and subject indexes.

369. Brimmer, Brenda, and others. *A Guide to the Use of United Nations Documents, Including Reference to the Specialized Agencies and Special U. N. Bodies*. New York University, Libraries, Occasional Papers, No. 3. Dobbs Ferry, N.Y.: Oceana, 1962. xv, 272 p.
    Based on the holdings of the UN collection of New York University Library. Although some sections are out-of-date, this handbook is still useful, especially the first part, 'Methods and Problems of Research'.

370. Cherns, J.J. *Official Publishing: An Overview; An International Survey and Review of the Role, Organisation and Principles of Official Publishing*. Guides to Official Publications, Vol. 3. Oxford: Pergamon, 1979. ISBN 0080233406.
    Surveys official (government) publishing in twenty countries and several organizations of the UN system (UN, Unesco, WHO, ILO, FAO, and the World Bank) as well as the OECD, the European Communities and NATO. Includes index.

371. Cholganskaia, Vera Leont'evna. *Publikatsii OON i Ee Spetsializirovannykh Uchrezhdenii: Istochnikovedcheskii Obzor za 1945-1975 gg.* 2d ed. Moscow: Nauka, 1977. 504 p.
   Bibliographical survey of documents and publications of the UN system. In three parts: 1, general publications of the UN; 2, UN and specialized agencies' publications on economic and social questions; 3, Unesco publications on education, science and culture. The text of the survey is Russian but the bibliography lists mostly English-language items.

372. *A Chronology and Fact Book of the United Nations, 1941-1985.* 7th ed. Edited by Thomas Hovet, Jr. Dobbs Ferry, N.Y.: Oceana, 1986. xi, 364 p. ISBN 0379206919.
   Chronological listing, subarranged by subject, of major events leading to the establishment of the UN, and of the main issues dealt with in the UN's various organs. Includes membership lists of the UN and its principal organs, UN budget and scales of assessment figures, and other data, as well as texts of the Charter and the GA rules of procedure, and an index.

373. Clews, John. *Documentation of the UN System: A Survey of Bibliographic Control and a Suggested Methodology for an Integrated UN Bibliography.* IFLA/UBC Occasional Papers, No. 8. London: IFLA International Office for UBC, 1981. 20 p.
   Outlines the pattern of documentation of the UN system and the state of bibliographic control, and makes recommendations for an integrated bibliographic system covering all UN organizations.

374. Commonwealth Secretariat. *Common Index and Glossary to the Brandt, Palme and Brundtland Reports of the Independent Commissions on International Development, Disarmament and Security, and Environment and Development.* London: Commonwealth Secretariat, 1990. 146 p.
   Combined subject index to the following four reports: *North-South: A Programme for Survival; Report of the Independent Commission on International Development Issues* (Brandt Report; #155); *Common Crisis North-South: Co-operation for World Recovery* (Brandt Memorandum; #154); *Common Security: A Blueprint for Survival* (Palme Report; #136); and *Our Common Future* (Brundtland Report; #237). Also includes name indexes to members and secretariats of the commissions and eminent persons, glossary, and an introduction by Shridath S. Ramphal.

375. *The Complete Reference Guide to United Nations Sales Publications, 1946-1978.* Edited by Mary E. Birchfield and Jacqueline Coolman. Pleasantville, N.Y.: UNIFO Publishers, 1982. 2 vols. ISBN 0891110119.
   Volume 1 of this cumulative guide lists sales publications by UN document series symbol, with full bibliographic information. Volume 2 contains indexes by keyword, title, and sales number.

376. Deardorff, John. *United Nations Security Council Index, 1946-1964.* Columbus: United Nations Collection, Ohio State University Library, 1969. vi, 100 leaves.
   Index to SC documents held in the Ohio State University Library. References are made to the Official Records or other sources where documents may be found. Partially fills the indexing gap for the period 1946-1949. *See also* John Deardorff, *United Nations Economic and Social Council Index, 1946-1965* (Columbus: United Nations Collection, Ohio State University Library, 1969; vii, 170 leaves).

377. *Documents of International Organisations: A Bibliographic Handbook Covering the United Nations and Other Intergovernmental Organisations.* Compiled and edited by Theodore D. Dimitrov. London; Chicago: International University Publications; American Library Association, 1973. xv, 301 p. ISBN 08390159X.
   Covers documents of the UN system and other IGOs. Also lists material about the agencies.

378.   *Documents of International Organizations: A Selected Bibliography.* Vol. 1-3, No. 4, November 1947-September 1950. Boston: World Peace Foundation.
     Covers material issued by IGOs within and outside the UN system. Partly fills the indexing gap for UN documents and publications prior to 1950. Includes cumulative table of contents.

379.   Fetzer, Mary K. *United Nations Documents and Publications: A Research Guide.* Occasional Papers, No. 76-5. New Brunswick, N.J.: Rutgers University, Graduate School of Library Service, 1978. 61 p.
     Describes basic resources (depository libraries and major indexes), types of UN documents and publications, and research problems. Discusses in some detail UN resolutions, voting records, speeches, and treaties. Includes bibliography and index.

          Fomerand, Jacques. *Strengthening the United Nations Economic and Social Programs: A Documentary Essay.* See #8.

380.   Food and Agriculture Organization of the United Nations. *FAO Books In Print.* 1973-1986. Rome : FAO. ISSN 02592665.
     Annual listing of FAO publications available for sale. Arranged by subject: agriculture, plant production and protection, animal production and health, forestry, fisheries, land and water development, economic and social development, statistics, food and nutrition, general. Includes author and title indexes and a list of FAO sales agents and booksellers. Continues *Bibliographic Catalogue of FAO Publications, 1945-1972* (Rome: FAO, 1973; viii, 151 p.) and is in turn continued by *FAO Publications Catalogue* (#381).

381.   Food and Agriculture Organization of the United Nations. *FAO Publications Catalogue.* 1987-88--. Rome: FAO.
     Lists in-print and out-of-print publications and documents. Arranged in ten subject categories: agriculture, plant production and protection, animal production and health, forestry, fisheries, land and water development, economic and social development, statistics, food and nutrition, and general. Includes alphabetical title index. Updated by quarterly and other periodic supplements. Continues *FAO Books in Print* (#380).

382.   Food and Agriculture Organization of the United Nations. *FAO Documentation: Current Bibliography = Documentation de la FAO: bibliographie courante = Documentación de la FAO: Bibliografia Corriente.* 1967-. Rome: FAO. ISSN 0304582X.
     Bimonthly index, with annual cumulation (the latter is now on microfiche) to FAO documents and publications. The fullest bibliography is arranged by accession number. Includes author, subject/geographic, project, and AGRIS/CARIS subject category indexes. Former title (1967-1971): *FAO Documentation: Current Index.*

383.   Food and Agriculture Organization of the United Nations. *Index [to] FAO Conference and Council Decisions, 1945-1972.* Rome: FAO, 1973. xxxvi, 498 p.
     Gives abstracts of operative paragraphs of decisions, arranged by subject and subarranged chronologically. An alphabetical table of contents lists entries and provides cross references and abbreviations.

384.   Food and Agriculture Organization of the United Nations. *List of Documents.* 1967-. Rome: FAO.
     Once monthly and annually cumulated, now irregular listing of FAO "main documents" by subject, available for sale. Includes title index and a list of FAO sales agents and booksellers.

          Food and Agriculture Organization of the United Nations. *Organization and Structure of FAO, Including Titles of Staff.* See #11.

385.	General Agreement on Tariffs and Trade. *Publications of the General Agreement on Tariffs and Trade.* 1966-. Geneva: GATT.
	In-print list, issued at irregular intervals, of GATT legal instruments, reports and studies on international trade, activity reports, and other GATT publications.

386.	Goehlert, Robert; and Marian Shaaban. "United Nations Documents and Bibliographical References." *News for Teachers of Political Science*, No. 24 (Winter 1980): 12-17.
	Brief review of the characteristics and types of UN documents and publications, and a selected, partly annotated guide to UN bibliographical guides and other reference tools.

387.	Haas, Michael. *International Organization: An Interdisciplinary Bibliography.* Hoover Institution Bibliographical Series, 41. Stanford: Hoover Institution Press, 1971. xxiv, 944 p.
	Lists some 8,000 monographs, journal articles and contributions to collective works on international organizations, including the League of Nations, the UN system, regional organizations, and NGOs. Includes author and subject indexes.

	Hajnal, Peter I. *Guide to Unesco.* See #16.

388.	Hajnal, Peter I. *Guide to United Nations Organization, Documentation and Publishing for Students, Researchers, Librarians.* Dobbs Ferry, N.Y.: Oceana, 1978. xxviii, 450 p. ISBN 0379202578.
	Overview of the structure, functions and evolution of the UN, and a detailed description of the pattern of UN documentation and publishing. Includes an annotated bibliography of works by and about the UN, a selection of major documents, and a brief survey of other organizations of the UN system.

389.	Hinds, Thomas S. "The United Nations as a Publisher." *Government Publications Review* 12 (July/August 1985): 297-303.
	Describes the production and dissemination of UN documents and publications.

390.	Hopkins, Michael. "The Documentation of Intergovernmental Organizations: A Critical Survey of Supply-and-Demand Situations in the United Kingdom." *International Social Science Journal* 32, No. 2 (1980): 371-82.
	Discusses the nature of documents and publications of international governmental organizations, and the availability and use of IGO information sources.

391.	Hüfner, Klaus; and Naumann, Jens. *The United Nations System: International Bibliography = Das System der Vereinten Nationen: Internationale Bibliographie.* München: Verlag Dokumentation; K. G. Saur, 1976-1979. 3 vols. in 5.
	Extensive bibliography of English-, French- and German-language monographs, journal articles and contributions to collective works on the UN system, with scantier coverage of items issued by the UN system itself. Volume 1 ("learned journals and monographs, 1945-1965," lv, 519 p.) has 5,545 entries; Volumes 2A ("learned journals, 1965-1970," xcii, 286 p.) and 2B ("learned journals, 1971-1975," lix, 436 p.) give a combined total of 8,342 entries; Volumes 3A ("monographs and articles in collective volumes, 1965-1970," xcii, 491 p.) and 3B ("monographs and articles in collective volumes, 1971-1975," lvi, 692 p.) provide a total of 13,394 entries. Each volume includes an author index.

	Index to International Statistics. See #298.

392.	International Atomic Energy Agency. *Index to Resolutions and Decisions of the General Conference.* 1957/1976-. Vienna: IAEA. GC/RES/INDEX/-.
	Alphabetical subject index, cumulative for 1957-1971 and 1977/1981. It is planned to keep it up to date by annual supplements.

393. International Atomic Energy Agency. *Information Circulars.* Vienna: IAEA, 1989. 66, 45 p. INFCIRC/1/Rev.9.

Lists information circulars of current interest, many of which provide texts of international treaties and agreements in the field of arms control, disarmament, nuclear weapons, and nuclear safety. An annex gives a full list of information circulars.

394. International Atomic Energy Agency. *INIS Atomindex: An International Abstracting Service.* Vol. 1-, 1970-. Vienna: IAEA. ISSN 00047139.

Classified index, with abstracts, to IAEA publications and to material issued by IAEA member states and other IGOs on nuclear science and its peaceful applications. Prepared from semimonthly magnetic tapes and available in paper and COM (computer output microfiche) versions. Issued semimonthly, with semiannual, annual, and multi-year cumulations. Includes subject, author, conference, report, and other indexes.

395. International Atomic Energy Agency. *International Atomic Energy Agency Publications; Catalogue.* 1958-. Vienna: IAEA.

Covers IAEA publications available for sale as well as some out-of-print material. In two parts: 1, list by subject (life sciences, nuclear safety and environmental protection, physics, chemistry/geology/raw materials, reactors and nuclear power, industrial applications, miscellaneous, periodicals); 2, series, title, and meetings indexes. Former title (1958-1970): *Publications in the Nuclear Sciences.* Kept up to date by supplements.

396. *International Bibliography: Publications of Intergovernmental Organizations.* Vol. 1-, March 1973-. Millwood, N. Y.: Kraus International Publications. ISSN 00000477.

Quarterly current-awareness bibliography of publications of organizations in the UN system and other IGOs. The section "Bibliographic Record" provides an annotated list, arranged by broad subject, of selected sales publications and free material. Excludes working documents, press releases and internal documents. A "Periodicals Record" gives annotated entries or tables of contents of current issues of selected IGO periodicals. Has organization, title, and subject indexes. Former title (1973-1982): *International Bibliography, Information, Documentation.*

397. International Centre for Settlement of Investment Disputes. *ICSID Bibliography.* Washington, D.C.: ICSID, 1989. 22 p. Doc.ICSID/13/Rev.1.

Guide to material published by or related to ICSID. In three parts: 1, texts of the ICSID Convention and publications of ICSID; 2, articles and books; 3, decisions.

398. International Civil Aviation Organization. *Catalogue of ICAO Publications.* 1946-. Montreal: ICAO.

Annual catalogue of publications and documents available for sale. Also lists out-of-print items. Arranged by ICAO activity, with numerical indexes to documents and circulars. Updated by supplements.

399. International Civil Aviation Organization. *Index of ICAO Publications.* Cumulated ed. 1947-. Montreal: ICAO. DOC. 9515.

Annual list of ICAO's basic documents as well as PICAO (Provisional International Civil Aviation Organization, 1945-1947) documents.

400. International Development Research Centre. *International Cooperative Information Systems: Proceedings of a Seminar Held in Vienna, 9-13 July 1979.* IDRC-156e. Ottawa: IDRC, 1980. ISBN 0889362521.

Includes papers on AGRIS, UNISIST, INFOTERRA, and other international cooperative information systems.

Catalogs, Indexes, Guides 71

401. ***International Documents for the 80's: Their Role and Use; Proceedings of the Second World Symposium on International Documentation, Brussels, 1980.*** Edited by Theodore D. Dimitrov and Luciana Marulli-Koenig. Pleasantville, N.Y.: UNIFO Publishers, 1982. xxxvi, 570 p., 5 microfiches in pocket. ISBN 0891110127.

Compendium of almost eighty papers grouped by panels of the symposium: 1, sources of international documentation; 2, acquisition and organization of international documents; 3, utilization of international documents; archives of international organizations. Includes subject and author indexes.

402. ***International Information: Documents, Publications and Information Systems of International Governmental Organizations.*** Edited by Peter I. Hajnal. Englewood, Co.: Libraries Unlimited, 1988. xxix, 339 p. ISBN 0872875016.

Compendium of essays examining the nature of IGOs, their role as publishers, the problems of bibliographic control, collection development and library arrangement of IGO documents and publications, reference and information work, citation forms, IGO documentation in microform, and computerized information systems. Concludes with case studies of use and users of IGO documentation. Includes bibliography and index.

International Labour Conference. *List of Ratifications of Conventions.* See #204.

403. International Labour Office. ***Bibliography of Published Research of the World Employment Programme.*** 7th ed. International Labour Bibliography, No. 4. Geneva: ILO, 1988. xi, 125 p. ISBN 9221063909.

Lists books and articles published by ILO, as well as ILO works issued by outside publishers and related non-ILO books and articles. Arranged by topic; for example: employment planning and promotion, basic needs, technology, migration, women. Updated by *Supplement* (1989; ISBN 9221069788.)

404. International Labour Office. ***Catalogue of Publications in English of the International Labour Office, 1919-1950.*** Geneva: ILO, 1951. 379 p.

In two parts: 1, author/title/subject list; 2, conference, organization, and series index.

405. International Labour Office. ***ILO Catalogue of Publications in Print.*** 1944-. Geneva: ILO. ISSN 10110569.

Covers monographs, periodicals, series, audiovisual material, microfiche items and magnetic tapes available for sale. The main part is alphabetical, by title, with separate lists of documents of the International Labour Conference, ILO regional conferences, industrial and statistical meetings, series, periodicals, conventions and recommendations. Includes author index. Updated by *ILO Publications*, issued three times a year.

406. International Labour Office. ***Industrial Meetings Catalogue, 1945-1983: Reports, Records and Other Publications.*** Geneva: ILO, 1984. vi, 53 p.

Catalog of ILO publications related to committee meetings and other meetings on inland transport, coal mines, iron and steel, metal trades, textiles, petroleum and other industries.

407. International Labour Office. ***International Labour Documentation.*** 1954- . Geneva: ILO. ISSN 00207756.

Subject list, with abstracts, of material in the areas of employment, industrial relations, labor law, working conditions and other labor-related fields acquired by the ILO central library, whether or not published by the ILO. Cumulative editions for 1965-1969, 1970-1971 and 1972-1976 (Boston: G. K. Hall). *LABORDOC*, an electronic version, is available online. An earlier version titled "Daily Reference List" [of journal articles] was issued by the ILO Library from 1949 to 1953[?].

408. International Labour Office. Central Library and Documentation Branch. *Subject Guide to Publications of the International Labour Office, 1919-1964*. Bibliographical Contributions, No. 25. Geneva: ILO, 1967. i, 478 p.

Lists sales and other publications. Supplemented by *Subject Guide to Publications of the International Labour Office, 1980-1985* (International Labour Bibliography, No. 1; Geneva: ILO, 1987; x, 614 p.; ISBN 9291060764); and *Geographic Index* (Geneva: ILO, 1968; 14 p.)

409. International Maritime Organization. *Index of IMO Resolutions, January 1959 to April 1987*. 1st ed. London: IMO, 1987. 98 p. Sales No. 126 87.14.E.

In three sections: 1, list of subject headings; 2, chronological list of resolutions adopted by the Assembly, Council, Maritime Safety Committee, Marine Environment Protection Committee, and Consultation Meeting of Contracting Parties to the London Dumping Convention; 3, subject list of resolutions.

410. International Maritime Organization. *Publications of the International Maritime Organization*. 1982-. London: IMO.

Annual in-print catalog, arranged in seven subject categories: general, cargoes, facilitation of travel and transport, legal matters, marine environment protection, marine technology, and navigation. Includes chronological and alphabetical indexes, and status of IMO conventions. Title varies: 1982-198?, *Publications Catalogue*. Continues *IMCO Publications* (1968-1981).

411. International Maritime Organization. *Publishing in the United Nations and Its Related Agencies*. [London:] IMO, 1988. vi, 57 p. Pub. 071/87.

Provides basic information on publications of twenty-seven agencies in the UN system. For each agency, gives address, subject categories of publications, information on availability of material, major catalogs, and names of responsible officers.

412. International Monetary Fund. *Catalogue of Publications, 1946-1971*. Washington, D.C.: IMF, 1972. viii, 104 p.

Lists publicly available publications and documents: general publications, periodicals, pamphlet series, books, items primarily for IMF use, and information for the press. Also covers material translated into French, Spanish, German and Portuguese. Appendices include a list of contents of the *Staff Papers* (#162). Updated by the IMF's annual *Publications Catalog*.

413. International Telecommunication Union. *Dissemination of Information and Documentation at the International Telecommunication Union in the '90s: A Paper Presented to the International Seminar on Information Management, Practice and Education, Budapest, 24-27 April 1990*. By A. G. El-Zanati. Geneva: ITU, 1990. iv, 104 p.

Outlines ITU's purposes, objectives, functions and methods of operation. Covers conferences and meetings, technical assistance and dissemination of information. Provides details on ITU documentation and suggestions for filing and maintenance of source material.

414. International Telecommunication Union. *List of Publications, September 1990*. Geneva: ITU, 1990. 54 p.

Latest issue of an annual list of ITU publications in print. Arranged by broad subject: publications common to telegraph, telephone and radio services; telegraphy and telephony; radio; publications of the ITU Administrative Council; miscellaneous; and general information.

415.   International Trade Centre (UNCTAD/GATT). *Compendium of Publications Prepared by ITC during Its First 20 Years, 1964-1984 = Répertoire des publications préparées par le CCI au cours de ses 20 premières années, 1964-1984 = Compendio de las Publicaciones Preparadas por el CCI durante sus Primeros 20 Años, 1964-1984.* [Geneva:] ITC, 1984. v, 75 p.

Lists some 550 titles. In three parts: 1, chronological listing of product/market-oriented publications, classified by type of study; 2, product/market studies classified by product category; 3, handbooks, directories, trade functions, training material, and miscellaneous publications.

416.   Inter-Organization Board for Information Systems [of the United Nations System of Organizations]. *Bibliography of United Nations Thesauri, Classifications, Nomenclatures.* Geneva: IOB, 1979. 252 p.

Covers linguistic tools used by the UN system. Arranged by broad subjects such as political affairs, general development issues, natural resources. Includes alphabetical index by agency.

417.   Joint FAO/WHO Food Standards Programme. *Codex Alimentarius.* Rome: Food and Agriculture Organization of the United Nations, 1981- . ISSN 02592916.

The Codex, a result of the work of the Joint FAO/WHO Codex Alimentarius Commission, is a compendium, in twenty-five looseleaf binders, of some 200 internationally acceptable food standards (seventeen numbered volumes, for example: Volume 5, Fish and Fishery Products; 14, Food Additives) and forty codes and guidelines (eight lettered volumes, for example: Volume A, General Principles of Food Hygiene; Volume J, Code of Ethics for International Trade in Food). They embrace food, raw materials, food processing and packing, consumer information, and verification of compliance. A handy overview is: Joint FAO/WHO Food Standards Programme, *Introducing Codex Alimentarius* (Rome: Food and Agriculture Organization of the United Nations, 1988; 23 p.)

Joint Inspection Unit [of the United Nations System of Organizations]. *Control and Limitation of Documentation in the United Nations System.* See #54.

Joint Inspection Unit [of the United Nations System of Organizations]. *Publications Policy and Practice in the United Nations System.* See #55.

418.   Marulli, Luciana. *Documentation of the United Nations System: Co-ordination in Its Bibliographic Control.* Metuchen, N.J.: Scarecrow Press, 1979. x, 225 p. ISBN 0810812339.

Surveys bibliographic policies and practices of seventeen organizations in the UN system, explores the status of bibliographic control and co-ordination, and makes recommendations. Includes bibliography.

419.   McConaughy, John Bothwell. *A Student's Guide to United Nations Documents and Their Use.* New York: Council on International Relations and United Nations Affairs, 1969. 17 p.

Concise guide to UN documents, with a selective bibliography of information sources about the UN. Includes a brief guide to suggested research methods.

420.   New Zealand. Ministry of Foreign Affairs. *United Nations Handbook.* 1961- . Wellington.

Concise annual survey of the constitutions, structure, membership and other characteristics of the UN system of organizations. Former titles: *United Nations and Specialized Agencies Handbook* (1961-1967); *United Nations and Related Agencies Handbook* (1968-1972).

421.   Organisation for Economic Co-operation and Development. *Handbook of Information, Computer and Communications Activities of Major International Organisations.* Information, Computer, Communications Policy, 4. Paris: OECD, 1980. 233 p. ISBN 9264120351.

Provides information about activities in forty-eight IGOs and NGOs, including the UN system. Gives name, objectives, structure, and other information for each organization. Includes a short bibliography.

422. Osmańczyk, Edmund Jan. *The Encyclopedia of the United Nations and International Relations*. 2d ed. New York; Philadelphia; London: Taylor and Francis, 1990. xvii, 1220 p. ISBN 0850668336.

Compendium of information on the UN system and other international organizations, on a large number of international treaties and agreements (providing many full or partial texts), on UN member states, and on political, economic, military, diplomatic and legal concepts. Includes bibliographic notes, world population statistics and projections, glossaries, acronyms and abbreviations, and subject, treaty, and name indexes.

423. Public Affairs Information Service. *Bulletin*. Vol. 1-, 1915-. New York: PAIS.

Subject index to English-language monographs, pamphlets, reports and periodical articles in the social sciences. Provides good coverage of important IGO publications, including those of the UN system. Semimonthly, with quarterly and annual cumulations. A cumulative subject index for 1915-1974 has been published by Carrollton Press.

424. Rothman, Marie H. *Citation Rules and Forms for United Nations Documents and Publications*. Brooklyn, N.Y.: Long Island University Press, 1971. 64 p.

Guide to citing UN documents and publications, including periodical articles, in footnotes, bibliographies and other references. See also Diane Garner's chapter, "Citation Forms," in *International Information* (#402).

425. Royal Institute of International Affairs. Library. *Index to United Nations Documents to December 1947*, and *Supplements* No. 1-3, January 1948-December 1949. London: RIIA, 1948-1950. 4 parts in 1 volume.

Alphabetical subject list of UN documents and periodicals, with more selective coverage for material of other organizations of the UN system. Partially fills the indexing gap for the period 1946-1949.

426. Schaaf, Robert W. "Information Policies of International Organizations." *Government Publications Review* 17 (1990): 46-91.

Discusses information, publication and dissemination policies and practices of the UN system and other IGOs.

427. Schaaf, Robert W. "International Organizations Documentation: Resources and Services of the Library of Congress and Other Washington Based Agencies." *Government Information Quarterly* 1, No. 1 (1984): 59-73.

Discusses the documentation of the UN system and other IGOs, with special emphasis on resources in the Washington area, especially at the Library of Congress.

428. Schopen, Lynn. *Nations on Record: United Nations General Assembly Roll-call Votes (1946-1973)*. Oakville; Dundas, Ont.: Canadian Peace Research Institute, 1975. x, 515, 19 p.

Chronological list of recorded votes in General Assembly plenary meetings. For each resolution, provides a summary of the substantive portion, a tally of "Yes" and "No" votes, abstentions and "Absent/Non-participating" responses, and an indication whether or not the resolution was adopted. Includes a voting chart for each GA session and a subject index. Updated by the following compilations by Hanna Newcombe: *Nations on Record; Supplement: United Nations General Assembly Roll-Call Votes (1974-1977)* (Dundas, Ont.: Peace Research Institute, 1981; vi, 131, 6 p.; ISBN 919117112); *Nations on Record: United Nations General Assembly Roll-Call Votes, 2d Supplement (1978-1983)* (Dundas, Ont.: Peace Research Institute, 1986; vi, 322 p.; ISBN 919117120); *Nations on Record: General Assembly Roll-Call Votes (1984-1986)* (Dundas, Ont.: Peace Research Institute, 1988; vii, 260 p.; ISBN 919117139).

429. *Sources, Organization, Utilization of International Documentation; Proceedings of the International Symposium on the Documentation of the United Nations and Other Intergovernmental Organizations, Geneva, 1972*. FID Publication No. 506. The Hague: International Federation for Documentation, 1974. 586 p.

Compendium of papers covering the production, distribution, acquisition, organization, bibliographic control and use of documents and publications of the UN system and other IGOs.

Catalogs, Indexes, Guides 75

430. Stevens, Robert D. and Helen C. Stevens. *Reader in Documents of International Organizations*. Reader Services in Library and Information Science. Washington, D.C.: Microcard Editions Books, 1973. xii, 410 p. ISBN 0910972400.
Collection of essays on the documentation of the League of Nations, the UN system, and other international organizations.

431. Unesco. *Bibliography of Publications Issued by Unesco or under Its Auspices: The First Twenty-five Years, 1946 to 1971 = Bibliographie des publications éditées par l'Unesco ou ses auspices: les vingt-cinq premières années, 1946 à 1971*. Paris: Unesco, 1973. xviii, 385 p. ISBN 9230010375.
Covers some 5,500 monographs and serials published by or with the assistance of Unesco. Lists official publications but excludes documents. Arranged by Universal Decimal Classification. Includes author and title indexes.

432. Unesco. *Catalogue 1989: Unesco Collection of Representative Works*. Paris: Unesco, 1989.
The "collection of representative works" is the result of Unesco's Literature Translations Programme, in operation since 1948; it comprises translations from lesser-known languages into English, French and, to a lesser extent, other major languages. Titles translated include scholarly texts of history, philosophy and religion; anthologies of national literatures; epics, sagas, novels, short stories, drama and poetry.

Unesco. *A Chronology of Unesco, 1945-1987*. See #63.

433. Unesco. *Film and Video Catalogue, 1987-1988*. Paris: Audiovisual Information Division, Office of Public Information, Unesco. 28 p.
Latest edition of a periodic guide. Lists sixty-seven programs in the fields of education, science, social sciences, culture, and communication. Each entry gives a brief description of the theme, and information on production, rights, duration, and language versions. Also provides technical specifications and conditions of purchase or loan, and a worldwide list of centers holding Unesco film and video programs.

434. Unesco. *Index Translationum: Répertoire international des traductions = International Bibliography of Translations = Repertorio internacional de Traducciones*. 1-, 1948-. Paris: Unesco.
Annual list of books translated around the world. Grouped by country of publication arranged in French alphabetical order and sub-arranged by Universal Decimal Classification. Identifies the author, translator, title of translation, imprint, language and title of original. Includes alphabetical index of principal authors and statistics of translations. Continues *Index Translationum: Répertoire international des traductions = International Bibliography of Translations*, issued 1932-1940 by the International Institute of Intellectual Co-operation.

435. Unesco. *International Directory of Youth Bodies 1990 = Répertoire international des organismes de jeunesse 1990 = Repertorio Internacional de Organismos de Juventud 1990*. Paris: Unesco, 1990. xviii, 477 p. ISBN 9230026735.
Lists over 550 international, regional and national youth organizations, and research, training and information centers, whether governmental or not. Provides information on research and other activities, and publications of each institution, as well as brief economic and social statistics for each of the 123 countries represented. Includes indexes by institutional name and acronym, programme, and subject field.

436. Unesco. *Inventory of General Conference Documents, 1946-1989*. Paris: Unesco, 1990. xxiv, 63 p. SID.78/WS/2 Rev.
Checklist of documents of the General Conference as well as those of the 1945 Conference for the Establishment of Unesco. Includes lists of General Conference sessions and senior officials.

437. Unesco. *List of Unesco Documents and Publications*. 1949-1973. Paris: Unesco.
Covers Unesco publications and main series (general distribution) documents. Excludes working series (limited distribution) documents. Overlaps with and is continued by *Unesco List of Documents and Publications* (#444). Former titles: *Subject List of Unesco Documents* (1949-1950); *Subject List of Publications and Documents of Unesco* (1951-1956); *Bibliographical List of Unesco Documents and Publications* (1957-1958).

438. Unesco. *List of Unesco Secretariat Main Series Documents, 1947-1971: In Chronological Order by Department/Sector = Liste des documents principaux du Secrétariat de l'Unesco, 1947-1971: dans l'ordre chronologique par département/sector [sic]*. Paris: Unesco, 1986. xiii, 87 p. LAD-86/WS/1.
Covers some 950 "main series" documents: meeting reports, surveys, analyses of replies to questionnaires, bibliographical works and other program documents. Includes references to finding aids.

439. Unesco. *A New World Information and Communication Order: towards a Wider and Better Balanced Flow of Information; A Bibliography of Unesco Holdings*. Paris: Unesco, 1979. 73 p. CC/80/WS/24.
Lists some 700 books, conference papers, documents, periodical articles and reports, including many issued by Unesco. Includes subject index. Updated by *Supplement, 1980-1981* (Paris: Unesco, 1982; 46 p.; COM/82/WS/12.) A related publication is United Nations, Dag Hammarskjöld Library, *The New World Information and Communication Order: A Selective Bibliography* (New York: UN, 1984; viii, 152 p.; ST/LIB/SER.B/35; Sales No. EF.84.I.15.)

440. Unesco. *The Newspaperman's United Nations: A Guide for Journalists about the United Nations and Specialized Agencies*. By Jerzy Szapiro. Paris: Unesco, 1961. 229 p.
Although much of the information is out-of-date, this guide presents its fifteen "courses" (the creation of the UN, political questions, cooperation with NGOs, and other topics) clearly, and includes good bibliographies, index and appendices.

441. Unesco. *Publications Catalogue*. 1947-. Paris: Unesco.
Annual list of books and periodicals issued by Unesco or co-produced with other publishers. Covers some "official publications" but no documents. Updated by *Just Published*.

442. Unesco. *Study Abroad = Etudes à l'étranger = Estudios en el Extranjero*. 1-, 1948-. Paris: Unesco. ISSN 0081895X.
Worldwide directory of international and transnational scholarships and courses offered by IGOs, NGOs and national institutions. Indicates subject field, level, location, cost, size of awards, conditions of eligibility, and practical information on applications. Includes indexes of international organizations, national institutions, and subjects of study.

Unesco. *World Directory of Human Rights Teaching and Research Institutions*. See #223.

Unesco. *World Directory of Peace Research and Training Institutions*. See #139.

Unesco. *World Directory of Social Science Institutions*. See #167.

Unesco. *World Directory of Teaching and Research Institutions in International Law*. See #210.

443. Unesco. *World List of Social Science Periodicals = Liste mondiale des périodiques spécialisées dans les sciences sociales = Lista Mundial de Revistas Especializadas en Ciencias Sociales*. 7th ed. World Social Science Information Services. Paris: Unesco, 1986. viii, 818 p. ISBN 9230024422. 1980.

Annotated bibliography of over 3,500 periodicals in the social sciences, including bibliographical and abstracting services. In four sections: 1, alphabetical index of titles; 2, full entry for each periodical providing title, starting date, publisher's name and address, periodicity, subject and geographical coverage, and other information; 3, subject index; and 4, geographical coverage index. Updated by lists in Nos. 1 and 3 of each volume of *International Social Science Journal* (#165).

444. Unesco. Computerized Documentation System. *Unesco List of Documents and Publications = Liste de documents et publications de l'Unesco = Lista de Documentos y Publicaciones de la Unesco*. 1972-. Paris: Unesco. ISSN 0377631X.

Covers Unesco publications as well as documents of the General Conference, Executive Board, "main series" and "working series" documents, and most other categories of Unesco material. Indicates availability of documents and publications on microfiche. The main listing is by "masterfile" (a computer-assigned sequence of entry numbers). Includes subject, personal name, meeting and corporate body, title and series, and conference indexes. Quarterly, with annual and multi-year (1972-1976, 1977-1980, 1981-1983, and 1984-1986) cumulations. Overlaps with and continues *List of Unesco Documents and Publications* (#437).

445. Unesco. Division of the Unesco Library, Archives and Documentation Services. *Bibliography of Publications on Unesco = Bibliographie des publications sur l'Unesco*. Paris: Unesco, 1984. xiv, 433 p. LAD-84/WS/3.

Lists over 3,300 monographs, theses, contributions to books, and periodical articles about Unesco but not issued by that organization. Arranged by country of publication. Includes subject and author indexes.

446. United Nations. Archives Section. *Index to Microfilm of United Nations Documents in English, 1946-1961*. Archives Special Guide, No. 14. New York: UN, 1963. v, 279 p.

Cumulative guide to microfilmed English-language UN documents. Partially fills the indexing gap for the period 1946-1949. Supplemented by *Index to Microfilm of United Nations Documents in English; Supplement, 1962-1967* (Archives Special Guide, No. 14, Supplement No. 1; New York: UN, 1970; v, 82 p.)

447. United Nations Centre on Transnational Corporations. *Transnational Corporations: A Selective Bibliography, 1983-1987 = Les sociétés transnationales: bibliographie séléctive, 1984-1987*. New York: UN, 1988. 2 vols. ST/CTC/76. Sales No. E.88.II.A.9. ISBN 9210040309, 9210040317.

Lists books and articles on TNCs: general studies; foreign direct investment; enterprise; TNCs in specific economic sectors; TNCs in specific countries and regions; economic, political, social and environmental issues; international and national legal and policy framework; TNCs and other actors; technical assistance; reference sources. Volume 1 (viii, 442 p.) contains the main list by category, and author and title indexes; volume 2 (vi, 463 p.) is an alphabetical subject index. Supplement for 1988-1990 in preparation.

448. United Nations Centre on Transnational Corporations. *UNCTC Bibliography, 1974-1987*. New York: UN, 1988. v, 83 p. ST/CTC/88; Sales No. E.87.II.A.23. ISBN 9211042186.

Partly annotated bibliography of documents and publications, including journal articles, issued by the UNCTC from its inception to 1987. Arranged by subject. Lacks index.

449. United Nations Children's Fund. *Geographical Index to UNICEF Documents, 1946 to 1972*. New York, 1974. 324 p. E/ICEF/INDEX/2.

Lists UNICEF documents related to various countries and regions. Arranged in six groups, each further subdivided by region. Lacks index.

78 United Nations Documentary and Archival Sources

450. United Nations Conference on Trade and Development. *Atlas of the Least Developed Countries = Atlas des pays les moins avancés*. New York: UN, 1990. vii, 43 p. UNCLDC II/10.
   Twenty maps, accompanied by brief explanations, presenting climate, natural hazards, population density and growth, GDP per capita, health, nutrition and educational data, and other development indicators for the forty-two least developed countries. Most of the data reflect the situation in 1987.

451. United Nations Conference on Trade and Development. *The Group of Seventy-Seven: A Bibliography*. Geneva: UNCTAD, 1987. 6 p. UNCTAD/CA/2858.
   Alphabetical list by author. Lacks index.

452. United Nations Conference on Trade and Development. *Guide to UNCTAD Publications, Covering the Period from the First Conference to the End of 1969*. Geneva: UNCTAD, 1970. 73 p.
   Partly annotated list of studies, reports and reference documents of UNCTAD, the Trade and Development Board and other UNCTAD subsidiary bodies. Continued by the annual *Guide to UNCTAD Publications = Guide des publications de la CNUCED = Guía de Publicaciones de la UNCTAD*, 1970- (ISSN 02525224).

453. United Nations Conference on Trade and Development. *UNCTAD 1983-1987: Bibliography*. New York: UN, 1987. iv, 38 p. UNCTAD/CA/2857.

United Nations. Dag Hammarskjöld Library. *See also* United Nations. Library.

454. United Nations. Dag Hammarskjöld Library. *Bibliographical Style Manual*. Bibliographical Series, No. 8. New York: UN, 1963. vi, 62 p. ST/LIB/SER.B/18; Sales No. 63.I.5.
   Bibliographic style manual for citing UN and League of Nations documents and publications as well as other sources. Although written before international rules for bibliographic citation became common, parts of it are still used in the preparation of UN bibliographies. See also *United Nations Editorial Manual* (#471).

455. United Nations. Dag Hammarskjöld Library. *Index to Proceedings ...* . New York: UN. ST/LIB/SER.B/-.
   Indexes to the proceedings and documentation of the General Assembly, the Security Council, the Economic and Social Council, and the Trusteeship Council. The two main parts of each are a subject index and an index to speeches.
Index to Proceedings of the Economic and Social Council. 14th- session, 1952- . New York: UN. ST/LIB/SER.B/E-. ISSN 00828084.
Index to Proceedings of the General Assembly. 5th- session, 1950/1951- . New York: UN. ST/LIB/SER.B/A-. ISSN 00828157. Beginning with the 30th session (1975), includes a voting chart for resolutions adopted by recorded vote.
Index to Proceedings of the Security Council. 1964- . New York: UN. ST/LIB/SER.B/S-. ISSN 00828408. Beginning with 1976, includes a voting chart for resolutions adopted.
Index to Proceedings of the Trusteeship Council. 11th- session, 1952- . New York: UN. ST/LIB/SER.B/T-. ISSN 00828491.
For earlier proceedings, see *Check List of United Nations Documents* (#490), part 2, No. 1 (Security Council, 1946-1949); part 4, Nos. 1, 2 and 3 (Trusteeship Council, 1947-1949); and part 5, Nos. 1, 2 and 3 (Economic and Social Council, 1946-1949).

456. United Nations. Dag Hammarskjöld Library. *Index to Resolutions* .... New York: UN. ST/LIB/SER.H/-.
Cumulative indexes to resolutions of the General Assembly, the Security Council, the Economic and Social Council, and the United Nations Conference on Trade and Development. The two main parts of each are a numerical list and a subject index.
United Nations. Dag Hammarskjöld Library. *Index to Resolutions and Other Decisions of the United Nations Conference on Trade and Development and of the Trade and Development Board, 1964-1972*. New York: UN, 1973. iv, 57 p. ST/LIB/SER.H/2; Sales No. E.73.I.5.
United Nations. Dag Hammarskjöld Library. *Index to Resolutions of the Economic and Social Council, 1946-1970*. New York: UN, 1981. iv, 207 p. ST/LIB/SER.H/4; Sales No. E.81.I.16.
United Nations. Dag Hammarskjöld Library. *Index to Resolutions of the General Assembly, 1946-1970*. New York: UN, 1972. ST/LIB/SER.H/1, parts 1 and 2; Sales No. E.72.I.3 (part 1: 146 p.) and E.72.I.14 (part 2: iv, 122 p.)
United Nations. Dag Hammarskjöld Library. *Index to Resolutions of the Security Council, 1946-1970*. New York: UN, 1973. iv, 39 p. ST/LIB/SER.H/3; Sales No. E.73.I.16.
Other indexes to resolutions include:
United Nations Conference on Trade and Development. *Index to Resolutions, Recommendations and Decisions of the United Nations Conference on Trade and Development and of the Trade and Development Board, 1964-1981*. Belgrade: UNCTAD, 1983. TD(VI)/Misc.2.
United Nations. Dag Hammarskjöld Library. *Cumulative Index to Resolutions of the Trusteeship Council, First to Tenth Sessions Inclusive, March 1947-April 1952*. New York: UN, 1953. ST/LIB/SER.D/45.
United Nations. Economic and Social Commission for Asia and the Pacific. *Index to Resolutions of the Economic and Social Commission for Asia and the Pacific, 1947-1978*. New York: UN, 1979. ST/ESCAP/LIB/SER.B/1; Sales No. E.80.II.F.3.
United Nations. Economic Commission for Latin America. *Indexes to Resolutions Approved by ECLA, 1948-1966*. Santiago, Chile: ECLA, UN, 1966 (supplement to *A Basic Guide to the Commission and Its Secretariat*).

457. United Nations. Dag Hammarskjöld Library. *Instructions for Depository Libraries Receiving United Nations Material*. New York: UN, 9 January 1981. 20, 4, 1 p. ST/LIB/13/Rev.4.
Sets out the conditions of deposit, extent of material deposited, payment of contributions, inspection of depository libraries, maintenance of depository collections, claiming and other procedures. Annexes provide the principles governing depository libraries, and a model request for documents. Certain provisions are updated by: *Corrigendum 1* (New York: UN, 27 April 1981; 1 p.; ST/LIB/13/Rev.4/Corr.1) and *Corrigendum 2* (New York: UN, 7 March 1986; 1 p.; ST/LIB/13/Rev.4/Corr.2).

458. United Nations. Dag Hammarskjöld Library. *List of Depository Libraries Receiving United Nations Material = Liste des bibliothèques dépositaires recevant les documents et publications de l'Organisation des Nations Unies = Lista de Bibliotecas Depositarias que Reciben Documentos y Publicaciones de las Naciones Unidas*. New York: UN, 1987. iv, 28 p. ST/LIB/12/Rev./7.
Directory of full and partial depository libraries, parliamentary libraries, and UN information centers or services. Each entry gives the name and address of the library, the extent and language of material deposited, and the date when depository status began. Another version is "List of Libraries and Information Centres Receiving United Nations Publications" (United Nations, Department for Disarmament Affairs, *Disarmament Fact Sheet*, No. 49, December 1986: 19-53.)

459. United Nations. Dag Hammarskjöld Library. *New World Information and Communication Order: A Selective Bibliography = Le nouvel ordre mondial de l'information et de communication*. Bibliographic Series, No. 35. New York: UN, 1988. viii, 152p. ST/LIB/SER.B/35.
In two parts: 1, periodical articles and monographs; 2, documents and publications of the UN system. Each part is arranged by broad subject, covering the New World Information and Communication Order, communications infrastructure, freedom of the press, broadcasting, and bibliographies. Lacks index.

460. United Nations. Dag Hammarskjöld Library. *UNBIS: An Overview of the Databases.* New York: UN, 1990. 7 p.

Brief description of eleven files in the United Nations Bibliographic Information System (UNBIS): United Nations Documents File (DOCFILE); the Library's External Materials File (CATFILE); full text of GA, ECOSOC and Security Council resolutions (RES); Index to Proceedings File (ITP); Index to Speeches File (ITS); GA and Security Council Voting Record File (VOTEREC); UNCTC (UN Centre on Transnational Corporations) Bibliographic File (TNCBIS); Trilingual Thesaurus File (THESAU); Name Authority File (ATHFILE); Series Symbol File (SERSYM); and Agenda Item File (AGENDA).

461. United Nations. Dag Hammarskjöld Library. *UNBIS On-line User's Manual, Version 5.0.* New York: UN, 1989. Loose-leaf.

Provides information on UNBIS, describes UNBIS files and common database operations, and gives detailed instructions for searching the files. Includes lists of codes and other appendices. The UN plans to make two UNBIS files (the United Nations Documents File, DOCFILE; and the Dag Hammarskjöld Library's External Materials File, CATFILE) available to outside institutions that are members of the RLIN network.

462. United Nations. Dag Hammarskjöld Library. *UNBIS Reference Manual for Bibliographic Description; A Manual for the Preparation of Bibliographic Data for Input into and Retrieval from the United Nations Bibliographic Information System.* New York: UN, 1985. viii, 212 p.

Standardized outline for the preparation and storage of bibliographic information for input and storage in UNBIS (United Nations Bibliographic Information System.)

463. United Nations. Dag Hammarskjöld Library. *UNDEX: United Nations Documents Index.* January 1970-January 1979. New York: UN. ST/LIB/SER.I/-.

Index to UN documents and publications other than restricted and internal material. Overlaps with and continues *United Nations Documents Index.* In three series:
Series A: Subject Index. 1970-1978. ST/LIB/SER.I/A/-. Alphabetical. Under each subject heading, shows type of document, author, date, and document series symbol. Does not cover certain types of documents indexed previously in *United Nations Documents Index* (#468) and subsequently in *UNDOC: Current Index; United Nations Documents Index* (#464); for example, excludes documents of the main committees of the GA.
Series B: Country Index. 1970-1978. ST/LIB/SER.I/B/-. Alphabetical, by name of country. Each entry gives type of action, subject, and document series symbol. Does not cover certain types of documents indexed previously in *United Nations Documents Index* (#468) and subsequently in *UNDOC: Current Index; United Nations Documents Index* (#464).
Series C: List of Documents Issued. 1974-January 1979. ST/LIB/SER.I/C/-. Arranged by document series symbol, with full bibliographic description of each document. Coverage is more complete than in Series A and B. There is a cumulative edition of Series C: 1974-1977 (3 volumes); 1978[-1979] (1 volume) (White Plains, N.Y.: UNIFO Publishers, 1979-1980). Overlaps with and is continued by *UNDOC.* Because of incomplete coverage in A and B, it is recommended that for the period 1970-1973 *United Nations Documents Index* (#468) be used instead of *UNDEX.*

464. United Nations. Dag Hammarskjöld Library. *UNDOC: Current Index; United Nations Documents Index.* Vol. 1- , 1979- . New York: UN. ST/LIB/SER.M/-. ISSN 02505584.

Covers non-restricted UN documents and publications much more extensively than its predecessor, *UNDEX: United Nations Documents Index* (#463). Consists of a checklist arranged by document series symbol and giving full bibliographic information, and author, title and subject indexes. Also includes lists of maps, sales publications and new document series symbols. Quarterly, with annual cumulations (cumulations on microfiche only as of 1984).

465. United Nations. Dag Hammarskjöld Library. *United Nations Document Series Symbols, 1946-1977; Cumulative List with Indexes*. Bibliographical Series, No. 5/Rev.3. New York: UN, 1978. iv, 312 p. ST/LIB/SER.B/5/Rev.3; Sales No. E.79.I.3.

Lists series symbols, with each entry providing the name of the issuing organ, period during which the symbol was used, restricted distribution of documents where applicable, and subsequent and other related symbols. Includes alphabetical subject/title index. Updated by: United Nations, Dag Hammarskjöld Library, *United Nations Document Series Symbols, 1978-1984* (Bibliographical Series, No. 5/Rev.4; New York: UN, 1986; vii, 160 p.; ST/LIB/SER.B/5/Rev.4; Sales No. E.85.I.2. Further updated by listings in *UNDOC* (#464).

466. United Nations. Dag Hammarskjöld Library. *United Nations Documentation: A Brief Guide*. New York: UN, 1981. 51 p. ST/LIB/34/Rev.1.

Practical guide to UN documents, their categories, numbering, distribution, availability and bibliographic control. Includes information about documents in microform, suggestions for organizing and maintaining UN document collections, and a select bibliography of guides to UN documentation.

467. United Nations. Dag Hammarskjöld Library. *United Nations Documentation News*. No. 1-, September 1981-. New York: UN. ISSN 02576260.

Contains announcements of UN activities and publications. Published at irregular intervals.

468. United Nations. Dag Hammarskjöld Library. *United Nations Documents Index*. Vols. 1-24, 1950-1973. New York: UN. ST/LIB/SER.E/-.

"UNDI" covers UN documents and publications other than restricted and internal material. Issues for 1950-1962 also indexed selected documents and publications of other organizations of the UN system. The main parts are: checklist arranged by document series symbol and giving full bibliographic information; and author/title/subject index (called "subject index") in a single alphabetical sequence. The first thirteen volumes (1950-1962) of the 'subject' (author/title/subject) indexes are cumulated in *United Nations Documents Index: Cumulated Index* (Millwood, N.Y.: Kraus-Thomson, 1974; 4 volumes) "UNDI" overlaps with and is continued by *UNDEX* (#463); it is recommended that for the period 1970-1973 *United Nations Documents Index* be used instead of *UNDEX* because of incomplete coverage in Series A and B of the latter.
For the period prior to 1950, see: Royal Institute of International Affairs, Library, *Index to United Nations Documents* (#425); United Nations, Archives Section, *Index to Microfilm of United Nations Documents* (#446); United Nations, Department of Public Information, *Ten Years of United Nations Publications, 1945 to 1955: A Complete Catalogue* (#474); United Nations, Library, *Check List of United Nations Documents* (#490); United Nations, Office of Conference Services, *Catalogue [of] United Nations Publications* (#491); and *Documents of International Organizations: A Selected Bibliography* (#378).

469. United Nations. Dag Hammarskjöld Library. *United Nations Sales Publications, 1972-1977: Cumulative List with Indexes*. New York: UN, 1978. v, 149 p. ST/LIB/SER.B/27; Sales No. E.78.I.10.

Chronological list of UN sales publications (except for mimeographed sales publications of the Economic Commission for Europe), subarranged by sales number. Includes subject, title, author, and UN document series symbol indexes.

470. United Nations. Dag Hammarskjöld Library. Reference and Bibliography Section. *United Nations Bibliographic Sources*. List of Selected Documents on Topics of Current Interest, New Series, No. 4/Rev. 1. New York: UN, 1986. 17 p. RBS/BIBL/SER.A/4/Rev.1.

Lists some 100 publications catalogs, indexes and compendia of the UN and its various bodies.

United Nations. Department of Conference Services. *A Guide to Writing for the United Nations*. See #255.

471. United Nations. Department of Conference Services. *United Nations Editorial Manual: A Compendium of Rules and Directives on United Nations Editorial Style, Publication Policies, Procedures and Practice.* New York: UN, 1983. ST/DCS/2; Sales No. E.83.I.16. vii, 524 p.

The UN's official statement of rules for drafting, editing and reproducing UN documents, publications and other written material. Includes a brief survey of UN documentation and publication patterns. Partly updated by United Nations, Department of Conference Services, *United Nations Editorial Manual, Revised Text of Articles A to D* (New York: UN, 5 March 1985; 203 p.; ST/DCS/5, part I.)

472. United Nations. Department of International Economic and Social Affairs. *Macrothesaurus for Information Processing in the Field of Economic and Social Development.* 3d ed. Prepared by Jean Viet. New York: UN; Organisation for Economic Co-operation and Development, 1985. xiv, 347 p. Sales No. E.85.I.15. ISBN 9211002729.

Lists economic and social terms, indicating broader, narrower and related terms, and other relationships. In four parts: 1, alphabetical list of terms in English, with French and Spanish equivalents; 2, descriptor groups; 3, hierarchical index; 4, KWOC (keyword-out-of-context) index. Fourth edition is in preparation.

473. United Nations. Department of International Economic and Social Affairs. Information Systems Unit. *Development Information Abstracts.* No. 1-, 1981-. New York: UN. ISSN 02542412.

Abstracts of unpublished studies, and mission and project reports written by or for the UN Department of International Economic and Social Affairs, Department of Technical Co-operation for Development and the United Nations Centre for Human Settlements. Reports abstracted, except for restricted items, are available from the Department of International Economic and Social Affairs.

474. United Nations. Department of Public Information. *Ten Years of United Nations Publications, 1945 to 1955: A Complete Catalogue.* New York: UN, 1955. 271 p. ST/DPI/SER.F/7; Sales No. 1955.I.8.

In addition to UN monographic and periodical publications, this sales catalog covers UN Official Records as well as selected League of Nations material.

475. United Nations. Department of Public Information. *United Nations Conferences and Special Observances.* Press Release: Reference Paper No. 28. New York: UN, 1989. 25 p.

Contains information on UN conferences and special observances scheduled for 1989, and internationally recognized decades, years, weeks and days such as Disarmament Week, the Third United Nations Development Decade, World Environment Day, and International Literacy Year. Latest edition of an annual list.

476. United Nations. Department of Public Information. *World Media Handbook: Selected Country Profiles.* 1990-. New York: UN.

Intended primarily for the use of the UN Department of Public Information, this serial publication (the plan is to issue it every two years) provides data on broadcasting, newspapers, periodicals, journalists' associations and other media-related information for countries that host UN information centers or services. Also gives basic population, media, cultural and telecommunications statistics.

477. United Nations Development Programme. Central Evaluation Office. *Directory of Central Evaluation Authorities in UNDP Participating Countries and Territories.* 3d ed. New York: UNDP, 1986. iv, 214 p.

478. United Nations. Economic and Social Commission for Asia and the Pacific. *Catalogue of ESCAP Population Publications through 1987.* Bangkok: ESCAP, 1987. 440 p.

Catalogs, Indexes, Guides 83

479. United Nations. Economic and Social Commission for Asia and the Pacific. *Index to Resolutions of the Economic and Social Commission for Asia and the Pacific, 1947-1978.* New York: UN, 1979. 2 vols. in 3. ST/ESCAP/LIB/SER.B/1; Sales No. E.80.II.F.3.
Compendium of texts of ESCAP resolutions, with index.

480. United Nations Environment Programme. *Environment in Print: 1990/91 Publications Catalogue.* Nairobi: UNEP, 1990. 44 p.
Annotated list of recent and important earlier publications, as well as forthcoming titles, on climate, atmosphere and air pollution, arid lands and desertification, soil, agriculture, forestry, conservation, wildlife, human settlements, toxic chemicals, monitoring and assessment, and other environmental issues.

481. United Nations Environment Programme. *An Index to the Decisions and Resolutions of the Governing Council of the United Nations Environment Programme: The First through the Fifteenth Session, the Session of a Special Character and the First and Second Special Session (1990).* Compiled by the Dag Hammarskjöld Library, United Nations. UNEP Library Series, C; UNEP Documents, No. 6. Nairobi: UNEP, 1991. iv, 166 p.

United Nations Environment Programme. *Register of International Treaties and Other Agreements in the Field of the Environment.* See #234.

482. United Nations. General Assembly. *Annotated Preliminary List of Items To Be Included in the Provisional Agenda of the 45th Regular Session of the General Assembly.* New York: UN, 1990. 442 p. A/45/100.
Latest edition of an annual guide to the agenda of the forthcoming GA session, issued mid-June. Gives a concise history of each agenda item, with copious references to related documents and meetings. Together with the preceding A/[session No.]/50 (preliminary agenda), and the subsequent A/[session No.]/150 (provisional agenda) and A/[session No.]/200 (supplementary list), provides an important guide to the deliberations of the GA.

483. United Nations Industrial Development Organization. *Documents List: Cumulative List for the Period 1 January 1967 to 31 December 1982.* New York: UN, 1983. xvi, 331 p. ID/SER.G/208/Rev.1.
Lists major printed publications, documents of the Industrial Development Board and its subsidiary bodies, and the information series. Excludes certain types of technical and other documents. Arranged by document series symbol. Entries give titles, and languages available. Includes subject index and list of sales publications. Updated by the annual *Documents List* (Vienna: UNIDO; ID/SER.G/208/Rev.1/Add.1-; ISSN 03798127).

484. United Nations Industrial Development Organization. *Industrial Development Abstracts.* 00001-, 1971-. Vienna: UNIDO. ID/-, UNIDO/LIB/SER.B/-. ISSN 03782654.
Quarterly guide to studies, reports, articles and other documents on industrial development. In three parts: subject index, author index, and abstracts. Has cumulative indexes.

United Nations Institute for Disarmament Research. *UNIDIR Repertory of Disarmament Research, 1990.* See #145.

485. United Nations Institute for Training and Research. *Directory of European Training Institutions in the Fields of Bilateral and Multilateral Diplomacy, Public Administration and Management, Economic and Social Development = Répertoire des institutions européennes de formation, dans les domaines de la diplomatie bilatérale et multilatérale, de l'administration publique et de la gestion, du développement économique et social.* New York: UN, 1987. ix, 496 p. UNITAR/EUR/87/06; Sales No. E/F.87.III.K.DS/7. ISBN 9210570065.
Compiled by the European Office of UNITAR, it describes institutions in twenty-four European countries, including universities, involved in direct training in the fields indicated by the title. Includes index, and a note on UNITAR's activities in Geneva.

486. United Nations. International Court of Justice. *Bibliography of the International Court of Justice = Bibliographie de la Cour internationale de justice*. 1946-. The Hague: ICJ. ISSN 00852139.
Annual list of national and international publications and documents concerning cases before the Court. Was part of the ICJ *Yearbook* for 1946-1964.

487. United Nations. International Court of Justice. *Publications of the International Court of Justice; Catalogue*. The Hague: ICJ, 1988. 29 p.
Lists publications of the ICJ from its establishment in 1946 until 30 June 1988. ICJ publications are issued in the following series: *Reports of Judgments, Advisory Opinions and Orders*; *Pleadings, Oral Arguments, Documents*; *Acts and Documents concerning the Organization of the Court*; *Yearbook*; and *Bibliography*. The *Catalogue* is arranged numerically, by ICJ sales number. Includes chronological index of *Reports of Judgments, Advisory Opinions and Orders*, and alphabetical index of cases.

488. United Nations. International Law Commission. *International Law Commission: A Guide to the Documents, 1949-1969*. Geneva: UN, 1970. 58 p. ST/GENEVA/LIB/SER.B/Ref.2.
Arranged by subjects such as arbitral procedure, law of treaties, and special missionsy. Under each topic, documents are listed by title in chronological order.

United Nations. Library. *See also* United Nations. Dag Hammarskjöld Library.

489. United Nations. Library. *A Bibliography of the Charter of the United Nations = Bibliographie de la Charte des Nations unies*. Bibliographical Series, No. 3. New York: UN, 1955. 128 p. ST/LIB/SER.B/3.
Lists some 3,000 books, documents, and periodical articles.

490.   United Nations. Library. *Check List of United Nations Documents*. 1946-1953. New York: UN. 20 vols. ST/LIB/SER.F/-.   Partially fills the indexing gap for the period 1946-1949.
Part 1: General Assembly and subsidiary organs -- not issued.
Part 2, No. 1: Security Council, 1946-1949.
Part 3: Atomic Energy Commission, 1946-1952.
Part 4, No. 1: Trusteeship Council, 1947-1948.
Part 4, No. 2: Trusteeship Council, 1948, 3d session.
Part 4, No. 3: Trusteeship Council, 1949.
Part 5, No. 1: Economic and Social Council, 1946-1947.
Part 5, No. 2: Economic and Social Council, 1948.
Part 5, No. 3: Economic and Social Council, 1949.
Part 6A, No. 1: Economic and Employment Commission, 1947-1949.
Part 6B, No. 1: Transport and Communications Commission, 1946- 1949.
Part 6C, No. 1: Statistical Commission, 1947-1949.
Part 6D, No. 1: Commission on Human Rights, 1947-1949.
Part 6E, No. 1: Social Commission, 1946-1949.
Part 6F, No. 1: Commission on the Status of Women, 1947-1949.
Part 6G: Commission on Narcotic Drugs -- not issued.
Part 6H, No. 1: Fiscal Commission, 1947-1948.
Part 6H, No. 2: Fiscal Commission, 1949.
Part 6J, No. 1: Population Commission, 1949-1949,
Part 7A: Economic Commission for Europe -- not issued.
Part 7B, No. 1: Economic Commission for Asia and the Far East, 1947-1949.
Part 7C, No. 1: Economic Commission for Latin America, 1948-1949.
Part 8, No. 1: UNICEF and United Nations Appeal for Children, 1946-1949.
Part 9: Secretariat -- not issued.
For general indexes to UN documents and publications after 1950, see *United Nations Documents Index* (#468), *UNDEX: United Nations Documents Index* (#463), and *UNDOC: Current Index; United Nations Documents Index* (#464).

491.   United Nations. Office of Conference Services. *Catalogue [of] United Nations Publications*. New York: UN, 1967. vi, 276 p. ST/CS/SER.J/9.
    Lists sales publications issued from 1945 to 1966, arranged by broad subject. Updated by: United Nations, Office of Conference Services, *Catalogue [of] United Nations Publications, 1968-1969* (New York: UN, 1969.)

492.   United Nations. Office of Conference Services. *United Nations Official Records, 1948-1962: A Reference Catalogue*. New York: UN, 1963. 107 p. ST/CS/SER.J/2; Sales No. 64.I.3.
    Covers the Official Records of the GA, the three Councils, the Atomic Energy Commission and the Disarmament Commission, as well as the *Yearbook of the International Law Commission* (#104). Also lists documents of the United Nations Conference on International Organization (1945) and the Preparatory Commission of the United Nations. Updated by: *United Nations Official Records, 1962-1981* (New York: UN, 1982) and *United Nations Official Records, 1981-1984* (New York: UN, 1984.)

493. United Nations. Office of General Services. *Catalogue of Sound Recordings in the Custody of the Sound Recording Unit of the Telecommunications Section of the United Nations as of 31 December 1972*. New York: UN, 1973. 75 p. ST/OGS/SER.F/1/Rev.1.

In three parts: A, list of recorded UN proceedings, by subject or name of body; B, list of recorded proceedings of other organizations of the UN system, by name of body; C, list by subject and name of sound recordings of special observances, ceremonies, and press conferences. See also United Nations, Sound Recording Unit, *Catalogue of Sound Recordings of United Nations Meetings Transferred to the Library of Congress of the United States* (New York: UN, 1974; iii, 81, 5 p.; ST/OGS/SER.F/5) and United Nations, Sound Recording Unit, *List of Speeches and Visits Made by Heads of State and Dignitaries, 1945-1972* (New York: UN, 1973; iii, 81, 6 p.; ST/OGS/SER.F/4.

United Nations. Office of Legal Affairs. *Multilateral Treaties Deposited with the Secretary-General*. See #215.

494. United Nations. Office of Legal Affairs. *Statement of Treaties and International Agreements Registered or Filed and Recorded with the Secretariat = Relevé des traités et accords internationaux enregistrés ou classés et inscrits au répertoire au Secrétariat*. February 1947-. New York: UN. ST/LEG/SER.A/-. ISSN 02517582.

Monthly list of treaties and agreements registered in pursuance of Charter Article 102 (1) or filed and recorded in accordance with GA resolutions. Has successively cumulating index (annual cumulation in the December issue.)

495. United Nations. Office of the United Nations High Commissioner for Refugees. *Refugee Abstracts: A Publication of the International Refugee Integration Resource Centre*. Vol. 1-, March 1982-. Geneva: Centre for Documentation on Refugees. ISSN 02531445.

Quarterly journal of abstracts of material on all aspects of refugee questions. Within topical categories, abstracts are arranged by continent and country, and subarranged alphabetically by title. Entries provide full bibliographic information and list terms under which each item is indexed. Titles covered are in English and French.

496. United Nations Population Fund. *UNFPA Publications and Audiovisual Guide*. New York: UNFPA, 1989. 55 p.

Latest issue of a generally annual list of printed material and films produced by UNFPA. Includes index.

497. United Nations Research Institute for Social Development. *Available Publications*. Geneva: UNRISD, 1988. 7 p.

498. United Nations. Sales Section. *United Nations Publications Catalogue, 1990-1991*. New York: UN, 1989. 144 p.

Latest issue of a periodic catalog of UN publications in print. Updated by monthly, semiannual, and other supplements.

United Nations. Secretariat. *Administrative Instruction: The United Nations Archives*. See #357.

499. United Nations. Secretariat. *List of Non-Governmental Organizations in Consultative Status with the Economic and Social Council.* Geneva: UN, 1988. 175 p. 1988/NGO List I/II.

Alphabetical list of 779 NGOs. In two parts: 1, organizations in consultative status (categories I, II, and Roster) by action of the Economic and Social Council and the Secretary-General; 2, organizations placed on the Roster because of their consultative status with the specialized agencies and other UN bodies. Each entry gives the organization's name in English and French when available, address, name of chief executive officer, consultative status category, and name and address of Geneva representative if any. Other lists of NGOs are issued from time to time; for example: United Nations, Economic and Social Council, *List of Non-Governmental Organizations in Consultative Status with the Economic and Social Council in 1989* (New York: UN, 1989; 30 p.; E/1989/INF/1.) For a listing of UN system bodies dealing with NGOs, see United Nations, Secretariat, Office of the Under-Secretary-General for Political and General Assembly Affairs and Secretariat Services, *Directory of Departments and Offices of the United Nations Secretariat, United Nations Programmes, Specialized Agencies and Other Intergovernmental Organizations Dealing with Non-Governmental Organizations* (New York: UN, 1989; 19 p.)

United Nations. Statistical Office. *Directory of International Statistics.* See #319.

500. United Nations. Translation Division. Documentation, Reference and Terminology Section. *Acronyms and Abbreviations Covering the United Nations System and Other International Organizations = Sigles et abréviations utilisés par les organismes des Nations Unies et d'autres organisations internationales = Siglas y Abreviaturas de las Organizaciones del Sistema de las Naciones Unidas y Otras Organizaciones Internacionales.* Terminology Bulletin No. 311/Rev.1. New York: UN, 1981. xix, 406 p. ST/CS/SER.F/311/Rev.1.

Includes 825 acronyms and abbreviations, mostly of bodies in the UN system and other international organizations. In three parts: 1, listing in English alphabetical order; 2, English, French, Russian, Spanish, Chinese, and Arabic organizational name indexes; 3, English-French-Spanish, Russian, Chinese, and Arabic indexes of acronyms and abbreviations. Includes bibliography.

501. United Nations. Translation Division. French Service. *Lexique général anglais-français avec suppléments espagnol-français et russe-français.* 3d, rev. ed. New York: UN, 1982. xiv, 886 p. ST/DCS/1/Rev.3.

Dictionary of some 25,000 general, procedural, budgetary, administrative, technical and other terms used by the UN system and other international organizations.

502. United Nations. Translation Division. German Section. *Dreisprachenliste Vereinte Nationen, Englisch-Französisch-Deutsch = Trilingual Compendium of United Nations Terminology, English-French-German = Compendium trilingue de terminologie des Nations unies, anglais-français-allemand.* 4 vols. New York: UN, 1986. GTS/4/Rev.1; Sales No. E/F/G.86.I.20. ISBN 9210020480.

Glossary of about 15,000 terms. Volume 1 (xxxiii, 561 p.) provides: general terms and names; organizational names of the UN system; names of conferences, declarations, action plans, international years and decades; names of international organizations outside the UN system and acronyms and abbreviations. Volume 2 (vii, 366 p.) contains English, French and German alphabetical indexes to Volume 1 and acronyms and abbreviations used in Volume 3. Volume 3 (xi, 571 p.) gives names of departments and offices of the UN Secretariat and other UN bodies in New York, Geneva and Vienna, with English, French and German alphabetical indexes. Volume 4 (v, 167 p.) presents selected general UN terminology.

503. United Nations University. *UNU Publications: Complete Listing, Including New Titles for 1989-1990.* Tokyo: UNU. 100 p.

Latest edition of a biennial catalog.

88   United Nations Documentary and Archival Sources

504. *United Nations: A Keyword Dissertation Bibliography.* Ann Arbor, Mich.: University Microfilms International. 1975? ii, 41 p.
    Lists 345 doctoral dissertations on the UN system. Provides name of author, title, degree earned, degree-granting institution, location of abstract in *Dissertation Abstracts*, and other information.

505. United States. Library of Congress. *Government Publications: A Guide to Bibliographic Tools.* 4th ed. By Vladimir M. Palic. Washington, D.C.: LC, 1975. 441 p.
    Part 2: International Governmental Organizations (pp. 151-192.)

506. Universal Postal Union. *List of Publications.* Bern: UPU, 1989. 39 p.

507. Universal Postal Union. *Liste des publications du Bureau international de l'UPU.* 1957-. Bern: UPU. ISSN 02523779.

508. Vambery, Joseph T. *Cumulative List and Index of Treaties and International Agreements Filed or Recorded with the Secretariat of the United Nations, December 1969-1974.* Dobbs Ferry, N. Y.: Oceana, 1977. 2 vols.
    Volume 1 (xi, 461 p.; ISBN 0379007401) indexes treaties and agreements registered with the UN Secretariat, and ratifications and other subsequent action, from 1 December 1969 to 31 December 1974 (treaties 10043-13731). Volume 2 (iii, 415 p.; ISBN 037900741X) indexes ratifications and other actions affecting treaties prior to 1 December 1969 (numbers up to 10043.)

509. *Who's Who in the United Nations and Related Agencies.* 1st ed., 1975. New York: Arno Press. ISBN 040500490X.
    Gives biographies of over 3,700 senior officials of the secretariats of organizations in the UN system. Also provides other reference material; for example, directory information about UN offices worldwide. No further editions have been published.

510. Winton, Harry N. M. *Publications of the United Nations System: A Reference Guide.* New York: Bowker, 1972. xi, 202 p. ISBN 0835205975.
    Overview of the structure, main activities and publications of the UN system, with annotated bibliography and subject index.

511. World Bank. *Catalog of Publications.* 1976-1984. Washington, D.C.: World Bank.
    Annual subject list of free and priced publications, with author/title index. Continued by World Bank, *Index of Publications* (#513).

512. World Bank. *Catalog of Staff Working Papers.* Washington, D.C.: World Bank, 1985. 64 p.
    Lists in-print and out-of-print Staff Working Papers up to No. 721 (of the total of some 800 issued.) Includes numerical, title, and author indexes. Many out-of-print Staff Working Papers are available in reprint or microfiche from National Technical Information Service.

513. World Bank. *Index of Publications.* 1986-. Washington, D.C.: World Bank. ISSN 02597357.
    Annual list of World Bank publications in print. Alphabetical by title. Includes author, country/region, and subject indexes. Continues World Bank, *Catalog of Publications* (#511). Kept up to date by the periodical *Publications Update.*

514. World Bank. *The World Bank Research Program: Abstracts of Current Studies.* 1977?-. Washington, D.C.: World Bank. ISSN 02583143.

Annual collection of centrally-funded and departmentally-funded studies in progress or completed during the report year. Topics covered are: adjustment and growth; private and public sector management; global outlook, debt management and trade; reform of financial systems; people and the development process; natural resource management; technology, productivity and development; and basic services.

515. World Bank. Depository Library Program. *Directory of Libraries.* 2d ed. Washington, D.C.: World Bank, 1990. vii, 63 p. ISBN 0821314513.

Worldwide listing of World Bank depository libraries, arranged by country. Includes criteria for selection as depository and list of distributors of World Bank publications.

516. *World Bibliography of International Documentation.* Compiled and edited by Theodore D. Dimitrov. Pleasantville, N.Y.: UNIFO Publishers, 1981. 2 vols. ISBN 0891110100.

Lists some 9,300 monographs, journal articles and other material by and about the UN system and other IGOs. Volume 1 (xii, 474 p.), international organizations: activities, structure, information policies, bibliographic control; Volume 2 (352 p.), multilateral diplomacy and international relations, international periodicals. Includes personal author, corporate author, and subject indexes.

517. World Health Organization. *Publications Catalogue, 1948-1989.* Geneva: WHO, 1989. v, 294 p.

Alphabetical title list of over 2,000 books, reports and periodicals, whether or not in print, issued at WHO's headquarters and regional offices other than the Pan American Health Organization (PAHO). Does not cover technical documents that are not formal publications. Includes author/editor, series, and subject indexes.

518. World Health Organization. *Publications Catalogue: New Books, 1986-1990.* Geneva: WHO, 1990. iv, 248 p.

Provides annotated entries for over 500 books and publications in series published by the WHO at its headquarters and regional offices, including a few items published before 1986. Arranged under fifty subject headings; for example: AIDS, cardiovascular diseases, disease classification, food safety, health policy and ethics, occupational health. Includes author/editor, title, and series indexes.

519. World Health Organization. *World Health Organization Publications: Catalogue, 1947-1979.* Geneva: WHO, 1980. v, 133 p.

Subject catalog of monographs, periodicals and publications in series. Includes alphabetical indexes by author and subject. Updated by *Supplement, 1980-1984.*

520. World Health Organization. *WHODOC: List of Recent WHO Publications and Documents = Liste des publications et des documents récents OMS = Lista de Publicaciones y Documentos Recientes de la OMS.* Vol. 1-, 1981-. Geneva: WHO. ISSN 10109056.

Bimonthly list of WHO documents and publications including articles in WHO periodicals, as well as selected non-WHO items of interest to WHO. Arranged by broad subject categories. Includes meeting, author, and subject indexes.

521. World Intellectual Property Organization. *Catalogue of Publications of the World Intellectual Property Organization, 1990.* Geneva: WIPO, 1990. 52 p.

Latest list of WIPO publications other than documents issued for meetings. Arranged in twelve categories, for example: general information; periodicals; conventions, treaties and agreements; records of diplomatic conferences; statistics. Includes alphabetical keyword index.

522. World Meteorological Organization. *Catalogue of Publications, 1951-1977: Meteorology and Related Fields Such As Hydrology, Marine Sciences and Human Environment.* Geneva: WMO, 1977. vi, 140 p.

Kept up to date by periodically issued *Catalogue of Publications* (latest: 1988; 120 p.) which itself is updated by a *Supplement*.

523. *Worldmark Encyclopedia of the Nations, Vol. 1: United Nations.* 7th ed. New York: Worldmark Press, John Wiley & Sons, distributor, 1988. xxii, 276 p. ISBN 0471624063.

Guide to the origins, structure, financing, functions and major activities of the UN, with briefer articles on other organizations in the UN system. Includes indexes, bibliographies, statistical tables, glossaries, and lists of abbreviations and acronyms.

524. *Yearbook of International Organizations.* 1st- ed., 1948- . Brussels: Union of International Associations.

The most important directory of IGOs and NGOs of all types. The 27th (1990/1991) edition lists over 26,000 entities, arranged in the following sections: federations of international organizations; universal membership organizations; intercontinental membership organizations; regionally-oriented membership organizations; organizations emanating from places, persons, other bodies; organizations of special form; internationally-oriented national organizations; dissolved or inactive organizations; recently reported, unconfirmed bodies; religious orders and secular institutes; autonomous conference series; multilateral treaties and intergovernmental agreements; currently inactive non-conventional bodies. Includes a discussion of international organizations, bibliographies, an elaborate index, and statistics. Supplemented by information in *Transnational Associations: The Review of International Associations and Meetings* (1-, 1949-; Brussels: Union of International Associations.)

INDEX

AUTHOR/TITLE INDEX
(References are to entry numbers)

100 ans de statistiques de propriété industrielle, 342
100 Years of Industrial Property Statistics, 342
1957-1982: 25 Years -- International Atomic Energy Agency, 21

Abi, Saab, Georges, 64
Accelerated Development in Sub-Saharan Africa: An Agenda for Action, 192
"Access to Archives of United Nations Organizations", 345
Access to the Archives of United Nations Agencies: A RAMP Study with Guidelines, 356
ACCIS Newsletter, 362
ACCIS Guide to United Nations Information Sources on International Trade and Development Finance, 364
Acronyms and Abbreviations Covering the United Nations System, 500
Administrative and Financial Reform of the United Nations: A Documentary Essay, 6
Administrative Committee on Co-ordination [of the United Nations System of Organizations], 1
  Secretariat, 361
Advisory Committee for the Co-ordination of Information Systems [of the United Nations System of Organizations], 362-367
Administrative Instruction: The United Nations Archives, 357
Aeronautical Agreements and Arrangements, 203
African Economic and Financial Data, 333
Aga Khan, Sadruddin, 2
Agreement Establishing the International Fund for Agricultural Development, 34
Agreements Registered with the International Atomic Energy Agency, 201
Alves, Péricles Gasparini, 145
American Statistics Index, 298
Annotated Preliminary List of Items To Be Included in the Provisional Agenda ... of the General Assembly, 482
Annuaire de statistiques sanitaires mondiales, 340
Annuaire démographique, 318
Annuaire des statistiques de l'énergie, 320
Annuaire des statistiques du travail, 302
Annuaire FAO de la production, 295

Annuaire international de l'éducation et de l'enseignement, 247
Annuaire statistique des télécommunications du secteur public, 305
Annuaire statistique du commerce international, 324
Annuaire statistique pour l'Asie et le Pacifique, 311
Annual Epidemiological and Vital Statistics, 340
Annual Report on the Activities of the International Trade Centre, UNCTAD/GATT, 164
Annual Report of the World Meteorological Organization, 131
Annual Report of UNIDO, 93
Annual Review of Project Performance Audit Results, 194
Annual Review of United Nations Affairs, 3
Anuario de Estadísticas del Trabajo, 302
Anuario estadístico de las telecomunicacioines del sector público, 305
Anuario FAO de Producción, 295
"Archival Finding Aids in International Organizations", 349
"Archives des organisations internationales: le point de vue du chercheur", 347
"Archives et documentation", 352
"Archives et droit d'auteur", 360
"Archives of International Organizations: Introductory Report", 358
"Archives of the United Nations", 343
Articles of Agreement of the International Bank for Reconstruction and Development, 23
Articles of Agreement of the International Development Association, 31
Assignment Children, 171
ATAS Bulletin, 254
Atherton, Alexine L., 368
Atlas des pays les moins avancés, 450
Atlas of the Least Developed Countries, 450
Atomic Energy Review, 239

Bailey, Sydney Dawson, 4
Balance of Payments Statistics, 304
Basic Documents on United Nations and Related Peace-keeping Forces, 134

Basic Facts about the United Nations, 77
Basic Texts of the Food and Agriculture Organization of the United Nations, 9
Bertrand, Maurice, 57, 59, 100
"Bertrand Report", 59
Bibliographic Catalogue of FAO Publications, 1945-1972, 380
Bibliographical List of Unesco Documents and Publications, 437
Bibliographical Style Manual, 454
Bibliographie de la Charte des Nations unies, 489
Bibliographie de la Cour internationale de justice, 486
Bibliographie des publications éditées par l'Unesco ou ses auspices, 431
Bibliographie des publications sur l'Unesco, 445
Bibliography of Publications Issued by Unesco or under Its Auspices, 431
Bibliography of Publications on Unesco, 445
Bibliography of Published Research of the World Employment Programme, 403
Bibliography of the Charter of the United Nations, 489
Bibliography of the International Court of Justice, 486
Bibliography of United Nations Thesauri, Classifications, Nomenclatures, 416
Birchfield, Mary E., 375
Black, Maggie, 173
Blue Helmets: A Review of United Nations Peace-keeping, 144
Bossuyt, Marc J., 219
"Brandt Memorandum", 154
"Brandt Report", 155
Brandt, Willy, 155
Brimmer, Brenda, 369
Browne, Marjorie A., 114, 119
"Brundtland Report", 237
Budgeting in the Organizations of the United Nations System, 52
Bulletin de l'Organisation mondiale de la santé, 266
Bulletin of Labour Statistics, 302
Bulletin of the World Health Organization, 266
Bulletin on Narcotics, 260

Can the Common System Be Maintained?, 94
Carnets de l'enfance, 171
Catalogue 1989: Unesco Collection of Representative Works, 432

Catalogue of ESCAP Population Publications through 1987, 478
Catalogue of ICAO Publications, 398
Catalogue of Publications of the World Intellectual Property Organization, 521
Catalogue of Publications in English of the International Labour Office, 1919-1950, 404
Catalogue of Sound Recordings in the Custody of the Sound Recording Unit ... of the United Nations, 493
Catalogue of Sound Recordings of United Nations Meetings, 493
Catalogue [of] United Nations Publications, 491
Cayuela, José, 85
Centenary of the Telephone, 242
CEPAL Review, 185
Changing Relationship between the World Bank and the International Monetary Fund, 72
Charte des Nations Unies: commentaire, article par article, 5
Charter of the United Nations: Commentary and Documents, 14
Charter of the United Nations and Statute of the International Court of Justice, 78
Check List of United Nations Documents, 490
Cherns, J.J., 370
Children and Development in the 1990s: A UNICEF Sourcebook, 172
Children and the Environment, 235
Children and the Nations: The Story of UNICEF, 173
Cholganskaia, Vera Leont'evna, 371
Chronicle of the World Health Organization, 267
Chronology and Fact Book of the United Nations, 1941-1985, 372
Chronology of Unesco, 1945-1987, 63
Citation Rules and Forms for United Nations Documents and Publications, 424
Civil Aviation Statistics: ICAO Statistical Yearbook, 299
Clews, John, 373
Codex Alimentarius, 417
Codex Alimentarius Commission (FAO/WHO), 417
Collected Resolutions on the International Development Strategy and the New International Economic Order, 286
Commemoration of the Twenty-fifth Anniversary of the United Nations Conference on Trade and Development, 73
Commission on International Development, 146

Commodity Trade Statistics, 314
Common Crisis North-South, 154, 374
Common Index and Glossary to the Brandt, Palme and Brundtland Reports, 374
Common Security, 136, 374
Commonwealth Secretariat, 374
Communication Policy Studies, 245
Compendio de Estadísticas Relativas al Analfabetismo, 306
Compendio de las Publicaciones Preparadas por el CCI durante sus Primeros 20 Años, 1964-1984, 415
Compendium des statistiques relatives à l'analphabétisme, 306
Compendium of Housing Statistics, 315
Compendium of Human Settlement Statistics, 315
Compendium of International Conventions concerning the Status of Women, 229
Compendium of Publications Prepared by ITC during its First 20 Years, 415
Compendium of Resolutions Adopted by the United Nations Economic Commission for Africa, 284
Compendium of Resolutions and Decisions of the Economic Commission for Europe, 285
Compendium of Statistics and Indicators on the Situation of Women, 316
Compendium of Statistics on Illiteracy, 306
Compendium trilingue de terminologie des Nations unies, anglais-français-allemand, 502
Compilation of Economic and Social Council and General Assembly Resolutions on UNICEF and the International Year of the Child, 174
Compilation of United Nations Resolutions and Decisions Relevant to the Struggle against Racism, Racial Discrimination and Apartheid, 293
Complete Reference Guide to United Nations Sales Publications, 1946-1978, 375
Composition de l'OMM, 132
Composition of the World Meteorological Organization, 132
Comprehensive Handbook of the United Nations, 271
Concept of International Organization, 64
Concluding Report on the Implementation of General Assembly Resolution 32/197 concerning the Restructuring of the Economic and Social Sectors of the United Nations System, 53
Conference Diplomacy: An Introductory Analysis, 95

Constitution de l'Organisation internationale du Travail et Règlement de la Conférence internationale du Travail, 37
Constitution of the International Labour Organisation and Standing Orders of the International Labour Conference, 37
Constitution of the United Nations Industrial Development Organization, 92
Construction Statistics Yearbook, 317
Control and Limitation of Documentation in the United Nations System, 54
Convenio sobre Aviación Civil Internacional, 30
Convention Establishing the Multilateral Investment Guarantee Agency and Commentary on the Convention, 24, 122
Convention Establishing the World Intellectual Property Organization, 129
Convention on International Civil Aviation, 30
Convention relative à l'aviation civile internationale, 30
Coolman, Jacqueline, 375
Copyright: Monthly Review of the World Intellectual Property Organization, 268
Cordier, Andrew W., 278
Cost of Social Security, 300
Costo de la Seguridad Social, 300
Cot, Jean-Pierre, 5
Coût de la sécurité social, 300
Credentials Considerations in the United Nations General Assembly: The Process and Its Role, 114
Cultures: Dialogue between the Peoples of the World, 246
Cumulative Index to Resolutions of the Trusteeship Council, 456
Cumulative Index to the General International Agreements in the United Nations Treaty Series, 211
Cumulative List and Index of Treaties and International Agreements Filed or Recorded with the Secretariat of the United Nations, 508
Cyprus. Press and Information Office, 272

De Gara, John, 6
Deardorff, John, 376
Demographic Yearbook, 318
Development Data Book: A Guide to Social and Economic Statistics, 334
Development Information Abstracts, 473

Developments in International Labour Statistics, 301
Diehl, John A., 15
Dimitrov, Theodore D., 377, 401, 516
Diplomat's Handbook of International Law and Practice, 213
Direction of Trade Statistics, 303
Directory of Central Evaluation Authorities in UNDP Participating Countries and Territories, 477
Directory of Departments and Offices of the United Nations Secretariat ... Dealing with Non-Governmental Organizations, 499
Directory of European Training Institutions in the Fields of Bilateral and Multilateral Diplomacy..., 485
Directory of International Statistics, 319
Directory of Selected Collections of United Nations System Publications, 363
Directory of United Nations Databases and Information Services, 364
Directory of United Nations Serial Publications, 365
Disarmament: A Periodic Review, 140
Dissemination of Information and Documentation at the International Telecommunication Union in the '90s, 413
Djonovich, Dusan J., 288, 292
Documentación de la FAO: Bibliografía Corriente, 382
Documentary Study of the Politicization of Unesco, 61
Documentation de la FAO: bibliographie courante, 382
"Documentation of Intergovernmental Organizations: A Critical Survey", 390
Documentation of the UN System: A Survey of Bibliographic Control, 373
Documentation of the United Nations System: Co-ordination in Its Bibliographic Control, 418
Documents of International Organisations: A Bibliographic Handbook, 377
Documents of International Organizations: A Selected Bibliography, 378
Documents on the International Court of Justice, 273
Dreisprachenliste Vereinte Nationen, Englisch-Französisch-Deutsch, 502

ECE 1947-1987, 84

ECLAC: 40 Years (1948-1988), 85
Economic and Social Survey of Asia and the Pacific, 183
Economic Bulletin for Asia and the Pacific, 185
Economic Bulletin for Europe, 185
Economic Bulletin for Latin America, 185
Economic Survey of Asia and the Far East, 183
Economic Survey of Europe, 186
Economic Survey of Latin America and the Caribbean, 180
ECOSOC: Options for Reform, 96
Effective Negotiation: Case Studies in Conference Diplomacy, 261
El-Zanati, A. G., 413
Elements of an International Development Strategy for the 1990s, 177
Emerging Stock Markets Factbook, 156
Encyclopedia of the United Nations and International Relations, 422
Energy Statistics Yearbook, 320
Environment in Print: 1990/91 Publications Catalogue, 480
Environment Statistics in Europe and North America: An Experimental Compendium, 312
Environmental Data Report, 233
Erlandsson, Alf M. E., 343, 344
ESCAP 1947-1987: Regional Co-operation for Development, 81
Estadísticas Agropecuarias Mundiales, 297
Estudios en el Extranjero, 442
Etudes à l'étranger, 442
Evans, F. B., 345
Evans, Luther H., 346
Evborokhai, A.O., 289
Everyman's United Nations, 107
Everyone's United Nations, 107
Evolving Role of IDA, 123

FAO Books In Print, 380
FAO Documentation: Current Bibliography, 382
FAO Documentation: Current Index, 382
FAO Production Yearbook, 295
FAO Publications Catalogue, 381
FAO Trade Yearbook, 296
FAO: Its Origins, Formation and Evolution, 1945-1981, 10
Feinberg, Richard E., 73
Fetzer, Mary K., 379

Final Report of the [ACCIS] Technical Panel on Database Access, 366
Finance & Development, 195
Finger, J. Michael, 195
Finley, Blanche, 7
Fomerand, Jacques, 8
Food and Agriculture Organization of the United Nations, 9-11, 147-148, 295-297, 380-384
    List of Documents, 384
Food and Nutrition, 147
Food and Nutrition Bulletin, 147
Foote, Wilder, 278
Four Decades of Achievement: Highlights of the Work of the World Health Organization, 127
Frei, Daniel, 262
From Semaphore to Satellite, 243
Fromuth, Peter J., 62
Future Role of the United Nations in an Interdependent World, 96

Garritsen de Vries, Margaret, 42-45
GATT Activities: An Annual Review of the Work of the GATT, 12
GATT Focus, 149
General Agreement on Tariffs and Trade, 12-13, 149-152, 200, 385
    Basic Instruments and Selected Documents, 274
    Status of Legal Instruments, 200
General Agreement on Tariffs and Trade: Text of the General Agreement, 13
Geographical Index to UNICEF Documents, 1946 to 1972, 449
Ghebali, Victor-Yves., 347
Global Environment Monitoring System (UNEP), 233
Global Outlook 2000: An Economic, Social, and Environmental Perspective, 168
Global Report on Human Settlements, 169
Glover, Frederick J., 50
Goehlert, Robert, 386
Goodrich, Leland M., 14
Gottschalk, Louis, 238
Government Finance Statistics Yearbook, 304
Government Publications: A Guide to Bibliographic Tools, 505
Great Britain. Department of the Environment, 233
"Group of 18", 8, 87
Group of Seventy-Seven: A Bibliography, 451

Group of High-level Intergovernmental Experts to Review the Efficiency of the Administrative and Financial Functioning of the United Nations, 8
Growth of World Industry, 322
Guia de Publicaciones de la UNCTAD, 452
Guide des publications de la CNUCED, 452
Guide to Delegate Preparation: UNA-USA Model U.N. Survival Kit, 15
"Guide to the Archives of International Organizations", 359
Guide to the Archives of International Organizations, Part 1: The United Nations System, 353
Guide to the Archives of International Organizations, Part 2: Archives of International Organizations, 354
Guide to the Archives of International Organizations, Part 3: Archives of Other International Inter-governmental Organizations, 355
Guide to the "Travaux préparatoires" of the International Covenant on Civil and Political Rights, 219
Guide to the Use of United Nations Documents, 369
Guide to UNCTAD Publications, 452
Guide to Unesco, 16
Guide to United Nations Organization, Documentation and Publishing, 388
Guide to Writing for the United Nations, 255

Haas, Michael, 387
Hajnal, Peter I., 16, 388, 402
Hambro, Edvard, 14
Handbook of Foreign Policy Analysis, 262
Handbook of Industrial Statistics, 313
Handbook of Information, Computer and Communications Activities of Major International Organisations, 421
Handbook of International Trade and Development Statistics, 309
Handbook on Social Indicators, 321
Harrelson, Max, 278
Hawkes, Jacquetta, 238
Herzstein, Robert Edwin, 348
Higgins, Rosalyn, 135
Hill, Martin, 153
Hindle, W.H., 255
Hinds, Thomas S., 389

History of Mankind: Cultural and Scientific Development, 238
History of UNCTAD, 1964-1984, 74
Holborn, Louise W., 17
Hopkins, Michael, 390
Horsefield, J. Keith, 43
Hovet, Thomas Jr., 372
Hüfner, Klaus, 391
Human Development Report, 182
Human Resources Development: A Neglected Dimension of Development Strategy, 178
Human Rights Teaching, 221
Human Rights: A Compilation of International Instruments, 225
Human Rights: Status of International Instruments, 226
Humphrey, John, 222

IAEA Yearbook, 19
ICAO Bulletin, 241
ICAO Journal, 241
ICAO Monthly Bulletin, 241
ICSID Basic Documents, 28
ICSID Bibliography, 397
IDA in Retrospect, 124
IFAD Annual Report, 35
ILO and the World of Work, 157
ILO Catalogue of Publications in Print, 405
IMCO Bulletin, 39
IMCO Publications, 410
IMF in a Changing World, 42
IMF Survey, 160
IMO News, 39
In the Minds of Men: Unesco, 1946 to 1971, 65
Independent Commission on Disarmament and Security Issues, 136
Independent Commission on International Development Issues, 154-155
Index of ICAO Publications, 399
Index of IMO Resolutions, 409
Index to International Statistics, 298
Index to Microfilm of United Nations Documents in English, 446
Index to Proceedings of the Economic and Social Council, 455
Index to Proceedings of the General Assembly, 455
Index to Proceedings of the Security Council, 455
Index to Proceedings of the Trusteeship Council, 455

Index to Resolutions and Other Decisions of the United Nations Conference on Trade and Development, 456
Index to Resolutions of the Economic and Social Commission for Asia and the Pacific, 456, 479
Index to Resolutions of the Economic and Social Council, 456
Index to Resolutions of the General Assembly, 456
Index to Resolutions of the Security Council, 456
Index to Resolutions, Recommendations and Decisions of the United Nations Conference on Trade and Development, 456
Index [to] FAO Conference and Council Decisions, 1945-1972, 383
Index to the Decisions and Resolutions of the Governing Council of the United Nations Environment Programme, 481
Index to United Nations Documents to December 1947, and *Supplements ... to December 1949*, 425
Index Translationum: Répertoire international des traductions, 434
Indexes to Resolutions Approved by ECLA, 456
Industrial Development Abstracts, 484
Industrial Meetings Catalogue, 406
Industrial Property Statistics, 341
Industrial Statistics Yearbook, 322
Industry and Development: Global Report, 188
"Information Policies of International Organizations", 426
Information Sources of Food and Agriculture, 364
INIS Atomindex: An International Abstracting Service, 394
Institute for Palestine Studies, 281
Instructions for Depository Libraries Receiving United Nations Material, 457
International Atomic Energy Agency, 18-22, 201-202, 239-240, 392-395
    Annual Report, 18
    Index to Resolutions and Decisions of the General Conference, 392
    Information Circulars, 393
    Resolutions and Other Decisions of the General Conference, 240
    Statute, 22
International Atomic Energy Agency Bulletin, 20
International Atomic Energy Agency Publications; Catalogue, 395

International Bank for Reconstruction and Development, 23-26
   Report of the Executive Directors on the Convention on the Settlement of Investment Disputes, 25
   Summary Proceedings of the Annual Meetings of the Boards of Governors, 26
International Bibliography, Information, Documentation, 396
International Bibliography of Translations, 434
International Bibliography: Publications of Intergovernmental Organizations, 396
International Centre for Settlement of Investment Disputes, 27-28, 397
   Annual Report, 27
International Civil Aviation Organization, 29-30, 203, 241, 299, 398-399
   Annual Report of the Council, 29
International Commission for the Study of Communication Problems, 248
International Cooperative Information Systems, 400
International Covenant on Civil and Political Rights, 219-220
   Optional Protocol, 219
International Development Association, 26, 31
International Development Research Centre, 400
International Digest of Health Legislation, 218
International Directory of Youth Bodies, 435
International Documents for the 80's: Their Role and Use, 401
International Finance Corporation, 26, 156
   Annual Report, 32
   Articles of Agreement, 33
International Financial Statistics, 304
International Fund for Agricultural Development, 34-36
   Governing Council. *Report*, 36
International Governmental Organizations: Constitutional Documents, 276
International Guide to Education Systems, 247
International Information: Documents, Publications and Information Systems, 402
International Institute for Environment and Development, 236
International Institute of Intellectual Co-operation, 434
International Labour Conference, 204
   List of Ratifications of Conventions, 204
   Record of Proceedings, 206

International Labour Conventions and Recommendations, 206
International Labour Documentation, 407
International Labour Office, 37, 157-159, 205, 300-302, 403-407
   Central Library and Documentation Branch, 408
   Legislative Series, 205
   Official Bulletin, 159
International Labour Organisation, 206
International Labour Review, 158
International Law Commission: A Guide to the Documents, 1949-1969, 488
International Law of Human Rights, 222
International Legal Materials, 207
International Maritime Organization, 38-39, 409-411
   Basic Documents, 38
   Status of Multilateral Conventions and Instruments, 208
International Meteorological Organization, 133
International Monetary Fund, 40-47, 160-163, 194, 303-304,
   Annual Report of the Executive Board, 40
   Articles of Agreement, 41
   Catalogue of Publications, 412
   International Monetary Fund, 1945-1965, 43
   International Monetary Fund, 1966-71, 44
   International Monetary Fund, 1972-1978, 45
   Publications Catalog, 412
   Staff Papers, 162
   Summary Proceedings of the Annual Meeting of the Board of Governors, 47
International Organizations: A Guide to Information Sources, 368
International Organization: An Interdisciplinary Bibliography, 387
International Organization and Integration: Annotated Basic Documents, 275
"International Organizations Documentation: Resources and Services of the Library of Congress", 427
International Refugee Organization, a Specialized Agency of the United Nations, 17
International Social Science Journal, 165
International Standard Industrial Classification of All Economic Activities, 323
International Symposium on the Documentation of the United Nations and Other Intergovernmental Organizations, Geneva, 1972, 429
International Telecommunication Convention, 48

International Telecommunication Union, 48-49, 242-244, 305, 413-414
List of Publications, 414
International Trade, 150
International Trade Centre (UNCTAD/GATT), 50, 164, 415
International Trade Centre, UNCTAD/GATT, 1964-1984: An Historical Account of Twenty Years of Service to Developing Countries, 50
International Trade Statistics Yearbook, 324
International Treaties Relating to Nuclear Control and Disarmament, 202
International Yearbook of Education, 247
Inter-Organization Board for Information Systems [of the United Nations System of Organizations], 416
Introducing Codex Alimentarius, 417
Inventory of Arrangements for Programme Co-ordination in the United Nations System, 1
Inventory of Population Projects in Developing Countries around the World, 189
Issues before the ... General Assembly of the United Nations, 51

Jackson, R. G. A., 80
"Jackson Report", 80
Järvinen, Markku, 349
Joint FAO/WHO Food Standards Programme, 417
Joint Inspection Unit [of the United Nations System of Organizations], 52-59
Journal UIT, 244
Journal of Development Planning, 75
Journal of the Preparatory Commission [of the United Nations], 277
Journal of World History, 246

Kapteyn, P.J.G., 275
Kaufmann, Johan, 261
Kaufmann, Johan, 95
Keeping Faith with the United Nations, 98
Ku, Min-chuan, 271

LABORDOC, 407
Labour Law Documents: Treaties and Legislation on Labour and Social Security, 205
Laws of Armed Conflicts: A Collection of Conventions, Resolutions and Other Decisions, 137
Le nouvel ordre mondial de l'information et de communication 459

Lexique général anglais-français avec suppléments espagnol-français et russe-français, 501
List of Depository Libraries Receiving United Nations Material, 458
List of Non-Governmental Organizations in Consultative Status with the Economic and Social Council, 499
List of Speeches and Visits Made by Heads of State and Dignitaries, 1945-1972, 493
List of Unesco Documents and Publications, 437
List of Unesco Secretariat Main Series Documents, 1947-1971, 438
Lista de Bibliotecas Depositarias que Reciben Documentos y Publicaciones de las Naciones Unidas, 458
Lista de Documentos y Publicaciones de la Unesco, 444
Lista de Publicaciones y Documentos Recientes de la OMS, 520
Lista Mundial de Revistas Especializadas en Ciencias Sociales, 443
Liste de documents et publications de l'Unesco, 444
Liste des bibliothèques dépositaires recevant les documents et publications de l'Organisation des Nations Unies, 458
Liste des documents principaux du Secrétariat de l'Unesco, 1947-1971, 438
Liste des publications et des documents récents OMS, 520
Liste mondiale des périodiques spécialisées dans les sciences sociales, 443

M'Bow, Amadou-Mahtar, 67
Mabbs, A.W., 355
"MacBride Report", 248
Macrothesaurus for Information Processing in the Field of Economic and Social Development, 472
Manning, Raymond, 350
Manuel de statistiques industrielles, 313
Many Voices, One World, 248
Marulli-Koenig, Luciana, 401, 418
McConaughy, John Bothwell, 419
McNamara, Robert, 155
Michaelis, Anthony R., 243
Moraze, Charles, 238
Moss, Alfred George, 290
Muldoon, James P. Jr., 15
"Multilateralism and the United Nations", 75
Multilateral Aspects of the Disarmament Debate, 141

Multilateral Investment Guarantee Agency. *Annual Report*, 60
Multilateral Treaties Deposited with the Secretary-General, 215
Multilateral Treaties in Respect of which the Secretary-General Performs Depositary Functions, 215
Multinational Corporations in World Development, 170

Narasimhan, C. V., 101
National Accounts Statistics, 326
Nations on Record: United Nations General Assembly Roll-Call Votes, 428
Naumann, Jens, 391
New International Economic Order: Selected Documents, 1945-1975, 290
New United Nations Structure for Global Economic Co-operation, 91
New World Information and Communication Order: ... A Bibliography of Unesco Holdings, 439
New World Information and Communication Order: A Selective Bibliography, 439, 459
New Zealand. Ministry of Foreign Affairs, 420
Newcombe, Hanna, 428
Newspaperman's United Nations: A Guide for Journalists, 440
No Distant Millennium: The International Law of Human Rights, 222
North-South: A Programme for Survival, 155, 374
Nouvelles de l'Unesco, 66
Nuclear Power and Fuel Cycle: Status and Trends, 19
Nuclear Safety Review, 19

Obzory po Atomnoi Energii, 239
Official Publishing: An Overview, 370
Olechowski, Andrzej, 195
One Hundred Years of International Co-operation in Meteorology (1873-1973), 133
Organisation for Economic Co-operation and Development, 421, 472
Organization and Structure of FAO, 11
Osmańczyk, Edmund Jan, 422
Oudraat, Chantal de Jonge, 145
Our Common Future, 237, 374
Overall Economic Perspective to the Year 2000, 187

Palic, Vladimir M., 505
"Palme Report", 136

Pareti, Luigi, 238
Partan, Daniel G., 61
Partners in Development: Report, 146
Pavesković, N., 351
Peace Research Institute (Dundas, Ontario, Canada), 428
Pearson, Lester B., 146
Pease, Mina, 205
Peaslee, Amos Jenkins, 276
Pellet, Alain, 5
Pérotin, Gilberte, 352
Phillips, Ralph W., 10
Population and Vital Statistics Report, 327
Population Policy Compendium, 190
Populi: A Journal of the United Nations Population Fund, 191
Preparatory Commission of the United Nations. *Handbook: A Delegation and Secretariat Directory*, 277
Publications, 277
Procedure of the UN Security Council, 4
Providing Access to United Nations Databases, 366
Provisional Rules of Procedure of the Security Council, 110
Public Affairs Information Service. *Bulletin*, 423
Public Papers of the Secretaries-General of the United Nations, 278
Publications in the Nuclear Sciences, 395
Publications of the General Agreement on Tariffs and Trade, 385
Publications of the International Court of Justice; Catalogue, 487
Publications of the International Maritime Organization, 410
Publications of the United Nations System: A Reference Guide, 510
Publications Policy and Practice in the United Nations System, 55
Publikatsii OON i Ee Spetsializirovannykh Uchrezhdenii, 371
Publishing in the United Nations and Its Related Agencies, 411

Ramcharan, B.G., 98
Reader in Documents of International Organizations, 430
"Recently Opened United Nations War Crimes Archives: A Researcher's Comment", 348
"Records of Conferences Resulting in the Foundation of Organizations", 350

Recueil des statistiques des établissements humains, 315

Recueil de statistiques et d'indicateurs sur la situation des femmes, 1986, 316

Refugee Abstracts, 495

Register of Development Activities of the United Nations System, 367

Register of International Treaties and Other Agreements in the Field of the Environment, 234

"Registry and Archives", 351

"Relations between Archives and Libraries within the UN Family", 344

Relevé des traités et accords internationaux enregistrés ou classés et inscrits au répertoire au Secrétariat, 494

Renninger, John P., 94, 96, 97, 99

Répertoire des institutions européennes de formation dans les domaines de la diplomatie..., 485

Répertoire des publications préparées par le CCI au cours de ses 20 premières années, 1964-1984, 415

Répertoire mondial des institutions de formation et de recherche en droit international, 210

Répertoire mondial des institutions de recherche et de formation sur la paix, 139

Répertoire mondial des institutions de recherche et de formation sur les droits de l'homme, 223

Repertoire of the Practice of the Security Council, 76

Répertoire international des organismes de jeunesse, 435

Répertoire mondial des institutions de sciences sociales, 167

Repertorio internacional de Traducciones, 434

Repertorio Internacional de Organismos de Juventud, 435

Repertorio Mundial de Instituciones de Ciencias Sociales, 167

Repertorio Mundial de Instituciones de Formación y de Investigación en Derecho Internacional, 210

Repertorio Mundial de Instituciones de Investigación y de Formación en Materia de Derechos Humanos, 223

Repertorio Mundial de Instituciones de Investigación y de Formación sobre la Paz, 139

Repertory of Disarmament Research, 145

Repertory of Practice of United Nations Organs, 71

Report of the Executive Committee of the Preparatory Commission of the United Nations, 277

"Report of the Group of High-level Intergovernmental Experts to Review the Efficiency of the Administrative and Financial Functioning of the United Nations", 87

Report of the Preparatory Commission of the United Nations, 277

Report on Autonomous Research Institutes of the United Nations, 56

Report on the Activities of the International Telecommunication Union, 49

Report on the World Social Situation, 179

Report to Congress on Voting Practices in the United Nations, 115

Reporting to the Economic and Social Council, 57

Reports and Papers in Mass Communication, 249

Reports and Papers in the Social Sciences, 166

Reports of the Committee on the Elimination of Discrimination against Women, 230

Resolutions Adopted by the Economic and Social Council, 184

Resolutions Adopted by the Economic Commission for Latin America, 287

Resolutions and Decisions Adopted by the General Assembly, 288

Resolutions Adopted by the United Nations on the Cyprus Problem, 1964-1988, 272

Resolutions and Decisions of the Security Council, 292

Resolutions and Statements of the United Nations Security Council, 1946-1989, 279

Review of Developments in the Trading System, 151

Review of the Efficiency of the Administrative and Financial Functioning of the United Nations, 89

Review of United Nations Public Information Networks: United Nations Information Centres, 58

Revista de Energia Atomica, 239

Revue d'énergie atomique, 239

Right to Adequate Food As a Human Right, 227

Role and Function of the International Monetary Fund, 46

Role of the International Civil Service Commission, '94

Rosenne, Shabtai, 214, 273

Rothman, Marie H., 424

Royal Institute of International Affairs. Library, 245
Rules of Procedure of the Economic and Social Council, 83
Rules of Procedure of the General Assembly, 90
Rules of Procedure of the Trusteeship Council, 113
Ruloff, Dieter, 262

Schaaf, Robert W., 426, 427
Schindler, Dietrich, 137
Schopen, Lynn, 428
Science Policy Studies and Documents, 250
Segura, Bodil Ulate, 357
Selected Decisions of the International Monetary Fund and Selected Documents of the International Monetary Fund, 161
Sen, B., 213
Série législative des Nations unies, 217
Shaaban, Marian, 386
Sharif, Regina S., 281
Siekmann, Robert C. R., 134
Siglas y Abreviaturas de las Organizaciones del Sistema de las Naciones Unidas, 500
Sigles et abréviations utilisés par les organismes des Nations Unies, 500
Simons, Anne Patricia, 14
Simpson, Michael, 281
Social Indicators of Development, 335
Sociétés transnationales: bibliographie séléctive, 1984-1987, 447
Some Reflections on Reform of the United Nations, 59
Sources, Organization, Utilization of International Documentation; Proceedings, 429
Standard International Trade Classification, 328
State of the Environment, 235
State of the World Environment, 235
State of the World's Children, 175
Statement of Treaties and International Agreements Registered or Filed and Recorded with the Secretariat, 494
Statistical Masterfile, 298
Statistical Reference Index, 298
Statistical Yearbook for Asia and the Far East, 311
Statistical Yearbook for Asia and the Pacific, 311
Statistics on Children in UNICEF Assisted Countries, 308
Statistique des services postaux, 332
Statistiques de propriété industrielle, 341
Statistiques mondiales des cultures et de l'élévage, 297

Stevens, Helen C., 430
Stevens, Robert D., 430
Strengthening the United Nations Economic and Social Programs: A Documentary Essay, 8
Strong, Maurice F., 2
Structure of the United Nations General Assembly: An Organizational Approach to Its Work, 1974-1990s, 7
Structure of the United Nations General Assembly: Its Committees, Commissions and Other Organisms, 1946-73, 7
Student's Guide to United Nations Documents and Their Use, 419
Studies and Documents on Cultural Policies, 251
Study Abroad, 442
Study of the Capacity of the United Nations Development System, 80
Sub-Saharan Africa: A Long-term Perspective Study, 192
Subject Guide to Publications of the International Labour Office, 408
Subject List of Publications and Documents of Unesco, 437
Subject List of Unesco Documents, 437
Successor Vision: The United Nations of Tomorrow, 62
Summary of World Trade Statistics, 314
Survey and Analysis of Evaluations of the United Nations Intergovernmental Structure and Functions in the Economic and Social Fields, 99
Survey of Economic and Social Conditions in Africa, 180
Survey of the Economic Situation and Prospects of Europe, 186
System der Vereinten Nationen: Internationale Bibliographie, 391
Szapiro, Jerzy, 440
T.M.C. Asser Instituut, 279
Tavernier, Paul, 5
Telecommunication Journal, 244
Ten Years of United Nations Publications, 1945 to 1955, 474
Tessitore, John, 51
Texts of the Tokyo Round Agreements, 152
Third Generation World Organization, 100
Three Decades of the United Nations Economic Commission for Europe, 84
Three-Yearly Report on the Development of the Postal Services, 265

Toman, Jiří, 137
Tomeh, George J., 281
Traffic, Commercial Air Carriers, 299
Transnational Associations: The Review of International Associations and Meetings, 524
Transnational Corporations: A Selective Bibliography, 447
Transnational Corporations in World Development: A Re-examination, 170
Transnational Corporations in World Development: The Third Survey, 170
Transnational Corporations in World Development: Trends and Prospects, 170
Trends in Developing Economies, 336
Trilingual Compendium of United Nations Terminology, English-French-German, 502
Turvey, Ralph, 301

UN Chronicle, 256
UN Monthly Chronicle, 256
UNBIS On-line User's Manual, Version 5.0, 461
UNBIS Reference Manual for Bibliographic Description;, 462
UNBIS: An Overview of the Databases, 460
UNCITRAL: The United Nations Commission on International Trade Law, 212
UNCTAD 1983-1987: Bibliography, 453
UNCTAD Commodity Yearbook, 310
UNCTC Bibliography, 1974-1987, 448
UNDEX: United Nations Documents Index, 463
UNDOC: Current Index; United Nations Documents Index, 464
Unesco, 63-70, 138-139, 165-167, 209-210, 221-223, 238, 245-253, 306-307, 353-355, 431-443
   Annuaire statistique, 307
   Anuario Estadístico, 307
   Basic Facts and Figures, 307
   Computerized Documentation System, 444
   Division of the Unesco Library, Archives and Documentation Services, 445
   Film and Video Catalogue, 1987-1988, 433
   General Conference
      Records of the General Conference, 69
      Report of the Director-General on the Activities of the Organization, 70
   General Information Programme and UNISIST, 356
   Intergovernmental Programme for the Development of Communication, 253

Unesco
   Inventory of General Conference Documents, 1946-1989, 436
   Just Published, 441
   Publications Catalogue, 441
   Statistical Yearbook, 307
***Unesco Associated Schools Project*, 258**
Unesco Chronicle, 66
Unesco Collection of Representative Works, 432
Unesco Courier, 252
Unesco List of Documents and Publications, 444
Unesco News, 66
Unesco on the Eve of Its 40th Anniversary, 67
Unesco Sources, 68
Unesco Yearbook on Peace and Conflict Studies, 138
Unesco's Standard-setting Instruments, 209
UNFPA Publications and Audiovisual Guide, 496
UNICRI: United Nations Interregional Crime and Justice Research Institute, 106
UNIDIR Repertory of Disarmament Research, 145
United Nations, 71, 168, 224
   Advance Technology Alert System, 254
   Annuaire statistique, 329
   Archives Section, 446
   Bulletin mensuel de statistique, 325
   Centre for Human Rights, 225-228
      Study Series, 227
   Centre for Human Settlements (Habitat), 169
   Centre for Science and Technology for Development, 254
   Centre for Social Development and Humanitarian Affairs, 229-230
   Commission on Human Rights, 231
      Report on the ... Session, 231
   Committee for Development Planning, 177-178
   Committee on the Elimination of Discrimination against Women, 230
   Dag Hammarskjöld Library, 439, 455-469
      Reference and Bibliography Section, 470
   Department for Disarmament Affairs, 140-143
   Department of Conference Services, 255, 471
   Department of International Economic and Social Affairs, 75, 177-180, 472
      Information Systems Unit, 473
   Department of Political and Security Council Affairs, 76
   Department of Public Information, 77-79, 107, 144, 256-259, 474-476

United Nations
- Division of Narcotic Drugs, 260
- Economic and Social Commission for Asia and the Pacific, 81, 183, 311, 456, 478-479
- Economic and Social Council, 82-83, 184
  - *Official Records*, 82
- Economic Commission for Africa, 284
  - Economic Commission for Europe, 84, 185-187, 285, 312
- Economic Commission for Latin America, 286-287
  - *Basic Guide to the Commission and Its Secretariat*, 456
- Economic Commission for Latin America and the Caribbean, 85
- General Assembly, 86-90, 168, 288, 482
  - *Audited Accounts*, 86
  - *Medium-Term Plan*, 86
  - *Official Records*, 86
  - *Programme Budget*, 86
  - *Report of the Secretary-General on the Work of the Organization*, 88
- Group of Experts on the Structure of the United Nations System, 91
- Human Rights Committee, 220
  - *Report*, 232
- International Court of Justice, 486-487
  - *Acts and Documents concerning the Organization of the Court*, 487
  - *Pleadings, Oral Arguments, Documents* 487
  - *Reports of Judgments, Advisory Opinions and Orders*, 487
  - *Yearbook*, 102, 487
- International Law Commission, 103-104, 488
- International Refugee Integration Resource Centre, 495
- Library, 489-490
- *Mimeographed and Printed Documents*, 280
- *Monthly Bulletin of Statistics*, 325
- Office of Conference Services, 491-492
- Office of General Services, 493
- Office of Legal Affairs, 215-217, 494
- Office of Public Information, 107
- Office of the United Nations High Commissioner for Refugees, 291, 495

United Nations
- Sales Section, 498
- Secretariat, 357, 499
- Security Council, 109-110, 292
  - *Official Records*, 109
- Statistical Office, 314-331
- *Statistical Yearbook*, 329
- Translation Division
  - Documentation, Reference and Terminology Section, 500
  - French Service, 501
  - German Section, 502
- *Treaty Series*, 211
- Trusteeship Council, 112-113
  - *Official Records*, 112
  - *Resolutions and Decisions*, 263
- World Conference to Combat Racism and Racial Discrimination, 2d, Geneva, 1983, 293

United Nations: A Keyword Dissertation Bibliography, 504
United Nations Action in the Field of Human Rights, 228
United Nations: An Inside View, 101
United Nations and Disarmament: A Short History, 142
United Nations and Related Agencies Handbook, 420
United Nations and Specialized Agencies Handbook, 420
"United Nations as a Publisher", 389
United Nations at Forty: A Foundation To Build On, 79
United Nations Bibliographic Sources, 470
United Nations Bulletin, 256
United Nations Centre on Transnational Corporations, 170, 447-448
United Nations Children's Fund, 171-175, 308, 449
United Nations Commission on International Trade Law, 212
United Nations Conference on International Organization, San Francisco, 1945. *Documents*, 283
United Nations Conference on Trade and Development, 72-74, 176, 309-310, 450-453, 456
United Nations Conferences and Special Observances, 475

Index 103

United Nations Development Programme, 80, 182, 333
Annual Report of the Administrator, 181
Central Evaluation Office, 477
United Nations Disarmament Yearbook, 143
United Nations Document Series Symbols, 465
United Nations Documentation: A Brief Guide, 466
United Nations Documentation News, 467
"United Nations Documents and Bibliographical References", 386
United Nations Documents and Publications, 282
United Nations Documents and Publications: A Research Guide, 379
United Nations Documents Index, 468
United Nations Economic and Social Council Index, 1946–1965, 376
United Nations Editorial Manual: A Compendium of Rules and Directives, 471
United Nations Environment Programme, 233-236, 480-481
United Nations Fellowship Programme for Educators, 258
"United Nations Financial Emergency: Crisis and Opportunity", 2
United Nations Focus: Notes for Speakers, 257
United Nations Handbook, 420
United Nations Industrial Development Organization, 92, 188, 313, 484
Documents List, 483
Industrial Development Board, 93
United Nations Institute for Disarmament Research, 145
United Nations Institute for Namibia, 289
United Nations Institute for Training and Research, 94-101, 153, 213-214, 261-262, 290, 485
United Nations Intergovernmental Structure and Functions in the Economic and Social Fields, 99
United Nations Interregional Crime and Justice Research Institute, 105-106
Statute, 105
United Nations Juridical Yearbook, 216
United Nations Legislative Series, 217
United Nations Official Records: A Reference Catalogue, 492
United Nations Peacekeeping, 1946-1967: Documents and Commentary, 135
United Nations Population Fund, 189-191, 496
United Nations Publications Catalogue, 498
United Nations Reform: Issues for Congress, 119

United Nations Relief and Rehabilitation Administration, 108
United Nations Research Institute for Social Development. *Available Publications*, 497
United Nations Resolutions and Decisions Relating to the Office of the United Nations High Commissioner for Refugees, 291
United Nations Resolutions on Namibia, 1946-1978, 289
United Nations Resolutions on Palestine and the Arab-Israeli Conflict, 281
United Nations Resolutions, Series 1: Resolutions Adopted by the General Assembly, 288
United Nations Resolutions, Series 2: Resolutions and Decisions of the Security Council, 292
United Nations Review, 256
United Nations Sales Publications, 1972-1977, 469
United Nations Security Council Index, 1946-1964, 376
United Nations Social Defence Research Institute, 111
United Nations System: Co-ordinating Its Economic and Social Work, 153
United Nations System: International Bibliography, 391
United Nations System of Organizations and Directory of Senior Officials, 361
United Nations University, 147, 503
Annual Report, 264
United Nations War Crimes Commission, 348
United States
  Congress. Senate. Committee on Foreign Relations, 114
  Department of State, 115-118
  Library of Congress, 505
    Congressional Research Service, 119
United States and the United Nations, 117
United States Contributions to International Organizations, 116
United States Participation in the UN; Report by the President to the Congress, 117
Universal Postal Union, 265, 332
  Annual Report on the Work of the Union, 120
  List of Publications, 506
  Liste des publications du Bureau international de l'UPU, 507
UNRRA: The History of the United Nations Relief and Rehabilitation Administration, 108
UNSDRI at Twenty: 1968-1988, 111

UNU Publications: Complete Listing, 503
Uruguay Round: A Handbook on the Multilateral Trade Negotiations, 195
Uruguay Round: Further Papers on Selected Issues, 176
Uruguay Round: Papers on Selected Issues, 176
Use of the Veto In Meetings of the Security Council of the United Nations, 118

Vambery, Joseph T., 508
Viet, Jean, 472

Walne, Peter, 354
Ware, Carolyn F., 238
Weather Reporting, 269
Welander, Sven, 358, 359
Wellens, Karel C., 279
WHO Chronicle, 267
Who's Who in the United Nations and Related Agencies, 509
WHODOC: List of Recent WHO Publications and Documents, 520
Wiet, Gaston, 238
Winton, Harry N. M., 290, 510
WIPO: General Information, 130
WMO Bulletin, 270
Woodbridge, George, 108
Wooley, Leonard, 238
Woolfson, Susan, 51
Work of CEDAW: Reports of the Committee on the Elimination of Discrimination against Women, 230
Work of the International Law Commission, 103
Work of WHO, 128
World Bank, 120-126, 192-199, 333-339, 511-514
    Annual Report, 121
    Annual Review of Project Performance Results, 193
    Catalog of Publications, 511
    Catalog of Staff Working Papers, 512
    Depository Library Program. *Directory of Libraries*, 515
    Index of Publications, 513
World Bank and the International Finance Corporation, 125
World Bank Atlas, 337
World Bank Economic Review, 196
World Bank Operations: Sectoral Programs and Policies, 126
World Bank Research News, 197

World Bank Research Observer, 198
World Bank Research Program: Abstracts of Current Studies, 514
World Bibliography of International Documentation, 516
World Commission on Environment and Development, 237
World Communication Report, 253
World Concerns and the United Nations: Model Teaching Units, 258
World Court: What It Is and How It Works, 214
World Crop and Livestock Statistics, 297
World Debt Tables: External Debt of Developing Countries, 338
World Development Report, 199
World Directory of Human Rights Teaching and Research Institutions, 223
World Directory of Peace Research and Training Institutions, 139
World Directory of Social Science Institutions, 167
World Directory of Teaching and Research Institutions in International Law, 210
World Economic Outlook: A Survey by the Staff of the International Monetary Fund, 163
World Economic Survey, 180
World Energy Supplies, 320
World Food Survey, 148
World Health Organization, 127-128, 218, 266-267, 340, 517-520
    Publications Catalogue, 1948-1989, 517
    Publications Catalogue: New Books, 518
World Health Organization Publications: Catalogue, 1947-1979, 519
World Health Statistics Annual, 340
World Intellectual Property Organization, 129-130, 268, 341-342, 360, 521
World List of Social Science Periodicals, 443
World Media Handbook: Selected Country Profiles, 476
World Meteorological Organization, 131-133, 269-270
    Basic Documents, 294
    Catalogue of Publications, 522
World Resources, 236
World Resources Institute, 233
World Statistics in Brief: United Nations Statistical Pocketbook, 330
World Summit for Children, 172
World Symposium on International Documentation, 2d, Brussels, 1980, 401
World Tables, 339

World Trade Annual, 331
Worldmark Encyclopedia of the Nations, 523

Xidis, Dorothy Peaslee, 276

Year Book of Labour Statistics, 302
Yearbook of Common Carrier Telecommunication Statistics, 305
Yearbook of Construction Statistics, 317
Yearbook of Food and Agricultural Statistics, 295, 296
Yearbook of Industrial Statistics, 322
Yearbook of International Commodity Statistics, 310
Yearbook of International Organizations, 524
Yearbook of International Trade Statistics, 324
Yearbook of National Accounts Statistics, 326
Yearbook of Public Telecommunication Statistics, 305
Yearbook of the Human Rights Committee, 220
Yearbook of the International Law Commission, 104
Yearbook of the United Nations, 259
Yearbook of World Energy Statistics, 320
Yearbook on Human Rights, 224

Zarb, M., 360